Alan Watts—
HERE and NOW

D0878649

SUNY SERIES IN TRANSPERSONAL AND HUMANISTIC PSYCHOLOGY

Richard D. Mann, editor

Alan Watts—HERE and NOW

contributions to psychology, philosophy, and religion

Edited by

Peter J. Columbus and Donadrian L. Rice

state university of new york press

Published by
STATE UNIVERSITY OF NEW YORK PRESS
Albany

© 2012 State University of New York

For information, contact
State University of New York Press
www.sunypress.edu

Production and book design, Laurie Searl
Marketing, Anne M. Valentine

Library of Congress Cataloging-in-Publication Data

Alan Watts—here and now : contributions to psychology, philosophy, and religion / edited by Peter
J. Columbus and Donadrian L. Rice.
    p. cm. — (SUNY series in transpersonal and humanistic psychology)
  Includes bibliographical references and index.
  ISBN 978-1-4384-4199-3 (hardcover : alk. paper)
  ISBN 978-1-4384-4200-6 (pbk. : alk. paper)
  1. Watts, Alan, 1915-1973. I. Columbus, Peter J. II. Rice, Donadrian L.
  B945.W324A65 2012
  191—dc23

                   2011021791

10   9   8   7   6   5   4   3   2   1

Contents

Acknowledgments

The inspiration and idea for this book came to light in the sacred clearing that is the Unitarian Universalist Rowe Conference Center in Rowe, Massachusetts. Sincere appreciation to Rev. Douglas Wilson, Pru Berry, Felicity Pickett, and the staff of the Rowe Center for maintaining a remarkable sanctuary.

Infinite gratitude goes to our contributors and their readiness to write substantive chapters in the midst of already hectic schedules.

The book was edited in several locales: The psychology departments at Union College (Kentucky) and University of West Georgia; Sandra Cohen's New York estate; and Jean-Claude van Itallie's Shantigar estate in Rowe, Massachusetts. Thanks to all for their kindness, generosity, and benefaction.

Thanks also to Dr. Jeffrey J. Kripal, an anonymous reviewer, and the editing staff at SUNY Press for helping to make a more perfect book; to Susan Mann for her troubleshooting and encouragement, and to Kevin Kent for his careful and astute attention to the process of indexing.

We are grateful to Chungliang Al Huang who kindly shared his calligraphic artwork.

Illustrations

Introduction: A New Look at Alan Watts

Peter J. Columbus and Donadrian L. Rice

> I am committed to the view that the whole point and joy of human life is
> to integrate the spiritual with the material, the mystical with the sensuous,
> and the altruistic with a kind of proper self-love——since it is written that
> you must love your neighbor as yourself.
>
> —*Alan Watts (1973b, p. ix)*

This book is a call to remembrance and an opportunity for reconsidering the life and work of Alan Watts. Writing a mere fifteen years after
Watts' untimely demise, Michael Brannigan (1988) suggested that Alan's "place in
our history remains to be ascertained. We are still too close to the events of his life
and to his writings to perceive their full impact, but his influence has thus far been
undeniable" (p. 2). Several decades have now passed beyond Alan's countercultural
zeitgeist, arriving at a pivotal vantage point in a new century from which to assess
and re-vision the enduring merit of his writings and lectures.[1] November 2008 sig-
nified the thirty-fifth anniversary of Watts' death, and this benchmark date served
as inspiration for making a new study of his scholarship. The chapters compiled in
this volume reconsider Watts' insights on the human condition in light of today's
discourse in psychology, philosophy, and religion.

A hint of Watts' contemporary relevance may be found at the beginning
of his essay on "Wealth versus Money." He wrote: "In the year of our lord
Jesus Christ 2000, the United States of America will no longer exist" (Watts,
1971b, p. 3). The previous sentence strikes a rather prescient tone given so-
called "post-9/11" sensibilities. Watts was reflecting on modern-day obsessions
with abstract monetary riches acquired at the expense of personal, social, and
environmental well-being. He wrote also of waning natural resources, nuclear
arms proliferation, biological and chemical warfare, and "maniacal misappli-
cations of technology." Nowadays, there are new variations on old themes:
preemptive wars, terrorism, torture, "ethnic cleansing," food and fuel short-
ages, catastrophic oil spills, and global climate change. Each is pushing human
civilization toward the brink of disaster. Yet, Watts always offered his audiences

propitious and uplifting insights on what it means to be human. He continually broached the possibility that greed, anger, and ignorance could be transformed, as Buddhists often suggest, into wisdom, compassion, and enlightenment. If it is true in the new millennium as it was during Watts' own day, that humanity is facing what Martin Luther King called the "fierce urgency of now" as some contemporary voices would imply, then all the more compelling reason to consider Alan Watts anew.

CURRICULUM VITAE

Alan Watts' resume is impressive. It reflects the depth, breadth, and variety of accomplishment afforded by his fifty-eight years of living. He was born on January 6, 1915, in Chislehurst, England, and graduated from the prestigious King's School on the grounds of Canterbury Cathedral in 1932. Eschewing a traditional undergraduate education in favor of tutorials on Buddhism with Zen scholar Christmas Humphreys, Watts eventually enrolled at Seabury-Western Theological Seminary where he was ordained an Episcopal priest in 1944 and awarded an S.T.M. in 1948. He served upon ordination as examining chaplain for the bishop of Chicago and as chaplain at Northwestern University until leaving the Episcopal Church in 1950. Watts subsequently held a professorship in comparative philosophy and psychology at the College of the Pacific's American Academy of Asian Studies (1951–1957), where he also served a stint as dean of the academy (1953–1956). In 1958, the University of Vermont bestowed an honorary doctorate of divinity for his learned offerings to the field of comparative religion. Watts then spent the remainder of his life as an independent scholar and freelance philosopher.

Watts served as editor of *Buddhism in England* (1936–1938; now *The Middle Way)*, and co-edited (with L. Cranmer-Byng) the *Wisdom of the East* series (1937–1941). In later years he edited the *Patterns of Myth* series (1963a), Herrigel's (1974) *The Method of Zen,* and served as editorial advisor to *The Psychedelic Review* and the *Journal of Transpersonal Psychology.* Watts' writings can be divided roughly into three clusters. His early works, between 1932 and 1940, include three books (Watts, 1936, 1937, 1940) and many articles in various periodicals for general readership (Watts, 1987, 1997a). These initial offerings were prodigious and insightful but somewhat derivative of psychologists Carl Jung and Eric Graham Howe, the mystic teacher Jiddu Krishnamurti, and philosophers Dimitrije Mitrinovic and D. T. Suzuki.[2] Still he showed from the beginning his genius for integrative thinking and clarity of expression (Watts & Snelling, 1997).

Watts' middle works, from 1941 to the late 1950s, exuded greater originality and sophistication for academic audiences as he was situated variously at Seabury-Western Seminary, Northwestern University, and the American Academy of Asian Studies. Sadler (1974) suggested that Watts' best efforts emerged out of a tension between the "institutional conventions" of academia and his free-spirited intellect. Among these writings were *Behold the Spirit* (1947), *The Supreme Identity* (1950), *The Wisdom of Insecurity* (1951), *Myth and Ritual in Christianity* (1953c), *The Way of Zen* (1957), and *Nature, Man and Woman* (1958b). He also published erudite papers in such venues as the *Review of Religion* (Watts, 1941), *Philosophy East and West* (Watts, 1953d), *Journal of Religious Thought* (Watts, 1953b), and the *American Journal of Psychoanalysis* (Watts, 1953a, 1956).

By the end of the 1950s, however, Watts saw a need for academic specialists to "communicate with the myriads of literate nonscholars who increasingly constitute our world" (Watts, 1973b, p. 344). Although this view is an astute insight given current editorial attitudes in the social sciences calling for accessibility of content sans technical and pedantic jargon, Watts at the time was chastised in academic circles for vulgarizing Asian spiritual traditions by, for example, writing essays in *Playboy Magazine*. His books in this period include *This is IT* (1960), *Psychotherapy, East and West* (1961), *The Two Hands of God* (1963b), *Beyond Theology* (1964), *The Book: On the Taboo Against Knowing Who You Are* (1966), *Does it Matter?* (1971a), and *Cloud-hidden, Whereabouts Unknown* (1973a). His popularity as a best-selling author and public speaker (e.g., Watts, 2006) inspired a generation of young people toward new ways of experiencing themselves and the world (Lawson, 1988).

Watts was awarded research grants by the Franklin J. Matchette Foundation in 1950 and the Bollingen Foundation in 1951–1953 and 1962–1964. He was a research fellow at Harvard University in 1962–1964, visiting scholar at San Jose State University in 1968, research consultant at Maryland Psychiatric Research Center in 1969, and guest lectured at leading universities and medical schools worldwide, including Stanford, Berkeley, Chicago, Yale, Cornell, Cambridge, and the C. G. Jung Institute in Zurich. Watts offered a weekly program on Pacifica Radio originating at KPFA-FM in San Francisco and broadcast nationwide, filmed a twenty-six-part series entitled "Eastern Wisdom for Modern Life" for National Educational Television, and narrated award-winning films on Zen Buddhism for the Hartley Film Foundation.[3] He was a member of the American Oriental Society, a board member of the Foundation for Mind Research, sat on the Executive Council of the World Congress of Faiths, was founder and president of the Society for Comparative Philosophy, and established the *Alan Watts Journal* as an outlet for his writings.

Watts died in his sleep on November 16, 1973. His ashes were interred within a Buddhist *stupa* erected at the San Francisco Zen Center's Green Dragon Temple (*Soryu-ji*) in Muir Beach, California (see Baker, 1974; Ferlinghetti, 1974). Numerous volumes of his recorded and transcribed talks, conference presentations, and manuscripts continue to be published posthumously. A library devoted to preserving and disseminating his works for future generations of students and scholars, called The Alan Watts Mountain Center, is now under construction north of San Francisco.

ON THE TABOO AGAINST KNOWING ALAN WATTS

A contemporary reflection on Alan Watts may profit from a look at portrayals of him in earlier times and other places. This consideration requires suspending two common tendencies of judgment: idolatry and iconoclasm. As evidenced by any number of obituaries and book jackets, aggrandizing Watts as a cultural idol, New Age guru, or Buddhist holy man is conventional practice. He has even been called a "guru for those who don't trust gurus" (Lott, 1999, p. 24). This idolatry may be traced to Watts' involvement with the 1950s Beat subculture and subsequent countercultural wave of the 1960s. In the 1950s, his riveting lectures at the American Academy of Asian Studies, together with his KPFA radio program, fueled the "San Francisco Renaissance." Watts' writings on Zen Buddhism gained national attention with coverage in various news magazines such as *Time* (Zen, 1958), *Life* (Eager Exponent, 1961), and *The Nation,* which called him the "brain and Buddha of American Zen" (Mahoney, 1958, p. 311). He was closely associated with many eminent Beat poets and writers including Gary Snyder, Allen Ginsberg, and Jack Kerouac. Kerouac (1958), in fact, included a portrayal of Watts as the character "Arthur Whane" in his novel *The Dharma Bums.* Watts' ubiquitous presence on the intellectual and cultural scene in 1950s San Francisco leads to perceiving him as a renowned participant in the Beat movement. Leary (1998) called him the "Lord High Admiral of the Beat" (p. 105). Yet Watts' outlook on life was not consonant with the worldview of the Beat Generation as a whole; their lifestyle was seen as "aggressively slovenly and dowdy" (Watts, 1973b, p. 359). He criticized the Beats' appropriation of Zen as a self-defensive revolt against traditional values rather than as a liberation (neither conforming nor rebelling) from social convention (Watts, 1958a). By his own account, Alan considered himself as situated "in" rather than being "of" the Beat subcultural milieu (Watts, 1973b).

Watts earned greater notoriety with the countercultural upsurge of the 1960s, becoming "one of the most magical, incantatory names" of that era (Beidler, 1995, p. 199). He was a key player in the psychedelic arena consulting for Timothy Leary's research at Harvard University and writing the classic text on *The Joyous Cosmology* (Watts, 1962). *Time Magazine* called him "the psychedelic generation's most revered and thoughtful guru" (The New Ministry, 1969, p. 6). Watts' advocacy for Zen Buddhism and other Asian spiritual traditions gained greater currency amid the countercultural shift away from Western technocratic values (Roszak, 1969). Alan, furthermore, had a compelling style of presentation placing him at the forefront of the "human potential movement" at Esalen Institute where he "dazzled audiences with his verbal bridge-building between Eastern religion and Western psychology" (Anderson, 1983, p. 16; Kripal, 2007). His charismatic persona made him a venerated public figure and he constantly encountered individuals seeking discipleship (Furlong, 2001). Through his vocation of conveying Asian mystical traditions to Western audiences, wrote Watts (1973b), "I was pressing a button in expectation of a buzz, but instead there was an explosion" (p. 359). The outcome was that his rise to prominence brought him "the kind of success that passes for greatness: He became a celebrity" (Stuart, 1983, p. xi). The saliency of Watts' celebrity status makes it easy to render him as a sort of "popular iconic metaphor" (Columbus & Boerger, 2002) reflecting the veneer of cultural or historical fads and thereby obscuring the substance of his contributions to psychology, philosophy, and religion. The point here is not to deny the magnitude of Watts' fame but merely to move it aside temporarily in order to shed light on the overshadowed aspects of his work.

Aggrandizing Watts inevitably invites critics to knock him off the figurative pedestal by engaging three common *ad hominem* arguments that summarily dismiss his writings and lectures. First, Watts is often discounted by pointing toward his lifestyle choices, such as his extramarital affairs and immoderate alcohol consumption, as contraindications of spiritual and philosophical insight. The assumption being that supposed sins of the flesh ought not to afflict those perceived as operating on a higher (or deeper) spiritual plane. As Sibley (1984) put it, many people viewed Watts' style of living "as the complete antithesis of all he had written or talked about" (p. 219). Harding (1984) therefore asked, was Alan a "sage or anti-sage?" (p. 221). Second, the veracity or profundity of his spiritual awakening is diminished by contending that he misunderstood his subjective mystical experiences. The tack here is to extend this "misunderstanding" to Watts' discussions of mysticism in general. Third, his ingenious capacity for rendering complex ideas in comprehensible fashion is interpreted as intellectual shallowness. Roszak (1969) described the latter two discounting maneuvers as "rather arrogant criticism":

> On the one hand from elitist Zen devotees who have found him to be too discursive for their mystic tastes (I recall one such telling me smugly, "Watts has never experienced *satori*"), and on the other hand from professional philosophers who have been inclined to ridicule him for his popularizing bent as being, in the words of one academic, "the Norman Vincent Peale of Zen." (p. 132)

Ironically, Watts (1973b) apparently invited and contributed to the above *ad hominem* arguments. Regarding his lifestyle, he described himself as a "disreputable epicurean" (p. x) and "an unrepentant sensualist" (p. 54) with robust appetites for sexuality and liquor.[4] Concerning his mystical experiences, there is speculation that his discussion of fraudulent mystics acting as master teachers— the so-called "trickster guru" (Watts, 1977b)—is a self-reference.[5] Moreover, he often maintained sharp criticisms of academic life by arguing that upstanding reputations in American universities require production of mediocre work. "You must be academically 'sound' which is to be preposterously and phenomenally dull" (Watts, 1973b, p. 114). According to Watts, he was never charged as being "scholarly" by critics because his style of writing avoids blatant pedantry.[6]

Watts (1977a) portrayed himself as an amalgam of contradictory and paradoxical aspects: a "coincidence of opposites" and "a joker" with reference to a wild card taking on a variety of qualities in various circumstances. He wrote, "I realize quite clearly that the ego-personality named Alan Watts is an illusion, a social institution (as are all egos), and a fabrication of words and symbols without the slightest substantial reality" (p. 17). Furlong (2001) concluded that "Watts is not a man on whom it is possible to deliver an easy verdict— he escapes labels" (p. xi). Nevertheless, by setting aside the usual inclinations toward idolatry, iconoclasm, and Watts' own self-depreciation, a perusal of the literature reveals a number of variations in depiction of Alan Watts in scholarly and popular writings during and after his lifetime. These variations include Watts as theologian, contemplative mystic, Zennist, philosopher, psychologist, and cultural symptom.

WATTS AS THEOLOGIAN

Watts (1973b) saw himself as writing four key texts on theology (Watts, 1947, 1950, 1953c, 1964). Yet theological classifications of Watts are based on various combinations of his writings. *Behold the Spirit: A Study in the Necessity of Mystical Religion* (1947) was Watts' "first full utterance in *propria persona*" (Wheelwright, 1953, p. 494). Episcopal Canon theologian, Bernard Iddings Bell, called it "one of the half dozen most significant books on religion published in the twentieth century" (cited in Stuart, 1983, p. 109). F. S. C. Northrop (1947) considered it "one of the best—in fact the only first-rate—books in recent years in the field of religion" (see also, Akhilananda, 1948). Hartshorne and Reese (1953) classified Watts (1947) as reflecting a "modern panentheism" that overcomes the boundary negations of pantheism and the categorical contingencies of dualism by viewing the notion of deity as eternal and temporal, conscious and omniscient, and world inclusive.[7] Clark (1978), in contrast, considered the entirety of Watts' theological works to be situated within a "monistic pantheism" defined as the "class of religions and metaphysical theories which hold that all levels of reality are related ontologically . . . and ultimately are one" (p. 15). Some critics interpret Watts (1950) as expressing an Asian normative theology because, they argue, Christianity is subordinated to an Eastern metaphysic (Christian, 1950; Fuller, 2008). Park (1974), on the other hand, judged *The Supreme Identity* (1950) as weighted by assumptions of Western dualism that ultimately prevented Watts from faithfully interpreting the nondual nature of Asian religious thought. Swearer (1973) called Watts a "metatheologian" defined as a "comparative, creative thinker whose theological synthesis is one very much his own even though particular strands of it may be identified in terms of Christianity, Zen Buddhism or Vedanta" (pp. 295–296).[8] Another variation is Keightley's (1986) reading of Watts as an apophatic theologian because his texts exhibit the intention of "an intellectual yoga" emancipating the mind from enslavement to conceptual thinking. Likewise, Smith (2010) contended that Watts' vital contemporary significance for religious and theological studies is with reference to the "negative canon."

WATTS AS CONTEMPLATIVE MYSTIC

Alan Watts engaged a spiritual formation involving studies of Christian mysticism while preparing for Episcopal ordination as a priest. This included his translation and commentary on *The Theologia Mystica of Saint Dionysius* (Watts, 1944). In his essay on "The Meaning of Priesthood," Watts (1946) said "the privilege of priesthood is simply to be able to have the joy of giving to others the supreme gift of the Incarnation—union with God" (p. 23). In an era populated by neopragmatists reducing contemplative experience to affect, and positivists denying the reality of mysticism all together, Wheelwright (1953) considered Watts to be one of the few contemporary philosophers for whom contemplative reflection precedes action in the world. Bancroft (1989) included Watts in her text on *Twentieth-Century Mystics and Sages*. Alan was portrayed as deeply moved by his own mystical experiences of ego transcendence from which he forged a unique contemplative approach that joined Eastern and Western religious traditions. Nordstrom and Pilgrim (1980) offered a dissenting view by contending that Watts' mystical experiences were shallow and his contemplative writings were off the mark and misinformed. He was therefore called a "wayward" mystic. In a similar vein, Krishna (1975) suggested that Watts' mystical consciousness was not fully complete, his lifestyle revealing certain "dangers of partial awareness" (p. 96). Weidenbaum (2008), moreover, complained that Watts romanticized mysticism. In contrast, Foster (1986) argued that Watts was "a Western Bodhisattva" serving as an example for individuals who are wrestling with their innermost spiritual wisdom. Along similar lines, Guy (1994) suggested that Watts was a mystic in spirit and had the incomparable aptitude for expressing mystical insights with utmost clarity. Thus, Creel (2001) described Watts (1975a) as a twentieth-century example of the "mystical motive" in scholarly discourse.

WATTS AS ZENNIST

Watts' reputation is closely tied to his writings and lectures on Zen Buddhism. *The Spirit of Zen* (Watts, 1936) is considered the "first major attempt by a Westerner to write on the subject" (Humphreys, 1994, p. 15). *The Way of Zen* (Watts, 1957) was called the most comprehensible introductory overview of Zen Buddhism in the English language (Ellwood, 1981). According to Ellwood, "we cannot think of . . . Zen in America without putting Alan Watts in the foreground" (p. 152). Labeling Alan Watts as a "popularizer" of Zen is common practice (e.g., Oldmeadow, 2004; Szasz, 2000). This popular connection to Zen afforded his guru status among the nonconformists of the 1950s and 1960s (Ballantyne, 1989). His take on Zen was one of three styles of Zen Buddhism in the United States in the 1960s, along side monastic Buddhism and Thomas Merton's "dialogical approach" (Swearer, 1973). Swearer said Watts' style of Zen was an "accommodation approach" derived from a fusion of Eastern and Western sources. This blended Zen was criticized as unfaithful to, and incompatible with, a traditional Japanese Zen Buddhist orthodoxy (Nordstrom & Pilgrim, 1980). However, a rejoinder to Nordstrom and Pilgrim emphasized that Watts' view of Zen was neither the bohemian affectation of American "Beat Zen" nor the monastic regimentation of Japanese "Square Zen," but instead reflected the Daoist inclinations of ancient Chinese Zen masters (Columbus, 1985). Watts is often ascribed the opinion that meditative discipline is not necessary for Zen realization, a position referred to as "the Alan Watts heresy" (Sharf, 2005, p. 284) and "freestyle Buddhism" (Anderson, 2003, p. 86). Given this apparent heretical approach, he is sometimes interpreted as propounding an "intellectual and theoretical" Zen (Yamada, 2009, p. 221). Despite its seeming intellectualism, Coleman (2002) described Watts as presenting "a sophisticated picture of Zen and its subversive view of human nature" (p. 188).

WATTS AS PHILOSOPHER

Watts (1973b) described himself as an "eccentric and non-academic philosopher" (p. 5). Yet he offered scholarly critiques of positivist philosophy (Watts, 1953b) and continued advocating for a "philosophy beyond words" (Watts, 1975a) amid the upsurge of postmodern philosophies of language in the 1960s and 1970s. He was offering, in Beidler's (1995) view, "a semiotic sense of understanding . . . at the phenomenological intersection of words and things" and thus providing an alternative to the crisis of "infinite indeterminacies" unfolding in postmodern Western philosophy (p. 199). In their "Framework for Comparative Philosophy," Gupta and Mohanty (2000) suggested that Watts construed Western philosophy as propounding an artifactual model of the world, whereas he saw Indian philosophy reflecting a dramatic model, and Chinese philosophy an organismic model. A study appraising the logical consistency within and between philosophical ideas contained in his writings concluded that Watts has too many unexamined assumptions in his works resulting in hasty jumps from limited data to across-the-board judgments (Suligoj, 1975). Another critical evaluation, informed by a fundamentalist Christianity, concluded that Watts' philosophy falls short of rational credibility (Clark, 1978). Clark contended that Watts rejected the primacy of reason in favor of mysticism and therefore had nothing relevant to say about reality because all significant communicative processes are governed by rules of logic. In contrast, Brannigan (1988) proposed that acts of systematizing Alan Watts' philosophical works are "presumptuous" and shallow arrangements at best. Watts, he pointed out, was a philosopher of the intangible. Brannigan moved instead to render the feeling of what Watts had to share with his audience. He saw in Watts' writings a nondual philosophy substantively informed by the doctrine of *advaita* from Hindu Vedanta and the concept of *polarity* found in Chinese philosophical thought. More recently, Smith (2010) considered Watts' philosophy to be optimally appreciated as a distinctly modern nondualism rather than as a conduit for the expression of traditional Asian thinking.

WATTS AS PSYCHOLOGIST

Alan Watts is considered "one of the first to publicly point out that useful links could be developed" between Asian religions and Western psychology (Watts & Snelling, 1997, p. 5). In the *Handbook of General Psychology*, Wolman (1973) described Watts as an "apostle of rapprochement" between East and West (p. 833). Watts' eloquent portrayals of Daoism, Buddhism, and Hinduism made him a "Titan" of the humanistic psychology movement in the 1960s (Klee, 1970). He was also a major "nascent" influence on the emerging field of transpersonal psychology (Ferrer, 2002, p. 6), where his writings became "bibles of the consciousness movement" (Taylor, 2000, p. 275). The field of clinical psychology felt his influence most deeply when his "pioneering work . . . brought Eastern ideas of consciousness into the world of psychotherapy" (Lebow, 2006, p. 80; Santee, 2007). The eminent psychotherapist, Jay Haley (1992), cited a series of Watts' lectures on Western psychology and Eastern philosophy as substantively informing the trajectory of his and others' professional development in the early 1950s (see also, Watts, 1953a, 1956). Likewise, the renowned Jungian analyst, June Singer, credited Watts as profoundly affecting her understanding of Analytic Psychology (Rountree, 2005; Singer, 1983). Moreover, Bankart (2003) identified the publication of *Psychotherapy East and West* (Watts, 1961) as a "foundational event" in the contemporary expression of Buddhism in Western Psychology:

> Psychotherapy East and West was a far-reaching call for psychology and psychotherapy to facilitate the liberation of individual souls from the suffering resulting from suffocating conformity of a joyless, sexless, over-analyzed and vastly over-controlling society. He rejected the Freudian call for what he had called the domination of Eros by reason, and called, in its place, for Eros expressing itself with reason. The book was, for all extents and purposes, a vivid and heartfelt rejoinder to Freud's Civilization and Its Discontents. (p. 62)

The *zeitgeist approach* to intellectual history indicates that eminent individuals yield vital contributions to various fields of study because of their historical context (Teo, 2005). A key issue is that social climate and cultural circumstance influence the structure, meaning, and relevance of any particular piece of work. Alan Watts is no exception to this *"spirit of the times"* view to understanding the emergence of intellectual products. A reviewer of *Myth and Ritual in Christianity* (Watts, 1953c), for example, described the text as indicative of the circumstances Western religions inhabit since the issues addressed in the text turn up repeatedly in contemporary examinations of the subject matter (H. Watts, 1954). Similarly, Perry (1972/2007) considered *Beyond Theology* (Watts, 1964) as "typically symptomatic" of its time. Roszak (1969) explained Watts' ascendance in the 1960s counterculture as an interaction between his uncanny ability to render Zen accessible and a population of young people imbued with a spur-of-the-moment yearning to oppose the cheerless, greedy, and self-obsessive inclinations of the modern technological world. Watts has been characterized as exhibiting a distinctly twentieth-century reading of Zen (Wright, 2000, pp. 126–127). Practitioners of Zen in the early twentieth-century West were looking to differentiate themselves against the ground of European Romanticism, and Zen readings were therefore interpreted through the lens of Western individualism. Wright identified the title of Watts' autobiography, *In My Own Way*, as an extreme case in point. Watts is therefore viewed as belonging to a lineage of scholars articulating a "modern Buddhism" (Lopez, 2002) and "Buddhist modernism" (McMahan, 2008). Moreover, Watts' considerations of Asian mysticism have been criticized as misappropriations imbued with the assumptions of Orientalism and neo-Orientalism (Bartholomeusz, 1998; Tong, 1981). A final example is Woodhead's (2001) consideration of Alan Watts' life and work as a revealing illustration of what she has termed the "turn to life" that is endemic to present-day spiritual and religious practice. Watts is described as rejecting a somber, guilt-ridden, and repressive Christian religion and turning instead toward a free-thinking, sensual, and affirmative spirituality. This "turn" is considered by Woodhead as indicating one of the most noteworthy developments in Western culture since World War II.

HERE AND NOW

This volume is a collection of original essays written by eminent scholars. The story of how the book unfolded has as much to do with intuition and spontaneity as with reason and logistics—a plot line that undoubtedly would have resonated deeply with Alan Watts. The idea for the book emerged when Peter Columbus was on sabbatical at the Unitarian Universalist Rowe Conference Center. An exchange of brainstorming emails with Don Rice led to questions about Watts' legacy in the twenty-first century. Conjecture emerged concerning Stanley Krippner's perspective given his position as Alan W. Watts Professor of Psychology at Saybrook Graduate School and long-time association with Watts. Ralph Metzner, another former colleague of Watts, was scheduled to give an invited address at the University of West Georgia where Rice is stationed as chair of psychology, and was immediately invited to participate in the book project. Metzner recommended contacting Chungliang Huang.[9] Alan Pope, the "resident Buddhist" in the Psychology Department at West Georgia, climbed on board as well. Michael Brannigan and Alan Keightley each authored outstanding books on Watts in the 1980s, which sparked curiosity as to their latest viewpoints in the new millennium. Likewise, Ralph Hood's renowned expertise with the psychology of mysticism, Miriam Levering's insightful research on women in religion, and Kaisa Puhakka's depth of experience with Zen Buddhism and clinical psychology came to mind at once.

The editors invited these esteemed colleagues to contribute original chapters with general thoughtfulness to the following questions regarding Alan Watts' legacy: How do his writings appear in the context of twenty-first–century scholarship? In what ways does Watts inform psychology, philosophy, and religion in the new millennium? Are there domains of his scholarship, or particular nuances of his work, that have heretofore been neglected, unrecognized, or ignored? Moreover, in what ways has Watts informed one's own scholarly sensibilities, perceptions, and activities? The resulting volume is less a systematic study than a compilation of individual chapters, each with a unique angle on the life and work of Alan Watts. Yet there is a pattern to the organization and trajectory of the text that emerged organically from the writings themselves, beginning with Ralph Hood's chapter. Hood contributed an insightful chapter on four key issues in the psychology of religion anticipated by Watts in his autobiographical writings about his personal spiritual journey. As it turned out, all of our contributors submitted chapters that fit, broadly speaking, into Hood's four themes. Following Hood's contribution, therefore, are chapters addressing (a) perennial philosophy and psychology (Keightley, Chapter 2 and Columbus, Chapter 3), (b) psychedelic research and experience (Krippner, Chapter 4 and Metzner, Chapter 5), (c) embodied consciousness (Rice, Chapter 6; Brannigan, Chapter 7; and Levering, Chapter 8), and (d) psychospiritual transformation (Pope, Chapter 9; Puhakka, Chapter 10; and Huang, Chapter 11).

Hood brings Watts' contemporary relevance immediately to the fore with his chapter entitled "Alan Watts' Anticipation of Four Major Debates in the Psychology of Religion." Hood maintains that Watts' personal spiritual quest, as expressed in his autobiography and reflected in his popular writings, presaged noteworthy topics currently interesting scholars focused on the psychological study of religion. The first topic concerns the veracity of perennial psychology. Watts, like William James before him, contended there are universal bases to mystical experiences independent of cultural and contextual interpretation. The second debate involves the degree of relationship between religion, psychedelic drugs, and mystical experience. Watts asserted that LSD and the like could afford experiences of mystical states indistinguishable from those attained by religious practice when a person has the appropriate mindset and socioenvironmental setting. The third debate is on the extent to which eroticism and mysticism are connected. Watts experienced an intimate connection and described it clearly in his writings. There is, finally, the religion versus spirituality debate about whether religious institutions constrain or enable spiritual experience. The trajectory of Watts' personal development was toward spiritual experience free from institutional control or code of belief. There is now a body of empirical research supporting Watts' positions on each of these debates. The quirk of fate in all this, suggests Hood, "is that academics whose disdain of popular works kept Alan from a broader appreciation among scholars nevertheless belatedly championed his views in the academy."

In "Alan Watts: The Immediate Magic of God," Alan Keightley traces a thread of "direct, immediate mystical realization" running through Watts' theological writings. By the 1940s, Watts was steeped in Christian mysticism and saw its apophatic approach to religious experience as commensurate with the negative metaphysics of Buddhism. He envisioned that Christianity could absorb and synthesize Asian spiritual traditions and thereby re-form itself anew as a truly "catholic" or universal religion. By 1950, however, Watts was disillusioned with the institution of the Episcopal Church and its orthodox views of Christian doctrine. He resigned from the church because of its declarations of exclusivity as the highest religion and its assertion of the total distinction between God and creation. A rapprochement occurred in the 1960s when Watts saw that Christianity could be interpreted in the context of Hinduism as a radical journey of God getting lost in a Self-made illusion or *Maya*. From this point of view the absolute distinction between the Creator and the created is less real than apparent. The mundane world is therefore wholly sacred. The sacred quality of the mundane world allowed Watts to espouse an "atheism in the name of God" in response to the "death of God" theology of the 1960s. Keightley concludes that Watts saw spiritual treasures in "the ordinary, everyday, which are transparent to the divine transcendence, for those who are awake."

In "Phenomenological Exegeses of Alan Watts: Transcendental and Hermeneutic Strategies," Peter Columbus outlines philosophical methods inherent to a pair of texts where Watts claimed to be presenting Asian wisdom traditions in styles accessible to contemporary Westerners. Watts implicitly used a Husserlian transcendental phenomenological method for exploring anxiety in *The Wisdom of Insecurity* (1951), and employed a tacit hermeneutic phenomenology for understanding identity in *The Book* (1966). Both embedded strategies were engaged toward facilitating mystical experiences for his readers. How is Watts to be understood as a purveyor of Eastern philosophies in light of his appropriation of Western phenomenology? The short answer is that *philosophia perennis* was a *point of departure* toward applying transcendental phenomenology in *The Wisdom of Insecurity*. In light of Christian claims to exclusivity, however, Watts saw perennialism as a *point of arrival* via the hermeneutic "fusing" of Eastern and Western perspectives in *The Book*. The notion of Watts as a "phenomenologist" is largely unrecognized but seeing him as such allows for reconsidering his antecedent and contemporary influence on humanistic and transpersonal psychology. He is usually recognized with reference to Buddhism and psychotherapy but can now be viewed in terms of his holistic approach, phenomenological methods of inquiry, and subject matters of anxiety and identity. Thus, contrary to Watts' often quoted recommendation to hang up the telephone upon receiving the message, Columbus concludes that his texts are rich with implicit influences that remain available for discovery by contemporary and future scholars.

Krippner documents "The Psychedelic Adventures of Alan Watts." Watts' perspective on psychedelics ranged from an initial esthetic-perceptual experience to an eventual recognition of the substances as religious sacraments, a view traced to his spiritual formation and training in the Anglican/Episcopal church. Krippner met Watts in the context of Timothy Leary's research at Harvard University. Krippner appreciates Alan's mentoring, details the influence of LSD on one of Alan's concurrent projects, and shares their mutual concerns about Leary's approach to psychedelics. Krippner submits that Watts' writings and lectures in the 1960s legitimized the ontological status of psychedelic experience and, by integrating psychedelics with Eastern thinking and Western science, laid a foundation for subsequent spectrums, models, and typologies of consciousness in psychology. Additionally, Watts anticipated the issue of *neuropolitics* in reference to the debate about who controls and dispenses psychedelic chemicals. He argued that psychedelic usage should be constitutionally protected as a religious practice and the substances made readily available to scholars and students of religious experience. Thanks in part to Watts' advocacy many years earlier, there is a resurgence of entheogenic research in the United States and around the world. Krippner goes on to contrast Watts' occasional use of psychedelics with his all-too-frequent use of alcohol. There is a curious paradox of alcohol, tobacco, and Eastern philosophy in Alan's adolescence and young adulthood that presaged his lifestyle in later years. But, Krippner writes, "while rife with contradiction, the complex interaction of his life in his work, and vice versa, was partially responsible for the fertility of his thought."

Metzner illuminates further details of Alan Watts' psychedelic journeys "From The Joyous Cosmology to The Watercourse Way." Metzner was a key member of Leary's psychedelic research team at Harvard University where he first met Watts in 1961. The chapter begins with a collation of recollections about the early associations among Watts, Metzner, and Leary. Metzner then details the "experiential riches" contained in *The Joyous Cosmology* (Watts, 1962). Watts' text on psychedelics remains a singular achievement in a research field marked by controversy. Indeed, Leary's research program at Harvard was

eventually wracked by accusations of supervisory negligence and lack of scientific rigor. Here Watts offered intellectual support for Leary's innovative
existential-transactional approach by arguing its consistency with cutting-edge
scientific theory and methodology. Metzner concludes by elaborating Watts'
transition away from psychedelics toward renewed interest in Daoist philosophy. Watts devoted a great deal of time at his mountain cottage to writing
his final essays and books, including *Tao: The Watercourse Way* (Watts, 1975b).
Metzner conveys his gratitude for Watts' mentorship at Harvard University
while continuing Alan's legacy at the California Institute of Integral Studies,
the outgrowth of the American Academy of Asian Studies where Alan served
as professor and academic dean in the 1950s.

In "Alan Watts and the Neuroscience of Transcendence," Rice considers
Watts' descriptions of transcendent or mystical experience, sometimes called
"cosmic consciousness," in relation to contemporary neuroscience research.
First, Rice sets the stage for his discussion by elaborating six variations of
research on the neuroscience of transcendence. Contemporary advancements
in neuroscience research technologies are allowing some adventurous neuroscientists to investigate transcendent/spiritual-like experiences and corresponding
changes in brain activity related to cognitive, emotional, and perceptual processes affected by meditation or ingestion of hallucinogenic substances. Yet these
research programs have been criticized for either reducing spiritual experience
to biology or, conversely, introducing supernaturalism into natural science. Rice
points out that Watts bypassed reductionism and supernaturalism by couching
his writings on the nature of transcendence in terms of Gestalt psychology.
The trajectory of Watts' Gestalt psychology of transcendent experience into the
twenty-first century is traced in relation to the body–mind problem, cognitive-
Gestalt neuroscience, quantum psychology, and reflections on the extent to
which a neuroscience of transcendence can fully know its subject matter.

Brannigan expands on the body–mind issue with his contribution entitled
"Listening to the Rain: Embodied Awareness in Watts." Brannigan draws the
distinction between the immediacy of pre-reflective bodily awareness and the
reflective processes about an experience. Pre-reflective and reflective modes of
awareness are intertwined in everyday experience but a problem arises when
the latter is confused with the former: We lose touch with the sensuality of our
lives. This problem is evident in "disembodied religions" of the Judeo-Christian
heritage, which emphasize dogma and liturgical regimen while considering
bodily experience as the basis for moral transgression. As exemplified by his
commentary on the erotic spirituality depicted on the ancient Hindu temple of
Konarak, Watts invited religious men and women to experience the wonders
of existence through sensitivity to bodily experience. Brannigan describes Watts
as advocating and living a "sensual mysticism" that informs a contemporary
critique of technological culture, especially communication technologies. Like
blurring the distinction between pre-reflective and reflective experience, Bran-

nigan suggests it is easy to get caught amid communications tools and lose sight of an embodied connection to immediacy and interpersonal relations. Hence, phenomena such as "phoneslaughter," referring to vehicular deaths related to use of cell phones while driving. Watts challenges us "to observe things simply *as they are* without imposing layers of interpretation and judgment, to cultivate an embodied awareness, a persistent mindfulness," like listening to the rain.

Miriam Levering offers a contemporary view of "Alan Watts on Nature, Gender, and Sexuality." She describes three themes from *Nature, Man and Woman* (Watts, 1958b) anticipating and informing trends in the North American counterculture of the 1960s and 1970s, and which remain relevant for current scholarly discourse:

1. The interrelations of nature and gender,

2. The polarity of men and women, and

3. The confluence of sexuality and spirituality.

Levering then offers critical reflections in light of present-day scholarship. Watts is seen as an important precursor of the eco-feminist movement despite the fact the Christian feminist theologians could not accept his unitive mysticism. The polarity of men and women is considered with reference to Luce Irigaray's notion of "at least two" sexes, which intimates that polarity is a premature delimitation. Finally, Watts' integration of sexuality and spirituality borrowed heavily from Asian tantric systems and is critiqued for inspiring a Western "neo-tantra," which glorifies sex experience rather than enriching spiritual development. Levering suggests that "Watts' introduction of serious Indian and Chinese cultural practices to a wide audience in *Nature, Man and Woman* risks being seen as an insufficiently respectful appropriation of expressions from another culture for purposes for which they were not intended."

Alan Pope reflects on "Contributions and Conundrums in the Psycho-spiritual Transformation of Alan Watts." In the first half of his chapter, Pope celebrates and reviews some of the major themes in Watts' elucidation of the nature of psychospiritual transformation. These themes include the following:

1. The cultural and historical myths that guide perceptual activity,

2. The value of poetic language for expressing that which otherwise could not be expressed,

3. The issue of death,

4. The illusion of the self,

5. The field of awareness, and

6. The nature of liberation.

The second half of the chapter is a critical assessment of "Watts in Practice," addressing his approach to psychospiritual transformation in relation to phenomenology, Buddhist philosophy, and the *zeitgeist* in which he lived and worked. Pope completes this section of his chapter with a consideration of "Watts as Conundrum." The term *conundrum* refers to the paradoxical and mysterious nature of Watts' bohemian lifestyle. To what extent was he personally transformed through his mystical studies and spiritual explorations? Was his lifestyle symptomatic of unresolved neurosis or akin to the *crazy wisdom* of Chogyam Trungpa? Regardless of the ambiguity, or perhaps because of it, concludes Pope, Watts' contributions to the contemporary understanding of psychospiritual transformation are "profound and far-reaching."

Kaisa Puhakka draws on many years of Zen study and expertise as a clinical psychologist to consider "Buddhist Wisdom in the West: A Fifty-Year Perspective on the Contributions of Alan Watts." Buddhism, especially Zen, was a spiritual tradition central to Watts' life and work. Although not always a disciplined practitioner of sitting meditation or koan study, he was instrumental in bringing it to America. The Zen experience is beyond words and concepts, but Watts was uniquely able to convey its essence to twentieth-century Western audiences through his eloquent oratory and writing style. Puhakka suggests that Watts saw Buddhism as primarily a critique of the culture in which it happens to be situated at any given time. He therefore offers a needed corrective to disconcerting trends in the twenty-first century West. Informed by the Middle Way teachings of Buddhism, Watts allows for deconstructing the extreme (absolute) relativism in academic and popular thinking that reduces people to their contexts. Puhakka writes: "The Middle Way teachings demonstrate again and again that there really is nothing that can be claimed as absolutely true," including the relativistic thinking of constructivist philosophy. Watts, moreover, offsets contemporary tendencies to see Buddhism as either an adjunct to psychotherapy or as a compartment of therapeutic technique. He instead embraced a larger understanding of Buddhism that expands the horizons of Western psychotherapies by exposing the cultural premises on which they are based.

Chungliang Al Huang fittingly concludes this volume with "Watercourse Way: Still Flowing with Alan Watts." Huang, of course, put the finishing touch on Watts' (1975b) final book, *Tao: The Watercourse Way*, after Watts died unexpectedly in autumn 1973. Huang's chapter contains personal stories and anecdotes counterbalancing the analytical papers by other colleagues. Watts' friendship and mentoring ushered Huang into the human potential movement of the 1960s. Huang recounts various episodes from their work together and highlights Watts' infectious enthusiasm for his subject matter. Watts' most poignant teachings concerned "the wisdom of insecurity"—the process of finding equanimity in situations and times of uncertainty. These teachings guided Huang along his own path of integrating his Eastern background with his

Western life, especially in appropriating a sense of competence with the English language as he embarked on writing his first book. Huang recounts with mirth and irony two of Watts' alcohol-inspired speaking engagements but laments that Watts too often used liquor to cope with his heavy work schedule and seemed to become a victim of a *"yang-*dominant world." However, Watts' "delight with life was founded on his willingness to acknowledge the faults underlying his footing in the world. He was a clay-footed Buddha, but those feet of clay were positioned directly on the path of life."

AN EMERGING LEGACY

Through the chapters in this volume, Watts' legacy may be seen with greater clarity and insight. This legacy embodies Watts' living expression of the human condition shared by all—from the depths of suffering exemplified by his struggles with alcohol to the heights of transpersonal awareness and mystical consciousness. Personal suffering brought him to "the wisdom of insecurity" that infused his writings and lectures toward overcoming the "taboo against knowing" a cosmic sense of identity. His legacy intertwines contemporary scholarship on mysticism, entheogens, embodied awareness and sexuality, ecofeminism, spirituality and neuroscience, humanistic and transpersonal psychology, phenomenology and hermeneutics, Buddhism and psychotherapy, Daoism in the West, and psychospiritual transformation. Alan was not an "organization man" but he nevertheless has an institutional legacy: the California Institute of Integral Studies, the Alan W. Watts Professorship at Saybrook Graduate School, Esalen Institute, and Huang's Living Tao Foundation. And then there is the genealogical legacy of the mystical counterculture: his friendship and mentoring of Krippner, Metzner, and Huang who, in turn, affect the lives of many students. Finally, there is Watts' body of work, an abundance of writings and lectures with continuing resonance for untold numbers of readers. Perhaps Watts is not the "be all" or "end all" of contemporary scholarship in psychology, philosophy, and religion, but his voice and words offer his audiences an opening to the next moment of their lives. This opening is a radically new beginning to personal and transpersonal experience. At this moment, here and now, the new beginning is "Alan Watts' Anticipation of Four Major Debates in the Psychology of Religion" in Chapter 1.

NOTES

1. One biographer, writing in the 1970s, suggested that Watts was "among the most enduring" writers of his time and continues to "live through a body of work that has a very high vitality" (Stuart, 1983, p. xii).

2. Howe and Mitrinovic are likely the least recognizable names on this list. See Edwards (2006) for an account of Howe's contributions to psychology, and Howe

(2009) for a selection of writings (see also, Watts, 1937/1997b). Rigby (2006) provides an exposition of Mitrinovic's life and philosophical ideas. Watts published in the *Alan Watts Journal* an essay by Rutherford (1973) outlining aspects Mitrinovic's views on Christianity.

3. Film prizes include a Blue Ribbon at the American Film Festival and an Award of Merit from *Landers Film Reviews* (Hartley & Watts, 1967) plus the Gold Award (Hartley & Watts, 1968) and Silver Award (Hartley & Watts, 1969) at the New York International Film Festival. *Alan Watts: Art of Meditation* (Hartley & Watts, 1971) was a Finalist at the American Film Festival.

4. The "sensualist" label on Watts seems to have lasting (although not necessarily *ad hominem*) currency in popular Buddhist literature. For example, see Tweti (2007).

5. In *The Joyous Cosmology*, Watts (1962) reported this psychedelic-induced insight:

> I began to see my whole life as an act of duplicity—the confused, helpless, hungry and hideously sensitive little embryo at the root of me having learned, step by step, to comply, placate, bully, wheedle, flatter, bluff and cheat my way into being taken for a person of competence and reliability. (p. 43)

6. Watts (1973b) referred to one particular professional academic organization as an "in-group of . . . philological nit-pickers and scholarly drudges" who "dissolve all creative interest into acidulated pedantry" (p. 165). Yet the following insight by Richard Quinney (1988) may point to the source of Watts' criticisms of academe:

> As we mature we move beyond the rational and linear mode of thought to a more intuitive and transcendent mode. As we make the shift we lose the grasping and craving self of the individualized ego and we find ourselves in the realm of the universal Self. It is not natural—it is unhealthy—for the academic, the intellectual . . . to continue strictly in the rational mode of speculative and dualistic thought as he or she matures, although this is the approved and rewarded form for the modern academic. To continue solely in the rational mode of thought is retrogressive for the maturing person. Yet we are expected to continue in a thought form that is appropriate only for the middle stages of a discipline and of life. (pp. 104–105)

7. However, a reviewer of the Hartshorne and Reese (1953) text lamented: "the allocation of space is not always proportionate to the significance of the thinker: for example, less than two pages are given to quotations from the Buddha and more than nine are accorded Alan Watts" (Nagley, 1955, p. 365).

8. Elsewhere Swearer (1970) suggested that "Alan Watts will never be a theologian's theologian" (p. 139) because his writings are too idiosyncratic.

9. Having the participation of Krippner, Metzner, and Huang in this volume is an opportune circumstance. Toward the end of his autobiography, Watts (1973b) commented:

> the closer I get to the present time, the harder it is to see things in perspective. . . . I feel I must wait another ten years to find out just what I was

doing, in the field of psychotherapy, with . . . Stanley Krippner. . . . and in the formation of the mystical counterculture with . . . Ralph Metzner . . . and Chung-liang Huang. (pp. 415–416)

Watts, of course, died in 1973 thus never offering extensive reflections on his later years.

REFERENCES

Akhilananda, S. (1948). [Review of the book *Behold the Spirit*]. *Journal of Bible and Religion, 16*(3),185–186.

Anderson, W. T. (1983). *The upstart spring: Esalen and the American awakening.* Reading, MA: Addison-Wesley.

Anderson, W. T. (2003). *The next enlightenment: Integrating East and West in a new vision of human evolution.* New York: St. Martin's Press.

Baker, R. (1974). One hundredth day ceremony for Alan Watts. In L. Ferlinghetti (Ed.), *City Lights anthology* (pp. 138–139). San Francisco: City Lights Books.

Ballantyne, E. C. (1989). Alan Watts. In C. H. Lippy (Ed.), *Twentieth-century shapers of American popular religion* (pp. 437–445). Westport, CT: Greenwood Press.

Bancroft, A. (1989). *Twentieth-century mystics and sages.* London: Arkana.

Bankart, C. P. (2003). Five manifestations of the Buddha in the West: A brief history. In K. H. Dockett, G. R. Dudley-Grant, & C. P. Bankart (Eds.), *Psychology and Buddhism: From individual to global community* (pp. 45–70). New York: Kluwer Academic Publishers.

Bartholomeusz, T. (1998). Spiritual wealth and neo-orientalism. *Journal of Ecumenical Studies, 35*(1), 19–32.

Beidler, P. D. (1995). *Scriptures for a generation: What we were reading in the '60s.* Athens: University of Georgia Press.

Brannigan, M. C. (1988). *Everywhere and nowhere: The path of Alan Watts.* New York: Peter Lang.

Christian, W. (1950). Some varieties of religious belief. *The Review of Metaphysics, 4*(4), 595–616.

Clark, D. K. (1978). *The pantheism of Alan Watts.* Downers Grove, IL: Inter-varsity Press.

Coleman, J. W. (2002). *The new Buddhism: The western transformation of an ancient tradition.* New York: Oxford University Press.

Columbus, P. J. (1985). A response to Nordstrom and Pilgrim's critique of Alan Watts' mysticism. *The Humanistic Psychologist, 13*(1), 28–34.

Columbus, P. J., & Boerger, M. A. (2002). Defining popular iconic metaphor. *Psychological Reports, 90,* 579–582.

Cranmer-Byng, L., & Watts, A. W. (Eds.). (1937–1941). *Wisdom of the East* (multiple volumes). London: John Murray.

Creel, R. (2001). *Thinking philosophically: An introduction to critical reflection and rational dialogue.* Oxford, UK: Blackwell.

Eager Exponent of Zen. (1961, April 16). *Life Magazine, 50*(16), 88A–93.

Edwards, I. C. (2006). *Truth as relationship: The psychology of E. Graham Howe*. Unpublished doctoral dissertation, Duquesne University, Pittsburgh, PA). Retrieved from http://etd1.library.duq.edu/theses/available/etd-03132006-144607/unrestricted/EdwardsDissertation.pdf.

Ellwood, R. (1981). *Alternative altars: Unconventional and eastern spirituality in America*. Chicago: University of Chicago Press.

Ferlinghetti, L. (1974). Riding notes. In L. Ferlinghetti (Ed.), *City Lights anthology* (pp. 136–137). San Francisco: City Lights Books.

Ferrer, J. N. (2002). *Revisioning transpersonal theory: A participatory vision of human spirituality*. Albany: State University of New York Press.

Foster, M. (1986). A Western Bodhisattva. In R. Miller & J. Kenny (Eds.), *Fireball and the lotus* (pp. 135–149). Santa Fe, NM: Bear.

Fuller, A. R. (2008). *Psychology and religion: Classical theorists and contemporary developments* (4th ed.). Lanham, MD: Rowan & Littlefield.

Furlong, M. (2001). *Zen effects: The life of Alan Watts*. Woodstock, VT: Skylight Paths.

Gupta, B., & Mohanty, J. N. (2000). General introduction: A framework for comparative philosophy. In B. Gupta & J. N. Mohanty (Eds.), *Philosophical questions: East and West* (pp. xi–xxiv). Lanham, MD: Rowan & Littlefield.

Guy, D. (1994). Alan Watts reconsidered. *Tricycle: The Buddhist Review, 4*(1), 10–15.

Haley, J. (1992). Zen and the art of therapy. In J. K. Zeig (Ed.), *The evolution of psychotherapy: The second conference* (pp. 24–38). New York: Brunner/Mazel.

Harding, D. (1984). Alan Watts—Sage or anti-sage? *The Middle Way, 58*(4), 221–223.

Hartley, E. (Director)., & Watts, A. W. (Narrator). (1967). *The mood of Zen* [Motion picture]. (Available from Hartley Film Foundation, 49 Richmondville Ave., Suite 204, Westport, CT 06880.)

Hartley, E. (Director)., & Watts, A. W. (Narrator). (1968). *Buddhism, man and nature* [Motion picture]. (Available from Hartley Film Foundation, 49 Richmondville Ave., Suite 204, Westport, CT 06880.)

Hartley, E. (Director)., & Watts, A. W. (Narrator). (1969). *Zen and now* [Motion picture]. (Available from Hartley Film Foundation, 49 Richmondville Ave., Suite 204, Westport, CT 06880.)

Hartley, E. (Director)., & Watts, A. W. (Narrator). (1971). *Alan Watts: Art of meditation* [Motion picture]. (Available from Hartley Film Foundation, 49 Richmondville Ave., Suite 204, Westport, CT 06880.)

Hartshorne, C., & Reese, W. L. (1953). *Philosophers speak of God*. Chicago: University of Chicago Press.

Herrigel, E. (1974). *The method of Zen* (A. W. Watts, Ed., R. F. C. Hull, Trans.). New York: Vintage Books.

Howe, E. G. (2009). *The druid of Harley Street: Selected writings of E. Graham Howe* (W. Stranger, Ed.). Berkeley, CA: North Atlantic Books.

Humphreys, C. (1994). *Zen comes West: The present and future of Zen in Western society* (2nd ed.). Surrey, UK: Curzon Press.

Keightley, A. (1986). *Into every life a little Zen must fall: A Christian philosopher looks to Alan Watts and the East.* London: Wisdom Publications.

Kerouac, J. (1958). *Dharma bums.* New York: Harcourt Brace.

Klee, J. B. (1970, September). *The humanist perspective.* Paper presented to the American Psychological Association, Miami Beach, FL. [Reprinted in I. D. Welch, G. A. Tate, & F. Richards (Eds.). (1978). *Humanistic psychology: A source book* (pp. 1–12). Buffalo, NY: Prometheus Books.]

Kripal, J. J. (2007). *Esalen: America and the religion of no religion.* Chicago: University of Chicago Press.

Krishna, G. (1975). The dangers of partial awareness: Comments on Alan Watts' autobiography. In *The awakening of Kundalini* (pp. 96–105). New York: Dutton.

Lawson, M. (1988). Growing up lightly: Rascal-gurus and American educational thought. *Educational Philosophy and Theory, 20*(1), 37–49.

Leary, T. (1998). *The politics of ecstasy.* Berkeley, CA: Ronin.

Lebow, J. (2006). *Research for the psychotherapist: From science to practice.* New York: Routledge.

Lopez, D. S. (2002). *A modern Buddhist bible: Essential readings from East and West.* Boston: Beacon Press.

Lott, T. (1999). A guru for those who don't trust gurus. *New Statesman, 128* (8/30), 24–25.

Mahoney, S. (1958). The prevalence of Zen. *The Nation, 187*(14), 311–315.

McMahan, D. L. (2008). *The making of Buddhist modernism.* New York: Oxford University Press.

Nagley, W. E. (1955). [Review of the book *Philosophers speak of God*]. *Philosophy East and West, 4*(4), 365–366.

The new ministry: Bringing God back to life. (1969, December 26). *Time.* Retrieved from http://www.time.com/time/magazine/article/0,9171,941816-6,00.html.

Nordstrom, L., & Pilgrim, R. (1980). The wayward mysticism of Alan Watts. *Philosophy East and West, 30,* 381–401.

Northrop, F. S. C. (1947, November 2). [Review of the book *Behold the spirit*]. *Church Times.*

Oldmeadow, H. (2004). *Journeys East: 20ᵗʰ century encounters with Eastern religious traditions.* Bloomington, IN: Wisdom Traditions.

Park, O. (1974). *Oriental ideas in recent religious thought.* Lakemont, GA: CSA Press.

Perry, W. N. (2007). Anti-theology and the riddles of Alcyone. In H. Oldmeadow (Ed.), *Light from the East: Eastern wisdom for the modern West* (pp. 50–65). Bloomington, IN: World Wisdom. (Original work published 1972)

Quinney, R. (1988). Beyond the interpretive: The way of awareness. *Sociological Inquiry, 58*(1), 101–116.

Rigby, A. (2006). *Dmitrije Mitrinovic: A biography* (2nd ed.). York, UK: Sessions.

Roszak, T (1969). *The making of a counter culture: Reflections on the technocratic culture and its youthful opposition.* New York: Anchor Books.

Rountree, C. (2005). Modern woman in search of soul: An interview with June Singer, February 12, 1999. *The San Francisco Jung Institute Journal, 24*(1), 54–72.

Rutherford, H. C. (1973). The religion of Logos and Sophia: From the writings of Dimitrije Mitrinovic on Christianity. *Alan Watts Journal, 2*(3), 1–20.

Sadler, A. W. (1974). The complete Alan Watts. *The Eastern Buddhist* (New Series), 7(2), 121–127.

Santee, R. G. (2007). *An integral approach to counseling: Bridging Chinese thought, evolutionary theory, and stress management.* Thousand Oaks, CA: Sage.

Sharf, R. H. (2005). Buddhist modernism and the rhetoric of meditative experience. In P. Williams (Ed.), *Buddhism: Critical concepts in religious studies* (pp. 255–299). New York: Routledge.

Sibley, D. T. (1984). The legacy of Alan Watts: A personal view. *The Middle Way, 58*(4), 219–220.

Singer, J. (1983). *Energies of Love: Sexuality re-visioned.* Garden City, NY: Anchor Press/ Doubleday.

Smith, D. (2010). The authenticity of Alan Watts. In G. Storhoff & J. Whalen-Bridge (Eds.), *American Buddhism as a way of life* (pp. 13–38). Albany: State University of New York Press.

Stuart, D. (1983). *Alan Watts.* Briarcliff Manor, NY: Stein & Day.

Suligoj, H. (1975). The mystical philosophy of Alan Watts. *International Philosophical Quarterly, 15,* 439–454.

Swearer, D. (1970). *Buddhism in transition.* Philadelphia: Westminster Press.

Swearer, D. (1973). Three modes of Zen in America. *Journal of Ecumenical Studies. 10*(2), 290–303.

Szasz, F. M. (2000). *Religion in the modern American west.* Tucson: University of Arizona Press.

Taylor, E. (2000). *Shadow culture: Psychology and spirituality in America.* Washington, DC: Counterpoint.

Teo. T. (2005). *The critique of psychology: From Kant to postcolonial theory.* New York: Springer.

Tong, B. (1981). Alan Watts was sure one strange kinda Chinaman! *Quilt, 1,* 29–33.

Tweti, M. (2007). The sensualist: The life of Alan Watts. *Tricycle: The Buddhist Review.* Retrieved from http://www.tricycle.com/issues/editors_pick/4029-1.html

Watts, A. W. (1936). *The spirit of Zen: A way of life, work, and art in the Far East.* London: John Murray.

Watts, A. W. (1937). *The legacy of Asia and Western man.* London: John Murray.

Watts, A. W. (1940). *The meaning of happiness: The quest for freedom of the spirit in modern psychology and the wisdom of the East.* New York: Harper & Row.

Watts, A. W. (1941). The problem of faith and works in Buddhism. *Review of Religion, 5*(4), 385–402.

Watts, A. W. (1944). *The theologia mystica of Saint Dionysius.* West Park, NY: Holy Cross Press.

Watts, A. W. (1946). The meaning of priesthood. *Advent Papers,* No. 7. Boston: Church of the Advent.

Watts, A. W. (1947). *Behold the spirit. A study in the necessity of mystical religion.* New York: Pantheon Books.

Watts, A. W. (1950). *The Supreme identity: An essay on Oriental metaphysic and the Christian religion.* New York: Pantheon Books.

Watts, A. W. (1951). *The wisdom of insecurity.* New York: Pantheon Books.

Watts, A. W. (1953a). Asian psychology and modern psychiatry. *American Journal of Psychoanalysis, 13*(1), 25–30.

Watts, A. W. (1953b). The language of metaphysical experience: The sense of non-sense. *Journal of Religious Thought, 10*(2), 132–143.

Watts, A. W. (1953c). *Myth and ritual in Christianity.* New York: Vanguard.

Watts, A. W. (1953d). On philosophical synthesis. *Philosophy East and West, 3,* 99–100.

Watts, A. W. (1956). Convention, conflict, and liberation: Further observations on Asian psychology and modern psychiatry. *American Journal of Psychoanalysis, 16*(1), 63–67.

Watts, A. W. (1957). *The way of Zen.* New York. Pantheon

Watts, A. W. (1958a). Beat Zen, square Zen, and Zen. *Chicago Review, 12*(2), 3–11.

Watts, A. W. (1958b). *Nature, man and woman.* New York: Pantheon.

Watts, A. W. (1960). *This is it, and other essays on Zen and spiritual experience.* New York: Pantheon.

Watts, A. W. (1961). *Psychotherapy, East and West.* New York: Pantheon.

Watts, A. W. (1962). *The joyous cosmology.* New York: Pantheon.

Watts, A. W. (Ed.). (1963a). *Patterns of Myth* (3 vols.). New York: G. Braziller.

Watts, A. W. (1963b). *The two hands of God: Myths of polarity.* New York: G. Braziller.

Watts, A. W. (1964). *Beyond theology: The art of godmanship.* New York: Pantheon.

Watts, A. W. (1966). *The book: On the taboo against knowing who you are.* New York: Pantheon.

Watts, A. W. (1971a). *Does it matter? Essays on man's relation to materiality.* New York: Pantheon.

Watts, A. W. (1971b). Wealth versus money. In *Does it matter? Essays on man's relation to materiality* (pp. 3–24). New York: Pantheon.

Watts, A. W. (1973a). *Cloud-hidden, whereabouts unknown.* New York: Pantheon.

Watts, A. W. (1973b). *In my own way: An autobiography.* New York: Vintage.

Watts, A. W. (1975a). Philosophy beyond words. In C. J. Bontempo & S. J. Odell (Eds.), *The owl of Minerva: Philosophers on philosophy* (pp. 191–200). New York: McGraw-Hill.

Watts, A. W. (with C. Huang). (1975b). *Tao: The watercourse way.* New York: Pantheon.

Watts, A. W. (1977a). Speaking personally. In *The essential Alan Watts* (pp. 13–22). Berkeley, CA: Celestial Arts.

Watts, A. W. (1977b). The trickster guru. In *The essential Alan Watts* (pp. 3–10). Berkeley, CA: Celestial Arts.

Watts, A. W. (1987). *The early writings of Alan Watts* (M. Watts & J. Snelling, Eds.). Berkeley, CA: Celestial Arts.

Watts, A. W. (1997a). *The seeds of genius: The early writings* (M. Watts & J. Snelling, Eds.). Shaftesbury, UK: Element.

Watts, A. W. (1997b). The whole and its parts. In *The seeds of genius: The early writings* (pp. 189–193). Shaftesbury, UK: Element. (Original work published 1937)

Watts, A. W. (2006). *Eastern wisdom, modern life: Collected talks, 1960–1969.* Novato, CA: New World Library.

Watts, H. H. (1954). [Review of *Myth and ritual in Christianity*]. *Journal of Bible and Religion, 22*(4), 265–266.

Watts, M., & Snelling, J. (1997). Introduction. *Seeds of genius: The early writings of Alan Watts* (pp. 1–37). Shaftesbury, UK: Element.

Weidenbaum, J. (2008). The philosopher and the neuroscientist: Dewey, Harris, and the nature of religious experience. *The Journal of Liberal Religion, 8*(1), 1–14.

Wheelwright, P. (1953). The philosophy of Alan Watts. *The Sewanee Review, 61,* 493–500.

Wolman, B. B. (1973). *Handbook of general psychology.* Englewood Cliffs, NJ: Prentice Hall.

Woodhead, L. (2001). The turn to life in contemporary religion and spirituality. In U. King (Ed.), *Spirituality and society in the new millennium* (pp. 110–123). Sussex, UK: Sussex Academic Press.

Wright, D. S. (2000). *Philosophical meditations on Zen Buddhism.* Cambridge, UK: Cambridge University Press.

Yamada, S. (2009). *Shots in the dark: Japan, Zen, and the West* (E. Hartman, Trans.) Chicago: University of Chicago Press.

Zen: beat and square. (1958). *Time, 72*(3), 49.

CHAPTER ONE

Alan Watts' Anticipation of Four Major Debates in the Psychology of Religion

Ralph W. Hood Jr.

It is appropriate in a volume dedicated to the work and influence of Alan Watts that academics evaluate a man who many in the academy dismissed as a mere popularizer of topics in religion, which some claimed he lacked the credentials to treat with proper depth. In his autobiography, Watts (1973) admitted to the charge of "popularizer" and to the horror of academics who largely ignored his work in Asian mysticism, seeing him as unschooled in the primary language of the traditions he explored (p. 262). Yet Watts emphasized repeatedly that his was less an academic pursuit than a personal quest (p. 316). The quest was lifelong and resulted in twenty published books by the time he began his autobiography. Other writings were to follow. However, Alan's pursuits, documented in a series of books for wide-ranging audiences, were far from aimless. In this chapter, I argue that Alan's personal quest resulted in discoveries that anticipated the findings of academics who largely ignored his popular works.

When offered a chance to contribute to this volume I looked over my library and found that I had sixteen of Alan's books. All have worn bindings and well-marked pages indicating a careful reading of admittedly popular works. I recalled that both as a college student and as a lifelong academic I had never seen Watts' works as required reading in courses in psychology (my general discipline) nor in the psychology of religion (my academic specialty). Yet, I also recalled seeing students and professors with various Watts' books. There was a virtual underground of collateral reading, much of it Watts' books, by students and professors of psychology whose academic interests did little to hide that there was a spiritual questing in the academy. As we see here, Alan Watts' personal quest was and still is widely shared by academics. However idiosyncratic Alan appeared to some, I argue that, in at least four areas, his own journey of discovery anticipated and then continued to parallel significant issues that occupy the contemporary academic study of the psychology of religion. The four issues championed by Alan Watts in his own journey can be identified as follows:

1. The claim to a perennialist philosophy rooted in mystical experience;

2. A cautious appreciation of the possibility that psychedelics can facilitate mystical experience;

3. The controversial claim of the relationship between eroticism and mystical experience; and finally,

4. The movement away from the study of religion to that of spirituality.

I rely on Alan Watts' autobiography, not the corpus of his published works, to show how his own quest was indeed one of genuine self-discovery that is available to all. The irony is that academics whose disdain of popular works kept Alan from a broader appreciation among scholars nevertheless belatedly championed his views in the academy.

THE PERENNIALIST THESIS

In the one undisputed classic text in the psychology of religion, *The Varieties of Religious Experience*, William James (1902/1985) noted:

> In Hinduism, in Neoplatonism, in Sufism, in Christian Mysticism, in Whitmanism, we find the same reoccurring note, so that there is among mystical utterances an eternal unanimity which ought to make a critic stop and think and which brings it about that the mystical texts have, as had been said, neither birthday or native land. (p. 324)

Alan Watts (1973), undoubtedly familiar with James' *Varieties,* noted early on in his autobiography that: "Taking the premises of Christian dogmatics, Hindu mythology, Buddhist psychology, Zen practice, psychoanalysis, behaviorism, or logical positivism, I have tried to show that all are aiming, however disputatious-ly, at one center" (p. 4). Academics have long challenged the "eternal unanimity" of James and the "one centeredness" of Watts' as popular ecumenical moves to seek a common core to what specialists say are distinct and often incommensurable faith and belief traditions (Katz, 1978a). Yet near the end of his autobiography, in reference to Dom Aelred's (a Benedictine from Ampleforth Abbey in Yorkshire) visit to see the Dalai Lama, Watts (1973) noted that Dom was "my idea of what a Benedictine should be" (p. 444). Aelred also illustrated for Alan a simple conclusion: "It seems that those who go deeply into any of the great spiritual traditions come to see the same place and find themselves talking the same language" (p. 445). Although not denying the particulars of any tradition that could be viewed as separating them, Alan sought and found a common ground. Midway in his autobiography this common ground was identified as:

> that mystical and perennial philosophy which has appeared in almost all times and places. One could get behind the screen of literal dogma to the inner meaning of symbols, to the level at which Eckhart and Shankara, Saint Teresa and Ramakrishna, Saint Dionysius and Nagarjuna are talking the same language. (p. 180)

The academic debate over the claim to a perennial philosophy has two major sources. One is the work of W. T. Stace. In *Mysticism and Philosophy*, Stace (1960) argued for what he termed a common core to mystical experience. Stace's common core thesis is based on several assumptions. Most important for the present discussion here are these four:

1. One can distinguish experience from interpretation of experience.

2. All mystical experiences are characterized as an experience of unity.

3. The experience of unity may be introvertive (a pure contentless consciousness) or extrovertive (experience of unity in diversity).

4. The ontological status of the unity in both introvertive and extrovertive mysticisms is the same "one."

I have defended the legitimacy of Stace's common core thesis in detail elsewhere (Hood, 1989, 2003a, 2006). Here it is sufficient to note that Stace's position quickly became the target of debate in academic circles (Gimello, 1978, p. 195). A rapidly rising tide of social constructionist thought in psychology argued that the experience/interpretation distinction was invalid (Hollenback, 1996; Proudfoot, 1985). Katz (1978b) launched an all-out attack on the common core thesis in a widely influential edited work. Arguing for the particularity of distinctive and different mystical experiences, Katz (1978a) declared forcefully: *"There are NO pure (i.e. unmediated) experiences"* (p. 26). He followed with two additional edited works, each heavily influenced by a social constructionist view (Katz, 1983, 1992).

As might be expected, none of the debate involved reference to Watts' popular works on the same topic. However, the presence of Alan's absence was obvious as academics began to appeal directly to experience, including their own, to support the common core thesis (Forman, 1990, 1998; Hood, 1989, 2003a, 2006; Parsons, 1999; Staal, 1975). As Watts had done, scholars turned East and found the commonality of thought supporting unmediated experience against the bias of Western academic social constructionist views. Authors writing from an experienced based view began to talk of a perennial psychology as opposed to philosophy. The focus was on mystical experience (psychology) and not its interpretation or social construction (philosophy). Allowing for unmediated experiences, academics began to follow a path already tread by Alan Watts.

Finally, the empirical psychology of religion began to provide systematic support for the common core or perennialist thesis. Much of this support is based on empirical research using a measure of reported mystical experience derived from Stace's work. Reviews of this research are readily available (Hood, 2005, 2006; Spilka, Hood, Hunsberger, & Gorsuch, 2003, pp. 290–340). Here I need but emphasize two facts about this research. First, both exploratory and confirmatory factor analytic studies support the claim that individuals reporting mystical experience can differentiate between the nature of the experience in phenomenological terms and various interpretations. Even when interpretations clash, experiences may be the same (Hood, 2003a, 2006). Second, in cultures as different as the United States and Iran, reports of mystical experience remarkably parallel Stace's common core delineation and the claim of perennialist psychologists (Hood et al., 2001). Watts must be smiling somewhere. His path demanded the practice and cultivation of mysticism. East or West he thought ultimately made little difference. It is useful to remember the subtitle to Watts' (1947) *Behold the Spirit: A Study in the Necessity of Mystical Religion.* Academics on both conceptual and empirical levels are coming to map this necessity in more scientific ways than Watts' own popularization of it demanded. Alan's reliance on the authority of personal experience rather than words or concepts about experience is what he referred to as "not *data* but *capta*" (1973, p. 5). Academics could treat Alan's data as capta and a source of hypotheses that could be empirically tested for those who demand objective evidence for what others know firsthand as William James (1902/1985) long ago recognized (pp. 335–339).

PSYCHEDELICS AND MYSTICAL EXPERIENCE

There is little extended discussion of what in the 1960s were generally referred to as "psychedelic" drugs in Watts' (1973) autobiography. One reason is that he admitted that he had learned all he could from his own experience with LSD, and "that when one has received the message one hangs up the phone" (p. 402.) The history over the debate on what to call these drugs such as LSD and psilocybin has been well documented (Forte, 1997; Nichols & Chemel, 2006). Here I am interested in Watts' basic thesis that these chemicals under appropriate set and setting can facilitate genuine mystical experiences.

To turn once more to his autobiography, Watts (1973) noted how in his youth he sensed his estrangement from modern culture: "I carry over from childhood the vague but persistent impression of being exposed to hints of an archaic and underground culture whose values had been lost to the Protestant religion and the industrial bourgeoisie, indeed to the modern West in general" (p. 37). Offering several possibilities for the source of this estrangement, he appealed to experiences modern culture ignores or represses. He went on to assert that:

> The *disciplinum arcanum* of this [rejected/repressed] culture, so easily mistaken in the child for idle reverie, was that intense contemplative watching of the eternal now, which is sometimes revived by the use of psychedelic drugs, but which came to me through flowers, jewels, reflected light in glass, and expanses of clear sky. (p. 37)

Alan Watts thereby anticipated an ongoing debate among academics on the relationship among religion, psychedelic drugs, and mystical experience that continues to provoke controversy.

One controversial issue is the claim that religion has its origin in primary experiences of the divine, a phrase essentially equivalent to mystical experience. Such experiences can occur spontaneously or more likely in set and settings conducive to facilitating these experiences. Exponents of the common core thesis and perennialist psychologists have long referred to the doctrine of causal indifference. The phrase suggests that a variety of conditions can facilitate mystical experience but the experience, once it occurs, may be identical regardless of differences in what we might call various facilitators or triggers of the experience. It may be that psychedelic drugs facilitate identical experiences triggered in Alan Watts by flowers or music, and by his experimentation with LSD. The issues can be made more complicated when given the fact that empirical studies document that people tend to differentially evaluate *identical experiences* based on differing triggers indicating that the principle of causal indifference is not a practice for the average person (Hood, 1980).

A second controversial issue is summarized under a term that Watts would surely see as academic obfuscation, *archeopsychopharmacology*. The term refers to interdisciplinary studies based on linking ancient texts and artifacts with the study of naturally occurring psychedelic substances to speculate on the origin of religions. It has led to the preference for the term *entheogens* to describe these substances among social scientists who study their ability to facilitate primary religious (mystical) experiences. Instead of mind manifesting (psychedelic), these substances are seen as God manifesting (entheogenic). (For reviews of this history see Forte, 1997; Nichols & Chemel, 2006; Spilka et al., 2003, pp. 283–289.) The nature of this debate centers on the claim that religions may have their origin in mystical experiences likely facilitated by the use of naturally occurring entheogens. For instance, Allegro (1971) argued that the Judeo-Christian tradition was heavily influenced by mystical states of consciousness facilitated by the mushroom *amantia muscaria*, a naturally occurring entheogen. Likewise, not only was the Judeo-Christian tradition influenced by Greek thought, Greek thought itself was heavily influenced by an ergot with entheogenic properties used in the Eleusinian mystery cults.

In a similar vein, Wasson (1968) argued that the sacred *soma* described in the *Reg Veda* was the *fly agaric* mushroom, another naturally occurring entheogenic substance. Merkur (2000) argued that the miraculous bread that the Israelites consumed in the wilderness contained a naturally occurring entheogen. He went on to argue that Philo of Alexandria, Rabbi Moses Maimonides, and St. Bernard of Clair Vaux all referred to special meditations to be performed when partaking of a naturally occurring entheogen (Merkur, 2001). Most strongly, Wasson, Kramrisch, Ott, and Ruck (1986) argued that *all* religions have their origin in the use of naturally occurring entheogenic substances whose use under religious set and settings accounts for the facilitation of primary religious experience that religions emerged to both explain and sustain. However, academics would go on to document what Watts' own journey discovered: Contemporary religions do less to sustain mystical experience than use theology to articulate the loss of the *disciplinum arcanum* that Watts found repressed or ignored among modern cultures, especially Western ones. This loss is also a fall into language that dismisses the possibility of a perennial psychology in favor of a social constructionist claim that overevaluates the role of language in mediating mystical experiences (Hood, 2006).

This "fall into language" leads to a third controversial issue in contemporary psychological studies of religion and entheogens anticipated by Watts: Entheogenic substances can be experimentally shown to facilitate mystical experiences that are identical in all respects to those occurring "spontaneously" or resulting from disciplined devotional practices. Here I need but mention three empirical studies relevant to Alan Watts' concern with the likelihood that mysticism is what is at the core of otherwise diverse religious and philosophical traditions. The studies I discuss either use criteria derived directly from Stace's common core theory already mentioned or used my *Mysticism Scale* (Hood, 1975), which is directly operationalized from Stace's common core. This scale is the most widely used measure of mysticism in empirical studies (Burris, 1999; Hood, 2002, 2005).

The first study of the uses of entheogens to facilitate mystical experience is the widely cited doctoral dissertation by Pahnke (1963, 1966). It has become widely known as the "Good Friday" experiment as twenty graduate students at Andover-Newton Theological Seminary met to hear a Good Friday service after they had been given either psilocybin (a known entheogen) or a placebo control (nicotinic acid). Participants met in groups of four, with two experimental and two controls all matched for compatibility. Each group had two leaders, one who had been given psilocybin. Immediately after the service and six months later, the participants were assessed on a questionnaire that included all of Stace's common core criteria of mysticism. Results were impressive in that the experimental participants scored high on all of Stace's common core criteria, whereas the controls did not. It was readily concluded that with appropriate set and setting, psilocybin did facilitate the report of mystical experiences. Watts, by the way, had already defended this thesis from the point of view of his first-person experience in *The Joyous Cosmology*, appropriately subtitled *Adventures in the Chemistry of Consciousness*, in 1962.

In what is also a widely quoted study, Doblin (1991) followed the adventures of the original Good Friday participants. He was able to locate and interview nine participants in the original experimental group and seven of the participants in the original control group. He also administered Pahnke's original questionnaire, including Stace's common core criteria of mysticism. In most cases, comparison of Doblin's results with both of Pahnke's (immediately after the service and six months later) indicate that participants in the experimental group showed *increases* on most of Stace's common core criteria of mysticism after almost a quarter of a century. Thus, as Alan Watts anticipated, once awakened to a mystical sense of the world, the experience continues to expand and to inform one's spirituality. Despite serious critiques of the Good Friday study (Doblin, 1991; Nichols & Chemel, 2006, pp. 10–11), it has until recently been the most significant study attempting to facilitate mystical experience in a religious setting.

The benchmark study in the tradition of the Good Friday experiment is the recent study by Griffiths, Richards, McCann, and Jesse (2006). They replicated Pahnke's original experiment with individual rather than group sessions, using a more rigorous experimental control and a more appropriate placebo (methylphenidate hydrochloride). The double-blind study was effective at two levels: first, the double-blind was not broken in what is a very sophisticated between-group crossover design that involved two or three eight-hour drug sessions conducted at two-month intervals. Although the complexity of the research design need not concern us here, suffice it to say that of thirty adult volunteers, half received the entheogen first, followed by the placebo control, and the other half received the placebo control first, followed by the entheogen. Six additional volunteers received the placebo in the first two sessions and unblinded psilocybin in the third session. The above procedures obscured the study design and protected the double-blind. Unlike the Good Friday experiment, the double-blind in this Johns Hopkins study was successful (Griffiths et al., 2006, p. 274). Although the Good Friday participants took psilocybin in a specifically religious setting, volunteers in the Johns Hopkins study had all sessions in an aesthetically pleasant living room-like setting. Although the volunteers had spiritual interests, the setting itself did not contain religious artifacts or cues. All sessions were monitored by an experienced male guide who had extensive experience with entheogens. However, unlike the Good Friday experiment neither the entheogenic experienced male guide nor a companion female guide took psilocybin while serving as guides. Second, numerous measures and observations were involved in this study, including Pahnke's original question-naire and my *Mysticism Scale* which, as mentioned earlier, is an operationalized measure of Stace's common core criteria (Burris, 1999; Hood, 1975; Hood et al., 2001). Thus, we have a direct measure of Alan Watts' claim that under appropri-ate set and setting conditions, psychedelics (entheogens) can facilitate mystical experiences. In this study, participants in the experimental conditions reported higher mysticism scores than those in the placebo-control conditions, despite the fact that all sessions (including placebo) were conducted in a supportive environment with participants who had no prior experience with entheogens but were interested in spiritual growth.

Thus, once again, the psychology of religion is "catching up" to Alan whose own personal religious quest suggested that mystical experiences facili-tated in some by such naturally occurring phenomena as flowers and light are for others facilitated by entheogens. Entheogens can clearly occasion mysti-cal insights as, if the archeopsychopharmacologists are correct, they perhaps have since the origin of religion. Entheogenic substances also can lead one on a spiritual quest where, to paraphrase Watts (1973), they can abandon their waterwings and learn to swim (p. 402).

EROTICISM AND MYSTICISM

Perhaps nothing Alan Watts championed raised as much debate as his views on eroticism and spirituality. We need not look here to entire books of his devoted to this relationship but again simply take from his autobiography what is more than simply a confession. Alan was explicit in his view that an enlight-ened person need not abstain from sex. His own spiritual path easily attested to that perspective. It is likely, for example, that *Erotic Spirituality* (Watts, 1971) is as autobiographical a book as any he wrote. He even boasted that "I once had the privilege of sharing a mistress with one of the holiest men in the land (1973, p. 423). However, here I want simply to focus on a comment in his autobiography where he noted that in a public lecture, "I let drop, as merely a passing remark, that there was some analogy between the ecstasy of *Sama-dhi*, or mystical experience, and sexual orgasm—not realizing that I had made myself the cat among the pigeons" (p. 274). Here Alan Watts both understood the long tradition of linking eroticism to mysticism in the conceptual literature, but also anticipated another focus in the psychology of religion.

There is a massive literature linking sexuality and mysticism in both West-ern and Eastern religious traditions (Hood & Hall, 1980). Watts knew this and in his own way explored various linkages both conceptually, and as always, as a questing practice in his own spiritual journey. Long before Watts, another popularizer of mysticism, Evelyn Underhill (1911/1970), gave her own under-standing of the analogical relationship between eroticism and mysticism. In language more religious than spiritual (discussed more fully below), she notes:

It was natural and inevitable that the imagery of human love and marriage should have seemed to the mystic the best of all images in his own "fulfillment of life." . . . It lay ready to his hand: it was understood of all men: and moreover, it certainly does offer, upon lower levels, a strangely exact parallel to the sequence of states in which man's spiritual consciousness unfolds itself, and which form the consummation of the mystic life. (pp. 133–137)

If Watts has some support from Underhill on the religious side, he also has support from one of the earliest psychologists of religion, J. B. Pratt. More cautious than either Underhill or Watts, Pratt (1920) argued that the link between eroticism and mysticism was merely metaphorical. In succinct terms he noted, "It is evident that the mystic must make use of expressions drawn from earthly love to describe his experience, or give up the attempt of describing it at all" (p. 418).

Yet we need not read too far between the lines to see that the "cat among the pigeons" was more radical than either Pratt supporting a metaphorical relationship between eroticism and mysticism or Underhill supporting an analogical relationship.

Erotic spirituality is not simply a title of one of Alan Watts' books; it is a declarative that they are and can be one and the same. As Alan sought deeper insights from Asian religions, he supported what elsewhere has been called the *identity view* (Hood & Hall, 1980, p. 196). It is expressed most clearly by Dimock (1966):

If one happens to hold to a doctrine which says there is no qualitative difference between the human and the divine, spiritual union of the two is possible, and fleshly union between the two is not only poetically but actually possible. The search and longing for this union are now the *means* to the ultimate experience, an actual union of flesh and spirit, of human and divine. (pp. 14–15)

Alan Watts did more than popularize the possibility of an erotic spirituality; he practiced it in his own life. In so doing, he also left a shadow that did not just cover the psychologists of religion but also showed how far behind him they were. However, the contemporary psychology of religion is now retracing the same path Alan trod. Here it suffices to but summarize three well-established findings in the empirical study of eroticism and mystical experience that were anticipated by Watts' own personal questing. First, accepting that mystical experience can be triggered by widely diverse occasions, there are consistent differences between those who do and those who do not cite sexuality as a trigger of their experience. More conservative and traditionally religious persons do *not* link sexuality to spirituality; those not religious often do link eroticism and spirituality (Spilka et al., 2003, pp. 328–331).

Second, for those who do experience an erotic spirituality, their actual sexual experiences and their mystical experiences run as parallel processes, different for males and females. Their mystical unions may be the same, but the process to that union is linked to their experience of sex. To focus on an Asian example we can do no better to sustain Watts' popularization of what is indeed an ancient understanding than to quote from the third-century *Kama Sutra of Vatsyayana* that confirms the identity of love and sex as ecstatic experiences:

> The difference in the ways of working, by which men are the actors, and women are the persons acted upon, is owing to the nature of male and female, otherwise the actor would be sometimes the person acted upon and, vice versa. And from this difference in the ways of working follows the difference in consciousness of pleasure, for a man thinks, "this woman is united to me," and a woman thinks, "I am united with this man. (Vatsyayana, 1981, pp. 130–131)

Those familiar with the range of Alan Watts' mixture of eroticism and spirituality might suspect that he had discovered for himself what has long been noted in the classic mystical literatures that refused to insist on linking enlightenment with celibacy: Mysticism and eroticism can be one and the same. Even from an evolutionary perspective it is clear that the neurophysiology of mystical experience and of sexual arousal overlap (Dawkins, 2006, pp. 185–186; Newberg, d'Acquili, & Rause, 2001).

Third, it is not accidental that Alan Watts spoke of erotic spirituality and not erotic religion. Alan progressed further from serious reflections on theology. His focus on aconceptual mystical traditions such as Zen and his own perennialist leanings made him, to use the title of another of his books, *Beyond Theology* (Watts, 1966a). Here is our final example of Alan Watts anticipating central issues in the academic psychological study of religion.

RELIGION AND SPIRITUALITY

Alan Watts' interest in religion waned as his spiritual journey found less and less worth in what in his autobiography he termed *talkative* institutions (1973, p. 55). Referring both to the Catholic Church and his own Church of England (insofar as he was reared in it) he noted that "impoverished Christians do nothing in their religious observances except chatter" (Watts, 1973, p. 56). As he progressed along his spiritual path he had much less concern with theology or dogma. It required neither response nor defense but more a simple recognition that it was merely "chatter." I noted previously how early on Watts' concern for a perennial psychology or philosophy sought the common core that implied a unity to diverse traditions. However, this unity was to be experienced and it could not be had by those caught in the "talk" or "chatter" of traditions.

Alan's well-documented Asian turn and his fondness for the more aconceptual traditions such as Zen (1957) and Tao (1975) favored a spirituality less fettered by institutional constraints and dogma. The distinction here is between one of religion and spirituality, an issue that is central in the current psychology of religion. Here I want to use this religion–spirituality distinction as a final example of how Alan Watts anticipated, in his personal quest and popularization, issues now central to the academic study of psychology of religion.

There are several excellent reviews of the conceptual and empirical issues in the religion versus spirituality debate (Hood, 2003b; Zinnbauer & Pargament, 2005). My concern here is to document Watts' anticipation that religious traditions can both foster and deny the spiritual expression. Insofar as what Watts referred to as "chatter" and "talk" are dominating religion, genuine spiritual expression may be hampered. The empirical data confirms that most individuals who identify themselves as religious also claim to be spiritual. Indeed, these are also in the majority of all religious believers. Here we have individuals whose spiritual life is either adequately constrained or expressed by the language of their faith tradition or who are satisfied with religious beliefs as guides to conduct and commitment. However, these individuals interested Alan less as he himself felt the increasingly unnecessary constraints of religion, including his own Anglican commitment, to be unacceptable to a spiritual life. Again, the common core thesis allows for the possibility of those who journey far along their own traditional religious path to arrive at the same place or, perhaps, to change metaphors, there is a horizon approached that allows some to see the transcendental unity to otherwise diverse religious traditions (Schuon, 1975). It is well established that mystics have often struggled to stay within their traditions (Katz, 1983). However, for most, the institutional binding of spirituality would seem to minimize their spirituality insofar as that spirituality is mystical. Reviews of the empirical literature indicate lower reports of mystical experience among those who identify themselves as both religious and spiritual (Hood, 2003b). These I must remind the reader, are mostly the majority, around three-fourths of the religiously self-identified in the United States (Zinnbauer & Pargament, 2005).

As Alan Watts anticipated his journey from religion to spirituality he left the chatter and talk of faith to a focus on experience that was as unifying as it was silent. Zen and Dao both show there is a way outside institutions that is, ironically, traditionally antitraditional. The empirical research shows that an emerging minority of persons identify themselves as "spiritual but *not* religious" (Hood, 2003b). Two facts about this emerging group (at least in the United States) must be noted. First, they have higher rates of the report of mystical experiences than persons who claim to be equally religious and spiritual. Their mysticism needs no religious interpretation, and certainly will not bend to any institutional demands for a "correct" interpretation. The old adage that "Those who talk, do not know" applies to this group, as does the corollary, "those who know, do not talk." Experience is not only distinguished from interpretation, but interpretation becomes mere "chatter" and "talk" that Alan Watts came to see is at best a comic defense of what needs none. A second fact that the empirical research reveals, especially qualitative studies based on in-depth open-ended interviews, is that those who identify themselves as "spiritual but not religious" place a heavy emphasis on "not." If Watts owed his early rearing to the Church of England, he came to realize, as noted above, that Luther's Reformation must occur once more. This new reformation is against any institutionalization of spirituality. Religion, as the institutional arbitrator of spirituality, has, simply put, got it wrong. They are part of "the taboo against knowing who you are," to closely paraphrase the subtitle on one of Alan's books (Watts, 1966b).

The empirical data have led many academics to defend the term *religion* as necessarily incorporating what others see as spirituality (the most common conservative move). A more common and liberal stance is to title books, chapters, or articles dealing with the psychology of religion with the caveat, "and spirituality." Few drop religion altogether and simply claim spirituality as their concern. This is no mere academic dispute but the use of "chatter" and "talk" to defend academic turfs and to control book marketing. It parallels Alan Watts' journey only in acknowledging that much of this is what Watts left behind. In a remarkable paralleling of Watts' own views, Day (1994) reveals some insightful words from a young woman he interviewed named Sandy whose views on religion illustrate Watts' own move from religion to spirituality:

> Religion tells you what is good or true and tells you who is favored and who is not. It operates in fixed categories. Spirituality is developed. You have to work hard at it and to be conscious about it and take time for it. Sometimes, in order to grow spiritually, you have to go beyond or even against religious doctrine. (p. 163)

Sandy's "beyond" favored silence and experience over "chatter" and "talk." She exemplifies what Watts anticipated in *Beyond Theology* noted previously and in the development of academic theories of religion. Two brief examples should suffice.

First, Emile Durkheim, surely one of the founders of the sociology of religion, if not of sociology itself, suggested in *The Elementary Forms of Religious Life* (1912/1995) that there were emerging "aspirations toward a religion that would consist entirely of interior and subjective states and be freely constructed by each one of us" (p. 44). However, his theory of religion demanded that it be essentially a collective phenomenon and hence needs a Church. He ends his major text on religion with the well developed assertion that insofar as religion is "a consciousness of consciousness" (p. 445) it is expressed in collective representations and hence is a permanent aspect of humanity.

Alan Watts would accept that "consciousness of consciousness," not as a social fact, but rather as a genuine sense of ontological wonder at being. Alan does not acknowledge that consciousness of consciousness needs collective representation. It is a primary experience, inherently mystical, natural to some childhood reveries, and elicited by phenomena ranging from flowers to entheogens to sex. As noted earlier, Alan had that sense of mystical wonder lost to modern culture. His mysticism needs no Church nor is it represented in or constructed by language. His turn to the aconceptual traditions of Zen and Dao was not only a personal quest, but a turning East that many today are following. It is a path of no path insofar as it rejects an appeal to church. It is not religious, but rather is spiritual.

If Durkheim virtually defined religion to require collective representations, he could not remove the talk and chatter from either the most primitive or any future church.

However, another scholar, Troeltsch, equally influential in the sociology of religion, used explicit Christian history to propose a universal tendency inherent in all religious traditions. His approach has been explored more fully elsewhere (Hood, 2003b; Spilka et al., 2003, pp. 334–339). Here it is sufficient to note that Alan Watts' religious quest ended where it started, to that mystical awareness beyond all talk and chatter. Troeltsch (1931), in *The Social Teachings of the Christian Churches*, proposed a threefold typology of forms of religious organization. H. R. Niebuhr (1929) popularized Troeltsch's typology in his *The Social Sources of Denominationalism* which antedated the English translation of Troeltsch's text by two years. Niebuhr was interested in religion and hence focused on only two of Troeltsch's types: (a) the church, open to all with minimal criteria of membership, and (b) the sect, demanding stricter criteria of admission and claiming a purer religious commitment. Although academics heavily relied on Niebuhr's popularization of Troeltsch's church/sect typology, Watts had already anticipated the neglected third aspect of Troeltsch's typology: mysticism.

Troeltsch had argued for two forms of mysticism, one being simply a demand for an inward appropriation of religion—to internalization of religious concepts in a deeply experiential sense. Insofar as this experience elicited by faith traditions is not simply interpreted in the language of the tradition, it allows for Watts' perennial philosophy. However, as already noted, Watts felt that traditions did less to foster a perennial philosophy than to defend a particular version of the elephant that each church in its blindness to the perennialist claims thought it had the only firm and proper hold on.

The proverbial blind persons debating the proper description of an elephant cannot even imagine what it is they are united to, each insisting their part, whether trunk, leg, or tail is the total reality. As Alan's journey moved away from church and religion, he illustrated Troeltsch's second sense of mysticism. This mysticism has no need of church and is independent of religion. It does not accept the constraints of religion that it tends to disdain. There is no more religious talk or defense of a faith. One can embrace eroticism and if necessary identify oneself not by a faith tradition, but simply as a mystic. Surely this is the final point that Alan reached in his own personal quest. He died "spiritual not religious."

If Watts' path took him away from mere religion, it was to deepen his spirituality. Alan knew the limitations and values of both religion and spirituality. Religions could rise to share in the perennial philosophy but were more likely to wallow in disunities created by their "talk" and their "chatter." Spirituality could also produce disunities instead of sharing in the perennial psychology championed by Watts, but Alan continued to speak freely to a mass audience and to academics and religious scholars who read his work though seldom quoting it; Watts' task was more poetic than the academic's prose that often became merely prosaic. In the prologue to his autobiography Alan told the reader what summarized his life's work, "basically an attempt to describe mystical experience . . . as seen and felt directly in a *silence* of words and mindings" (1973, p. 5, emphasis added). The "silence" of Watts now speaks loudly among academics who in the four areas noted earlier are trying to investigate and document the truth of Alan's own personal quest that should we desire, is available to us all, whether we are religious, spiritual or both.

REFERENCES

Allegro, J. M. (1971). *The sacred mushroom and the cross.* New York: Bantam.

Burris, C. T. (1999). The mysticism scale: Research form D (M Scale) (Hood, 1975). In P. C. Hill & R. W. Hood Jr. (Eds.), *Measures of religiosity* (pp. 363–367). Birmingham, AL: Religious Education Press.

Dawkins, R. (2006). *The God delusion.* Boston: Houghton-Mifflin.

Day, J. M. (1994). Moral development, belief, and unbelief: Young adult accounts of religion in the process of moral growth. In J. Corveleyn & D. Hutsebaut (Eds.), *Belief and unbelief: Psychological perspectives* (pp. 155–173). Atlanta, GA: Rodopi.

Dimock, E. D. Jr. (1966). *The place of the hidden moon.* Chicago: University of Chicago Press.

Doblin, R. (1991). Pahnke's "Good Friday" experiment: A long-term follow-up and methodological critique. *Journal of Transpersonal Psychology, 23,* 1–38.

Durkheim, E. (1995). *The elementary forms of religious life* (K. E. Fields, Trans). New York: The Free Press. (Original work published 1912)

Forman, R. K. C. (1990). *The problem of pure consciousness.* New York: Oxford University Press.

Forman, R. K. C. (1998). *The innate capacity: Mysticism, psychology, and philosophy.* New York: Oxford University Press.

Forte, R. (Ed.). (1997). *Entheogens and the future of religion.* San Francisco: Council on Spiritual Practices.

Gimello, R. M. (1978). Mysticism and meditation. In S. T. Katz (Ed.), *Mysticism and philosophical analysis* (pp. 170–199). New York: Oxford University Press.

Griffiths, R. R., Richards, W. A., McCann, U., & Jesse, R. (2006). Psilocybin can occasion mystical-type experience having substantial and sustained personal meaning and significance. *Psychopharmacology*, 187, 268–283.

Hollenback, J. B. (1996). *Mysticism: Experience, response, and empowerment*. University Park: The Pennsylvania State University Press.

Hood, R. W. Jr. (1975). The construction and preliminary validation of a measure of reported mystical experience. *Journal for the Scientific Study of Religion*, 14, 29–41.

Hood, R. W. Jr. (1980). Social legitimacy, dogmatism, and the evaluation of intense experiences. *Review of Religious Research*, 21(2), 184–194.

Hood, R. W. Jr. (1989). Mysticism, the unity thesis, and the paranormal. In G. K. Zollschan, J. F. Schumaker, & G. F. Walsh (Eds.), *Exploring the paranormal: Perspectives of belief and experience* (pp. 117–130). New York: Avery.

Hood, R. W. Jr. (2002). *Dimensions of mystical experiences: Empirical studies and psychological links*. Atlanta, GA: Rhodopi.

Hood, R. W. Jr. (2003a). Conceptual and empirical consequences of the unity thesis. In J. Belzen & A. Geels (Eds.), *International series in the psychology of religion*, Vol. 13. *Mysticism: A variety of psychological perspectives* (pp. 17–54). New York: Rodopi.

Hood, R. W. Jr. (2003b). The relationship between religion and spirituality. In A. L. Griel & D. G. Bromley (Eds.), *Religion and the social order*, Vol. 10. *Defining religion: Investigating the boundaries between the sacred and the* secular (pp. 241–264). Oxford, UK: Elsevier Science.

Hood, R. W. Jr. (2005). Mystical, spiritual, and religious experiences. In R. F. Paloutzian & C. L. Parks (Eds.), *Handbook of religion and spirituality* (pp. 348–364). New York: Guilford.

Hood, R. W. Jr. (2006). The common core thesis in the study of mysticism. In P. McNamara (Ed.), *Where God and science meet: How brain and evolutionary studies alter our understanding of religion*, Vol. 3. *The psychology of religious experience* (pp. 119–138). Westport, CT: Praeger.

Hood, R. W. Jr., & Hall. J. R. (1980). Gender differences in the description of erotic and mystical experiences. *Review of Religious Research*, 21, 195–207.

Hood, R. W. Jr., Ghorbani, N., Watson, P. J., Ghramaleki, A. F., Bing, M. B., Davison, H., et al. (2001). Dimensions of the mysticism scale: Confirming the three--factor solution in the United States and Iran. *Journal for the Scientific Study of Religion*, 40, 691–706.

James, W. (1985). *The varieties of religious experience*. Cambridge, MA: Harvard University Press. (Original work published 1902)

Katz, S. T. (1978a). Language, epistemology, and mysticism. In S. T. Katz (Ed), *Mysticism and philosophical analysis* (pp. 22–74). New York: Oxford University Press.

Katz, S. T. (1978b). *Mysticism and philosophical analysis*. New York: Oxford University Press.

Katz, S. T. (1983). *Mysticism and religious traditions*. New York: Oxford University Press.

Katz, S. T. (1992). *Mysticism and language*. New York: Oxford University Press.

Merkur, D. (2000). *The mystery of manna: The psychedelic sacrament of the bible*. Rochester, VT: Park Street Press.

Merkur, D. (2001). *The psychedelic sacrament: Manna, meditation, and mystical experience*. Rochester, VT: Park Street Press.

Newberg, A., d'Aquili, E., & Rause, V. (2001). *Why God won't go away: Brain science and the biology of belief.* New York: Random House.

Nichols, D. E., & Chemel, B. R. (2006). The neuropharmacology of religious experience: Hallucinogens and the experience of the divine. In P. McNamara (Ed.), *Where God and science meet: How brain and evolutionary studies alter our understanding of religion,* Vol. 3. *The psychology of religious experience* (pp. 1–34). Westport, CT: Praeger.

Niebuhr, H. R. (1929). *The social sources of denominationalism.* New York: Holt, Rinehart, & Winston.

Pahnke, W. N. (1963). *Drugs and mysticism: An analysis of the relationship between psychedelic drugs and the mystical consciousness.* Unpublished doctoral dissertation, Harvard University, Cambridge, MA.

Pahnke, W. N. (1966). Drugs and mysticism. *International Journal of Parapsychology, 8,* 295–320.

Parsons, W. B. (1999). *The enigma of the oceanic feeling: Revisioning the psychoanalytic theory of mysticism.* New York: Oxford University Press.

Pratt, J. B. (1920). *The religious consciousness: A psychological study.* New York: Macmillan.

Proudfoot, W. (1985). *Religious experience.* Berkeley: University of California Press.

Schuon, F. (1975). *The transcendental unity of religion* (Rev. ed., P. Townsend, Trans). New York: Harper & Row.

Spilka, B., Hood, R. W. Jr., Hunsberger, B., & Gorsuch, R. C. (2003). *The psychology of religion: An empirical approach* (3rd ed.). New York: Guilford.

Staal, F. (1975). *Exploring mysticism: A methodological essay.* Berkeley: University of California Press.

Stace, W. T. (1960). *Mysticism and philosophy.* London: MacMillan.

Troeltsch, E. (1931). *The social teachings of the Christian church* (Vols. 1–2). (O. Wyon, Trans.). New York: Macmillan.

Underhill, E. (1970). *Mysticism.* New York: World. (Original work published 1911)

Vatsyayana, M. (1981). *The Karma Sutra of Vatsyayana.*(R. Burton & F. F. Arbuthnot, Trans.). London: Unwin Paperbacks.

Wasson, R. G. (1968). *Soma: Divine mushroom of immortality.* The Hague: Mouton.

Wasson, R., Kramrisch, S., Ott, J., & Ruck, C. (1986). *Persephone's quest: Entheogens and the origin of religion.* New Haven, CT: Yale University Press.

Watts, A. W. (1947). *Behold the spirit: A study in the necessity of mystical religion.* New York: Random House.

Watts, A. W. (1957). *The way of Zen.* New York: Pantheon Books.

Watts, A. W. (1962). *The joyous cosmology: Adventures in the chemistry of consciousness.* New York: Pantheon Books.

Watts, A. W. (1966a). *Beyond theology: The art of Godmanship.* New York: Meridian.

Watts, A. W. (1966b). *The book: On the taboo against knowing who you are.* New York: Collier.

Watts, A. W. (1971). *Erotic spirituality: The vision of Konarak.* New York: Macmillan.

Watts, A. W. (1973). *In my own way: An autobiography*. New York: Vintage.

Watts, A. W. (1975). *Tao: The watercourse way*. New York: Pantheon.

Zinnbauer, B. J., & Pargament, K. I. (2005). Religiousness and spirituality. In R. F. Paloutzian & C. L. Parks (Eds.), *Handbook of religion and spirituality* (pp. 21–42). New York: Guilford.

CHAPTER TWO

Alan Watts: The Immediate Magic of God

Alan Keightley

Alan Watts had an abiding fascination with Rowan Tree Cottage in Holbrook Lane, Chislehurst, in the county of Kent, his home for more than twenty years before he left England for the United States. The drawing room in the cottage was a place of sheer magic for him long before he learned a language to explain its fascination. His mother taught the children of missionaries and this room contained gifts from their parents, Asian treasures gathered on their travels. The room gave Alan an interior compass that led him to the East through the West; through New York, Chicago, and finally, San Francisco.

I located the cottage some years ago. The rowan tree had long since gone. As the owner led me into the small drawing room she commented that she had just a few callers interested in Alan Watts' origins. She was puzzled by their particular interest in the bathroom upstairs and was surprised to learn that "upstairs" was a place of punishment for the young Alan. I explained that the "miserable bathroom" was where he was taught his prayers. She knew nothing about Alan Watts and directed me across the road to an elderly woman who had cared for Alan's father in his final illness. She too had no awareness that his son had touched the lives of millions. The topography of Rowan Tree Cottage was an enduring metaphor for Alan's changing relations with the Christian tradition. "Upstairs" was the realm of Christianity in its Anglican form. "Downstairs" was the domain of freedom and adventure, particularly the drawing room, the very presence of the mysterious East in Holbrook Lane, of all places.

There were four phases of Watts' descents and ascents on the metaphorical stairs. As a schoolboy he found Christianity to be an impossible religion, having concluded that there could be no high form of religion without mysticism at its center. Without this, Christianity was either a political ideology or a mindless fundamentalism. He thus declared himself a Buddhist. In the 1940s, he had second thoughts. A more mature Watts felt and thought that Christianity was plausible and became an Episcopalian priest. However, he left the church in

1950 having concluded for a second time that Christianity was an impossible religion. A decade before Watts' death, the mood of the times had changed radically to the degree that Christianity became an option again for those who were spiritually awake. He endorsed this view by claiming, characteristically, that Christianity was now a "possible" religion by virtue of the very fact that it *was* "impossible." Alan Watts was so prolific in books and recorded talks and the subject of his engagement with Christianity is so vast that a brief account can only sketch an outline of this. There is, however, a continuous thread running through all of Watts' writings on religion. This is the assertion of the possibility of a direct, immediate, mystical realization of reality, before thought and words; before it is classified conceptually and vocalized.

TOWARD AN APOPHATIC THEOLOGY

During my visit to Rowan Tree Cottage, I sat for a few minutes in Watts' cramped bedroom thinking of a passage in his autobiography:

> I especially remember that bedroom on Sunday twilights. . . . Alone in that bedroom I would hear the bells of Saint Nicholas [Church] falling down the major scale, ringing the changes forever downwards, to summon the faithful to Evensong, to the closing service of the day, with, as John Betjeman has put it, undertones of "death and hell at last." (Watts, 1973b, p. 46)

Alan Watts had been immersed in the Anglican tradition from birth until his late teens to a degree that is hardly imaginable today. He attended one of the oldest schools in England, King's School, adjacent to Canterbury Cathedral, the worldwide Mecca of Anglicanism under the very wing of the archbishop himself. A photograph shows the thirteen-year-old Alan carrying the train of Cosmo Gordon Lang during his enthronement ceremony in 1928.

Watts (1973b) recalled that he and his fellow pupils felt that they were being introduced to a very clear, perfectly logical cosmological order. God was supreme. Then Christ, who conferred spiritual power on his apostles. Finally there was the archbishop himself, an immediate descendent of those very apostles through ecclesiastical tradition. Watts commented that they knew their place and where they were and what the order of things was. Nevertheless, he became a Buddhist at age fifteen. He had discovered the Tao and Lao-tzu's teaching: "The Tao flows everywhere. It loves and nourishes all things, but does not lord it over them." As a boy, dragooned with the rest of the school into the cathedral services, the words from the throne of the Almighty jarred with those of the Chinese sage: "I am the Lord and there is non-else. Me only shalt thou serve, for there are no other gods beside me." The Anglican God was, in the language of King's School playground, a monster and a bore. Canterbury Cathedral with its looming Bell Harry Tower symbolized for Alan the overwhelming didactic ethos of the Anglican tradition. Watts (1973b) reflected on those times and admitted that traditional Christianity was still in his blood and that he was often haunted by the patriarchal images of the old religion.

The young Watts hungered for a mystical approach to Christianity as a non-verbal spiritual experience of the divine rather than mere doctrines or precepts. For Alan, the Christian tradition did indeed have beauty, for example, Solemn High Mass and Gregorian chant, but it lacked depth: "I wanted to plumb and understand *being* itself, the very heart and ground of the universe, not to control it, but simply to wonder at it" (Watts, 1973b, p. 92). Watts was later to read Eckhart, St. Teresa, and most of the great Christian mystics, but his childhood in Anglicanism gave no hint of mystical experience: "We were told only that Jesus, and Jesus alone, was one with God. But it was all talk—no vision, no feeling, no sensation, except a certain awe and military grandeur" (p. 93). The religion of the Church of England was "pious archaeology," a sense of continuity with the glorious past almost unknown in the New World (Watts, 1964/1973a).

By the 1940s, Watts was living in the New World, first in New York and then in Chicago. Wide reading in comparative religion and theology had shown Watts that Christian belief was by no means the shallow mythology that he had supposed it to be in his youth. His writings in this period indicate that he was still half way down the metaphorical stairs of Rowan Tree Cottage. He was not completely free of Chislehurst and had not yet fully discovered San Francisco. Thus Watts' new involvement with the Christian tradition was only possible through his realization that the Asian wisdom he had embraced in his youth could be *absorbed* into Christianity. What contemporary form of Christianity could embody the mystical traditions of Asian faiths? For Watts it would be Catholicism in the broadest sense, containing the Roman Catholic Church, Eastern Orthodox and Anglican churches.

These traditions center their worship around the altar as distinct from the pulpit. They were still fundamentally mystery religions and not merely societies for listening to lectures and promoting good works. Watts (1947/1971a) explained:

> Every great advance in Christian theology has involved absorption of an alien philosophy, to mention only the debt of Origen, Clement and St. Augustine to Platonism and of St. Thomas Aquinas to Aristotle. It is not too much to predict that the next great step in Christianity will be due, in part, to the absorption of Hinduism, Buddhism, Taoism, and, perhaps, Mohammedan Sufism, all of which are profoundly *mystical* religions. (p. 53)

Christianity had not merely to absorb but to create a synthesis with these unitive mystical traditions. Theoretically, the proposed accommodation of these divergent traditions would be expressed through the medium of that *philosophia perennis*, the perennial philosophy, which was the "gold within the sectarian dross of every great religion" (Watts, 1971c, p. xi). It was a medium associated with the writings of Guenon, Schuon, and Coomaraswamy, the "traditionalist" school, interpreting orthodox spiritual tradition as a considered adaptation of the perennial philosophy to the circumstances of various cultures. A "universal feature" of this tradition "is that what we experience as the succession of time, is an abstraction rather than a reality and that the real state of the universe is eternal or timeless—a 'moment' without past or future" (Watts, 1953/1968, p. 29).

Alan Watts was ordained an Episcopalian priest in 1944 and became chaplain at Northwestern University after theological studies at Seabury-Western Seminary. From the outset, he was embarrassed by the task of preaching and delivering optimistic, positive declarations about God and Jesus while affirming the faith of the students in his charge. Watts' years of studying Buddhism had convinced him that discovering the fundamental truth of existence was not afforded by learning something new, but by untruth dropping away: the cessation of delusion. He also knew of a very old and respected mystical tradition that readily practiced precisely this in Christian terms: the way of "remotion." This was the "apophatic" tradition, complemented by the "cataphatic." The former is the negative theology of saying what God is *not* like, while the latter says what God *is* like. Watts called the apophatic way "spiritual window cleaning" (1952,1960s/2006) or "atheism in the name of God" (1983, 2002). It was seeing through the conceptual images of God that contaminate our direct perception and experience of the divine. The only God you can cling to is the *idea* of God. Faith begins when clinging ceases.

Watts knew that few people he encountered in his role as chaplain were likely to be aware of the apophatic tradition, sanctified though it was via the work of a few theologians through the centuries. As a gesture in making this tradition more accessible, Watts translated the classic, *Theologia Mystica*, attributed to St. Dionysius (1944/1972). He also wrote two books in this period, bringing clarity to the affinity of the unitive mysticism in Asian religions to a comparable dimension in Christianity: *Behold the Spirit* (Watts, 1947/1971a) and *The Supreme Identity* (Watts, 1950/1973c). A third book, *Myth and Ritual in Christianity* (Watts, 1953/1968), explored the same premise shortly after he left the church and joined the American Academy of Asian Studies in San Francisco.

How did Alan Watts envision the role of formal religion within an apophatic theology? To respond to such a question we have to refer briefly again to Watts' central affirmation of the possibility of nonverbal religious realization, the experience he hungered for as a schoolboy. Watts (1960s/2006) insisted that there is no necessity for a word for this state; no need for a language for the "unsayable." Yet he added that you can have a word for this state if you know someone who shares the same experience. Lao Tzu wrote: "One who knows does not speak; one who speaks does not know." But he *said* that. Watts claimed that any vocalization of this in the context of the outward manifestation of religion is "pure gravy" after the realization, and secondary. But if you want a religion you can have one. It's a free world. Have ritual, so long as you don't take it seriously. Watts, in fact, was himself an accomplished liturgist as *Myth and Ritual in Christianity* (1953/1968) clearly shows. The latter expounded Christianity as the ritual reliving of the Christ story through the seasonal cycle of the ecclesiastical year. The marking of time was the appropriate and wholly absorbing ritual with which one watched over eternity.

Earlier, in *Behold the Spirit*, Watts described the characteristic of religion that, indeed, was given formal expression. It had three functions. First: "For those who *cannot* at present understand anything beyond forms, it is a way of speeding up and intensifying the attempt to possess God until they become quite convinced by experience that he cannot be possessed." Second: "It imparts a symbolic analogical knowledge of God which gives them courage to venture into the Reality beyond symbols." Third, there is a difficult intermediate state, that of those "who can go beyond forms but hesitate to do so through fear or ignorance, and the state of those for whom the forms have lost all real meaning, or for whom they have become positively misleading" (Watts, 1947/1971a, p. 104). One of his earliest books shows that his convictions did not fundamentally change in later years. He acknowledges that most people will need a verbalized, formal manifestation of the nonverbal experience:

> not specifically Eastern and it does not use the alien terms of exotic faiths but the language of ordinary life. In substance it appears to be the pure religious experience apart from any creed, and in form the pure everyday experience, common to all men apart from any nation or race. . . . Ideas and symbols are necessary, for their study is like the Prodigal's journey into a far country. In the end we return to the home from which we started, but it comes before our eyes in a new light. (Watts, 1937, p. 158)

Although the immediate, nonverbal experience may be the purest form for rare mystics, for most individuals Christianity is essentially a *story* and not a system of *ideas*. Is this story a reciting of historical events, the force of which depends on their factual accuracy? After all, the central figure in the Christian story is Christ who was, it is claimed, given bodily form in Jesus bar Joseph, the carpenter from Nazareth, doctrinally the incarnation of God on earth. It is probably true to say that for those who experience the intensity of the immediate realization before concepts and words, if such an experience is possible, the "present moment" itself is the incarnation, beyond words. The majority, of course, needs such a realization to be clothed, embodied; a story to hear and celebrate.

Watts (1953/1968), therefore, drew a distinction between two senses of the Incarnation of Christ. One is the "historical abnormality" (p. 129) interpretation: the orthodox view. The second, which was his own position, is the Incarnation understood as the "Christening of mankind" (p. 133).

For those who take the first view, the very center of Christian faith is that the world has been redeemed by a temporal and historical event: the crucifixion of Jesus Christ under Pontius Pilate. Jesus is the crucified one, the man with tangible wounds in hands and feet, convincing Christianity's first empiricist, doubting Thomas. Watts (1964/1973a) claimed that in its Protestant form, Christianity had increasingly rationalized Christ. Theologians and biblical scholars were pursuing the "quest for the historical Jesus" (p. 115). Watts found the products of this endeavor to demythologize Christ as dreary and unproductive, revealing Jesus to be "a rather boring prophet or messianic fanatic" (p. 111). Watts commented that he never warmed to the personality of Jesus as it comes to us through history and tradition. To ask in what sense Jesus is the answer to the contemporary human predicament is to see that he clearly has no relevance as a practical preacher offering guidance that we have simply to put into practice:

> Safely tucked away in ancient history . . . Christ can never be the beggar that comes to the door; and it was nothing more than a *figure of speech*, when he said, "Inasmuch as you have done unto one of the least of these my brethren, you have done it unto me." To insist on the historicity of the Christian myth is to remove Christ to the sterile distance of archaeological curiosity." (Watts, 1964/1973a, p. 113, emphasis added)

Indeed, the notion of God underlying this version of the Incarnation is itself archaeological. Watts (1947/1971a) called it the idolatrous "petrifaction" of God: solid but dead. If there ever *was* a god made of stone it was this one. It is reinforced in popular Christian spirituality: the "rock of ages" and the "rock that doesn't roll." The "mighty fortress" incarnated itself into the Christ who has "laid a sure foundation," and the "stone which the builders rejected, who has become the corner stone." These images are a denial of "Incarnation." The Word became *flesh*; soft, tender and utterly un-rock-like.

By contrast, Watts (1953/1968) interpreted the "Christening of mankind" by referring to St. Paul's "No longer I, but Christ" and argued that these words focus, in a very clear sense, the whole symbolism of the Incarnation. The "gospel," in the deepest mystical sense must be the communication of Christ's own experience of Godhood. It's hardly the case that Jesus accepted himself as his personal Savior, but instead realized he was, and always had been, united with God. The whole point of the gospel, for Watts, is that everyone may experience union with God in the same way and to the same degree as Jesus himself. It is barely good news, "gospel," to be urged to simply imitate "the actions of a man who had the unique advantage of being God. . . . It is thus that the "saving truth" of the gospel appears, not as Jesus' experience of Godhood, but as his punishment for proclaiming it" (Watts, 1971c, p. xvi). The "Christ of Catholic dogma" was a more profound comprehension than the simplified "Jesus of history" (Watts, 1953/1968). Liturgy then, for Watts, was not a merely memorialized aspect of the life of Christ. Through the cycle of the church year, through the daily celebration of the liturgy, these saving events were constantly relived in the present. Thus, in *Behold the Spirit,* Watts (1947/1971a) had set himself "the incarnational task of so uniting religion with ordinary life that ordinary life becomes religious itself" (p. 233).

CHRISTIANITY RECONSIDERED

In writing *Behold the Spirit* in 1947, Watts was "bending over backwards to speak from within the Christian tradition and to use theologically acceptable language" (Watts, 1973b, p. 228). But by 1950, he was at odds with the church and the orthodox interpretation of its doctrines. Conservative Christian thinkers were claiming that his use of the perennial philosophy implied syncretism and pantheism (see Clark, 1978). Even more seriously, Watts had undermined the church's teaching about the uniqueness of Jesus. In *The Supreme Identity,* for example, he suggested, "Christ will seem unique" to Asian minds "only if it can be made certain that his life and death, his resurrection and ascension, constitute the supreme analogy of his metaphysical realization" (Watts, 1950/1973c, p. 140).

Watts continued to delight in the formal rituals of the liturgy, but the Christian style of the inner life, with the "feeling of 'I' " as the "sensation of the soul," went completely against his innate sensibilities. He observed, "Christians hardly ever considered changing consciousness itself" (Watts, 1973b, p. 227). Watts (1973d) described the problem as follows:

> Our difficulty in talking about this is that our word "God" is so loaded . . . and our relationship to God . . . is blocked by the phenomenon of excessive reverence. I also call it "pedestalization"—Put that fellow high enough in your estimation and you can't reach him. This is a way of kicking him upstairs so he won't bother you. So, with this attitude of "God," we have lost the sense of *God* as the *"immediate magic:"* the absolute "inside" of everything. The "inside" is only used metaphorically for the most obvious "what there is," so screamingly obvious that only a well-educated person can miss it. You didn't see it because you were looking for something more recondite. So, when you've got this pedestalization, this great phenomenon of excessive reverence that prevents you from seeing the obvious, you think, surely,

it couldn't be that! Surely, it cannot be that simple. (emphasis added; see also, Watts, 1995)

This was one of the primary reasons for his leaving the priesthood in 1950. Another was that he could not defend the claim that Christianity was unique:

My previous discussions did not take proper account of that whole aspect of Christianity which is uncompromising, ornery, militant, rigorous, imperious and invincibly self-righteous. There is not a scrap of evidence that the Christian hierarchy was ever aware of itself as one among several lines of transmission for a universal tradition. (Watts, 1964/1973a, p. xii)

In the 1960s, however, Christianity became once more a plausible religion for Alan Watts who by then had encountered the "fog-cloud horizon" at "the end of the West" near San Francisco Bay (1973b, p. 31). As described earlier, Watts dissociated himself from Christianity in the 1950s because of its objectionable facets, among them being the church's imperious claims to be the supreme religion and its insistence on the absolute distinction between Creator and creature. Watts (1964/1973a) commented:

These objectionable facets were not temporary distortions or errors. They play an essential part in the Christian way of life, though in a manner that must necessarily be surprising and unexpected . . . only such a uniquely "impossible" religion could be the catalyst for the remarkable developments of human consciousness and self-knowledge which distinguish Western culture since 1500. (p. xiii)

Whereas Watts' first positive embrace of Christianity in the 1940s had sought to make it plausible by its absorption of the unitive mysticism in Asian traditions, the reverse is the case in the 1960s. Now other religious traditions could absorb Christianity and thus make it plausible in a different, unfamiliar setting. How might Christianity appear, for example, in the light of an interpretive context other than Western theology? Thus, in *Beyond Theology* Watts (1964/1973a) wrote: "Christianity is one thing in the context of Mediterranean and European culture, of Judaism and Islam. But in the context of Taoism and Confucianism, Hinduism and Buddhism, it may be quite another" (p. 12). Now, in his later attempts to speak positively about Christianity and give it a more intelligible sense, it would be in the framework of Asian wisdom traditions.

Situating Christianity, for example, in the context of Hinduism, it appears as "the extreme adventure of God into his own *maya.*" Thus in Christianity "as nowhere else is the good so gracious and the evil so blackly malignant" (Watts, 1964/1973a, p. 20). In biblical imagery, God breathed the *ruach Adonai* into Adam and sees the world through Adam's eyes. He forgot he was God. He was formless up to this point but from then on sees "forms." He looks back at himself and from Adam's eye. In theological terms, this "self-othering" in God is, in St. Paul's words, the act of self-emptying, "kenosis." Yet at this point, the formless God who now sees forms, acts also as a guru through the prophets and Jesus. The "original Self," then, appears in the human perspective as a Zen master or some other mystic teacher. Watts suggested that Christianity, on the surface, with its claims of distinction between Creator and created, appears to be making impossible, double-binding demands on individuals such as commanding or obliging spontaneous love of God. However, if we see these commands in the context of the Hindu world, it makes a great deal of sense. The double-bind "carries the sense of separate individuality and conscious will-power to a critical, and absurd, extreme—at which point the illusion explodes into the discovery of our original and eternal Identity" (p. 131). Thus in the beginning, dismemberment of the unity of things and the play is that the One is really many. Later on, when it is time to wake up, you remember in the sense of re-member.

Christianity so interpreted becomes an initiation, a method of liberation. God as the giver of grace has therefore the same function as the guru or spiritual guide in Hinduism. Thus, the means of grace would be the correct equivalent of *upaya* in Buddhist terms. That is, the "merciful technique" to awaken the sleeper. One of the Christian means of grace is the Holy Communion. Some early texts refer to the wheat scattered over the hills and then gathered together and made into one bread, so may we all, who have been scattered, become one body with Christ. The one body refers to the cosmological body of the universe and realizing the universe is one body and you are a member of it—not merely "members" in the sense of being "parts." In Protestant forms of the Holy Communion, the elements "represent" and therefore deny the union of spirit with matter. By contrast, the Catholic mass reflects the Hindu idea of *annam Brahman*, "God-food," the food of Brahman. So when the grape is crushed, that in the life in the grape is the supreme Lord offering himself to himself in the individual. He is always giving himself away and making whole—holy. Christ's words may express this: "Unless you eat the flesh of the Son of man and drink his blood, you have no life in you." The command to "eat this in re-membrance of me" is the Lord putting himself together again. We become whole by being dismembered—getting lost. To convert bread and wine into the body and blood of Christ is to divinize the material world. The Word became flesh, the Incarnation. Watts comments that Christian history has been humanity's resistance to that idea; to not let the miracle happen, not seeing the truth of it. Never was there a moment when "spirit" said to "matter," "I love you" (Watts, 1964/1973a).

As mentioned earlier, Watts' claims about the plausibility of an immediate, mystical realization of reality, before thought and words, is too large a subject here for a detailed discussion, but a few brief comments can be made. In psychological terms, Watts (1971b) admits: "It is not, today, either a respectable or popular notion that to be aware of reality is ecstasy. We speak, rather, of grim realities, harsh truths, and hard facts" (p. 72). In religious terms, Watts (1953/1968) likewise confessed:

> It seems quite incongruous to use the name "God" to signify *that* which we experience immediately, before thought has sundered it into a world of things. . . . The problem arises, however, because the theologians really want to say that God is a fact, a thing—albeit the first fact and the first thing, the Being before all beings. (p. 61)

Yet the question that confronts Watts here is "how *immediate* is the 'immediate' magic of God?" The contemporary phenomena of postmodernism and deconstruction (see Altizer, 1982) have remorselessly questioned the assumptions of any position of the kind that is the core of Watts' version of direct, nonverbal realization. Two useful discussions are *The Problem of Pure Consciousness* (Forman, 1990) and *Mysticism and Philosophical Analysis* (Katz, 1978). In a more general and literary area is *Languages of the Unsayable* (Budick & Iser, 1987).

Don Cupitt's (1998) *Mysticism After Modernity* is a very skeptical treatment of the position Watts advocated. Cupitt argues that there is no meaningfulness and no cognition prior to language. His book is an attempt to write the transition from a late modern to a fully postmodern understanding of religious experience and mysticism. He claims that even our own knowledge of ourselves is never immediate but corrigible, disputable, language-dependent. Cupitt's (1998) one solace for Christianity is that "it provides us with a language to live by, and a set of model narratives for us to draw upon in building our own life-stories" (p. 2). However, as Cupitt makes clear, the price to be paid for this slender form of meaning for Christianity is that this "adds up to the 'death of God.' " Cupitt insists that such a position, which he calls the "mysticism of secondariness," is the only religious option, a mysticism that has lost any noetic sense, or a special knowledge that transcends the everyday. In *The Old Creed and the New*, Cupitt (2006) reflects on the possible form Christian thought would take in the light of his analysis: "It offers the individual something more like psychology and 'life coaching' " (p. 49).

Cupitt's conclusion would have been a completely unacceptable reductionism for Watts. Fifty years before this most recent philosophical debate, Watts (1953) had discussed how logical philosophies of language had made a most vital contribution to religious faith in showing the impossibility of saying or thinking what reality *is*. Watts pointed out that logical philosophy was confirming the same Asian theme, for example, we find in the *Kena Upanishad*: "Brahman is unknown to those who know It, and is known to those who do not know It at all" (p. 143). Perhaps the most likely position Watts would have taken in the light of contemporary postmodern intellectual upheavals is expounded in the writings of his friend, Huston Smith (1992, 2003; Griffin & Smith, 1989; Rosemont & Smith, 2008). Some clues that give plausibility to this comparison can be seen in Watts' rejoinders to the "new theology" and the "death of God" movement in his own time.

I was a theology student at the height of the radical ferment in Christianity that was the midwife for the "new theology" that spanned a decade from its appearance in the 1960s. The implications of this wind of change were felt acutely in theological colleges. Many of my fellow students were tormented by the question of whether God was a transcendent reality or a three-letter word. I remember a senior student coming to my room at midnight and confessing, "I'm so relieved that I don't have to believe in God any more." There was no suggestion that he would have to give up his vocation to be a minister because of this. Such was the primacy of merely social radicalism of those times; a primacy of the secular pulpit over the mystical altar. It was during this period that I read Alan Watts for the first time. It was *In My Own Way* and I found one sentence arresting: "I have come to the place where I see through ideas, beliefs and symbols" (1973b, p. 6). It was a breath of fresh air. Here we were, students losing sleep over our tortured obligation to believe in belief. Watts' words could be taken, at a superficial level, to mean that he, too, was relieved of an obligation to believe in God. Closer attention, of course, revealed that Watts did not empty the world of transcendence. Quite the contrary. Watts confidently said, as discussed earlier, that this was a reality that could be experienced directly without the doubt and angst of the belief that you could only hope to believe. What's more, I learned that Watts had been saying so, in various contexts, throughout his adult life.

I dutifully read the books by Thomas Altizer (see Altizer, 2006), William Hamilton (e.g., Altizer & Hamiliton, 1966; Hamilton, 1966), and many other scholars of the "new theology" who caught the mood of the times. They were clearly reductionist and revisionist despite their claims to be expounding the essence of Christianity. Watts (1960s/2006, 1977, 1983) had entered into dialogue with them. He concluded that they wanted to get rid of God, not just a conception of God. There was nothing more they appeared to offer than the ordinary, everyday reality—life as it comes into view on a dreary Monday morning. Watts (1971c) regarded their alternative to "God" as "insipid humanism" (p. xiii) spectacularly devoid of imagination. Joseph Campbell, a friend of Watts, often observed that we have the kind of God we are capable of having. Watts' (1960s/2006) view was that when the radical theologians claim that God is dead, they are saying nothing more than the only kind of God they know is dead. But, said Watts, you don't have to settle for the notion that life is just "a trip from the maternity ward to the crematorium." If the theologians do so, they make the best of it and apply the gospel to that, and we have simply arid "secular" Christianity.

Alan Watts (1960s/2006) argued, as he had done even as a schoolboy, that the "God" who is dead is the "political" God, the divine paternalist, and the authority that rules the universe and to whom we are related as a subject to a king by analogy. The God who had died is a *conception* of God; an idol, a thought-graven image, the most beguiling of all idolatrous images of God. Watts raises the question: If the crude, monarchical-political God is defunct, what is the alternative? One possibility, of course, is none. He concluded that the mainstream death of God and secular theologians adopted this view. What they were neglecting was the opportunity of having a more refined understanding of God. This, Watts suggested, could be called, as we saw earlier, "atheism in the name of God," in the apophatic tradition that is centuries old. The heart of the latter is the realization of God at first hand, the very thing itself.

Characteristically, Watts' (1960s/2006, p. 201) immediate response to the "new" theology's consensus that the ordinary, everyday reality is all there is, was: "Haven't I heard something like this before?" It was, of course, the exchange between a student and a Zen master. The student asks, "What is Buddha?" The master replies, "It's windy again this morning." Does this exchange say what it appears to mean? No, said Watts. There is something different happening. The exchange may culminate:

> in a completely shattering experience that is very difficult to talk about, but generally speaking, it is the encounter with eternity, with the eternal—not necessarily in the sense of that which goes on and on through time, but the eternal in the timeless. That which transcends time is beyond measurement in hours or days. When someone has been through that state of consciousness and looks at the ordinary everyday world, it's true, they see the ordinary everyday world as we see it, but with a very extraordinary difference. (pp. 201–202)

That difference is "the immediate here and now, as when the meaning of the universe is realized 'in the clatter of a broken tile'" (Watts, 1964/1973a, p. 120). Ninian Smart (1970/2009) too drew on Buddhism to cast a different perspective on the new theology in a lecture on Buddhism and the death of God. He said "Christianity will ultimately be tested not in the secular city, whose prototype is Chicago and New York, but in the hearts of those who have tested the canned fruits of the post-Christian West and found them tasteless." He adds that the Buddhist tradition, with no God, "can tell us something which transcends the vulgarity of the new moral radicalism afflicting secularizing Christian theologians" (p. 163).

CONCLUSION

My present conclusion on Alan Watts' significance for Christianity is one that I made in my earlier study of his thought, when we ask whether life remains in the words of the particular Christian themes and analogies: "The analogies can hardly appear rich and evocative to individuals who have no feeling of transformed identity and consciousness" (Keightley, 1986, p. 171). As already acknowledged, Watts said that Christians hardly ever consider changing consciousness itself. The price would be giving up believing in belief. Watts' life and work addresses this observation to the tradition that nurtured him from childhood and still haunted him long after he had cut the ties that bound him to it. The change in consciousness even now can still be clothed in the garments of Christian symbolism as of every other tradition that still has its mysterious treasures. As St. Paul wrote, "We have this treasure in earthen vessels." In Alan Watts' case, the earthen vessels are the life and language of what we call the ordinary, everyday, which are transparent to the divine transcendence, for those who are awake:

> For we have to live the Christian story, and this is not done simply by remembering its events on the days of the year set apart for each. The task is not so much to think of the present meaning of what happened in the past, as to think of those past events as symbols of what is happening in the present. (Watts, 1937, p. 157)

Those words are from one of his earliest publications. Watts was twenty-two when he put pen to paper in Rowan Tree Cottage—probably in the drawing room. He later described the book as "immature," yet there are parts of it that are as profound as anything he wrote in later years. Not least the final paragraph of the book:

> Between the greatest height of spirituality and the most ordinary things of the world there is no division. We shall study every philosophy, search through all spiritual exercises until our minds are swollen with the whole wisdom of the world. But in the end we shall return to the surprising fact that we walk, eat, sleep, feel and breathe, that whether we are deep in thought or idly passing the time of day, we are alive. And when we can know *just that* to be the supreme experience of religion we shall know the final secret and join in the laughter of the gods. For the gods are laughing at themselves. (Watts, 1937, pp. 158–159)

REFERENCES

Altizer, T. J. J. (Ed.). (1982). *Deconstruction and theology.* New York: Crossroad.

Altizer, T. J. J. (2006). *Living the death of God.* Albany: State University of New York Press.

Altizer, T. J. J., & Hamilton, W. (1966). *Radical theology and the death of God.* Indianapolis, IN: Bobbs-Merrill.

Budick, S., & Iser, W. (Eds.). (1987). *Languages of the unsayable.* New York: Columbia University Press,

Clark, D. (1978). *The Pantheism of Alan Watts.* Downers Grove, IL: Inter-Varsity Press.

Cupitt, D. (1998). *Mysticism after modernity.* Oxford: Blackwell.

Cupitt, D. (2006). *The old creed and the new.* London: SCM.

Forman, R. K. C. (Ed.). (1990). *The problem of pure consciousness.* New York: Oxford University Press.

Griffin, D. R., & Smith, H. (1989). *Primordial truth and postmodern theology,* Albany: State University of New York Press.

Hamilton, W. (1966). *The new essence of Christianity* (Rev. ed.). London: Danton, Longman, & Todd.

Katz, D. (Ed.). (1978). *Mysticism and philosophical analysis.* London: Sheldon.

Keightley, A. (1986). *Into every life a little Zen must fall: A Christian philosopher looks to Alan Watts and the East.* London: Wisdom.

Rosemont, H. Jr., & Smith, H. (2008). *Is there a universal grammar of religion?* Chicago: Open Court.

Smart, N. (2009). Buddhism and the death of God. In J. J. Shepherd (Ed.), *Ninian Smart on world religions: Selected papers Vol. 1. Religious experience and philosophical analysis* (pp. 151–163). Burlington, VT: Ashgate Publishing. [Reprinted from Eighth Montefiore Memorial Lecture delivered on February 5, 1970, University of Southampton.]

Smith, H. (1992). *Forgotten truth.* San Francisco: HarperCollins.

Smith, H. (2003). *Beyond the postmodern mind* (3rd ed.). Wheaton, IL: Quest Books.

Watts, A. W. (1937). *The legacy of Asia and Western man.* London: John Murray.

Watts, A. W. (1952). Introduction. In F. Spiegelberg, *Spiritual practices of India* (2nd ed., pp. vii–xv). San Francisco: Greenwood Press.

Watts, A. W. (1953). The language of metaphysical experience: The sense of non-sense. *Journal of Religious Thought, 10*(2), 132–143.

Watts, A. W. (1968). *Myth and ritual in Christianity.* Boston: Beacon Press. (Original work published 1953)

Watts, A. W. (1971a). *Behold the spirit: A study in the necessity of mystical religion.* New York: Vintage. (Original work published 1947)

Watts, A. W. (1971b). *Erotic spirituality.* New York: Collier Macmillan.

Watts, A. W. (1971c). Preface to the new edition. In *Behold the spirit: A study in the necessity of mystical religion* (pp. xi–xxiv). New York: Vintage.

Watts, A. W. (1972). *The theologia mystica of Saint Dionysius.* Sausalito, CA: Society for Comparative Philosophy. (Original work published 1944)

Watts, A. W. (1973a). *Beyond theology: The art of Godmanship.* New York: Vintage. (Original work published 1964)

Watts, A. W. (1973b). *In my own way: An autobiography, 1915–1965*. New York: Vintage.

Watts, A. W. (1973c). *The supreme identity*. London: Wildwood House. (Original work published 1950)

Watts, A. W. (Speaker). (1973d). *Taoism: The watercourse way* (cassette recording). Sausalito, CA: MEA.

Watts, A. W. (1977). God. In *The essence of Alan Watts* (M. J. Watts, Ed., pp. 25–42). Millbrae, CA: Celestial Arts.

Watts, A. W. (1983). The relevance of Oriental philosophy. In *The Way of Liberation: Essays and lectures on the transformation of the self* (M. Watts & R. Shropshire, Eds., pp. 39–53). New York: Weatherhill.

Watts, A. W. (1995). Jesus: His religion or the religion about him. In *Myth and religion: A thorn in the flesh* (M. Watts, Ed., pp. 39–54). London: Eden Grove Editions.

Watts, A. W. (2002). Images of God. In *Tao of philosophy* (A. W. Watts, Ed., pp. 53–62). Boston: Tuttle.

Watts, A. W. (2006). Democracy in the kingdom of heaven. In *Eastern wisdom, modern life: Collected talks, 1960–1969* (pp. 191–207). Novato, CA: New World Library. (Original work presented 1960s)

CHAPTER THREE

Phenomenological Exegeses of Alan Watts: Transcendental and Hermeneutic Strategies

Peter J. Columbus

The sensibilities of twenty-first–century scholarship seem to require a statement of reflexivity by the author of a text. This means readers should be advised that information is being rendered to effectively structure the manuscript they are perusing, and this interpreted knowledge may be an artifact of an approach that is nuanced by personal experience, social and cultural context, or historical and political dynamics. My claim of interest in Alan Watts has been neither neutral nor objective since first encountering his writings during a three-year segment of adolescence and young adulthood in the 1970s when my parents were dying from extended illnesses. His books were pivotal in helping me to traverse that precarious terrain of life. The old cliché about teachers appearing on the scene when students are ready for learning proved to be auspiciously apropos of my situation. The attention to Alan Watts afforded by the events of living and dying subsequently informed my decision to study humanistic and phenomenological psychologies in graduate school where my first academic publication (Columbus, 1985) was a rejoinder to Nordstrom's and Pilgrim's (1980) critique of Watts' mysticism.

The original intent with this chapter was to reconsider my response to Nordstrom and Pilgrim in light of middle-aged professional and personal experience. This initial project was envisioned as a kind of midlife exploration on the well-worn theme of "if I only new then what I know now," not in the sense of regret about the past, but rather in terms of clarity about the subject matter. When rereading after many years two of Watts' texts in preparation for the new paper, I realized that he was employing, in implicit fashion, what appeared as contemporary Western philosophical strategies while claiming to profess the insights of ancient Asian wisdom. In other words, Watts used phenomenological methods without either informing his readers that he was doing so or engaging the technical language of phenomenological philosophy. In one of these texts (Watts, 1951b), it seemed that Watts used a Husserlian transcendental phenomenological method to consider the experience of insecurity, whereas the other book (Watts, 1966/1989) reflected hermeneutic phenomenological strategies in addressing the question of identity. The final product of this chapter thus emerged from a recognition of Watts' uses of phenomenology in *The Wisdom of Insecurity* and *The Book: On the Taboo Against Knowing Who You Are.*

Saying that Watts (1951b, 1966/1989) was engaging phenomenological *exegeses* is not to suggest that he was only explaining, interpreting, or analyzing particular domains of knowledge. He was instead calling his readers toward transfigured experiences of themselves and the world. Indeed, a key theme in the writings of Alan Watts is the notion that people are caught in the illusion of their egos as separate and isolated from the rest of the universe. Amid this illusion of separateness, our egos engage in futile attempts at controlling our bodies, other people, and nature. Watts, moreover, identified the philosophies of Daoism, Buddhism, and Vedanta as recognizing that the "I" is not an "individualized consciousness alone, but the matrix from which it arises" (Watts, 1953a, p. 100), and the point is not merely to intellectually understand the concept of this unity of person and world, but to experientially know it as such. Watts saw the main intention of his overall work as imparting the realization that a sense of disjunction from the integrated ground of creation is but a mere by-product of conceptual thinking. He sought to afford this insight for his readers via a direct and transformative experience of reality beyond the words and concepts expressed on the written page (Watts, 1953b, 1975).

Watts (1951b, 1966/1989) claimed to be offering ancient Asian wisdom via special styles that are accessible to contemporary Western readers. Despite acknowledging stylistic presentations of these writings, however, he did not offer any detailed discourses on the methods he used to afford transformative experiences in the readers of these texts. As this chapter proceeds, the phenomenological strategies employed by Watts will be sketched and followed by a consideration of how he may be understood as a philosopher of Asian mysticism in light of his use of Western philosophical methods. Finally, I explore the question of Alan Watts as an antecedent and contemporary influence on the development of humanistic/transpersonal psychology beyond the usual references to Zen and psychotherapy.

TRANSCENDENTAL PHENOMENOLOGY AND
THE WISDOM OF INSECURITY

At the risk of sounding overly pedantic to some readers and excessively remedial or cursory to others, it may nevertheless be useful at the outset to offer a brief (and thus incomplete) description of transcendental phenomenology defined as the systematic study of *intentionality* developed by Husserl (1913/1962) via Brentano. *Intentionality* is the term used by phenomenologists to describe the basic relational processes of consciousness. In phenomenology, consciousness is always an awareness of something beyond the act of being conscious, and the way the object for consciousness appears is contingent on one's orientation toward it. Husserl called the act of being conscious the *noesis* and the object for consciousness the *noema*. A phenomenology of intentionality begins with a consideration of the *natural attitude*. The natural attitude refers to the naive assumption in everyday life where what appears to consciousness is considered to be unrelated to the act of being conscious. The assumption of the natural attitude is subsequently *bracketed*, or put in abeyance, toward identifying and examining the intentional processes of consciousness. The bracketing procedure allows the phenomenologist to consider how appearances of things (the noema) are constituted by acts of consciousness (the noesis). Other bracketing procedures can subsequently be applied toward identifying alternative possibilities for experience.[1]

Alan Watts appears to have employed an implicit transcendental phenomenology in *The Wisdom of Insecurity* (1951b). This book was an exploration of the "quest for psychological security" and humankind's "efforts to find spiritual and intellectual certainty in religion and philosophy" (p. 9). The text, subtitled as *A Message for an Age of Anxiety*, was written in the dusk of World War II and at the dawn of the Cold War. The manuscript was penned with the sentiment that no composition could be more fitting in a period where human existence looked to be so "peculiarly insecure and uncertain" (p. 9). Indeed, W. H. Auden's poem, *The Age of Anxiety: A Baroque Eclogue*, was published in 1947 and won the Pulitzer Prize in 1948. Leonard Bernstein's Symphony No. 2, also with the title "Age of Anxiety" premiered in April 1949. In 1950, Jerome Robbins choreographed his "Age of Anxiety" ballet to Bernstein's music. In *The Wisdom of Insecurity* (1951b), Watts offered a description of the natural attitude of insecurity, suggested a bracketing procedure toward identifying the intentional character of insecure experience, and applied a second bracketing procedure, thus affording his readers an alternative and possibly transformative experience of the world: "to be aware of life, of experience as it is at this moment, without any judgments or ideas about it" (p. 75). What follows is a brief explication of this phenomenological process employed by Watts.

THE NATURAL ATTITUDE OF INSECURITY

Watts (1951b) described the taken-for-granted feeling that we live in a time of unusual insecurity due to the increased pace and hostility of modern living brought about with the emergence of science, technology, and industry. These trends are seen as leading to dysfunctions in customary cultural and family structure, economic and political organization, and religious practice. Science, as described by Watts, has relegated religion to the status of fictional myth and diluted the power of religious conviction to offer plausible relief in fixed things such as the notion of Deity, the idea of everlasting spirit, and divine justice (a sort of "disenchantment of the world" *a la mode de* Max Weber). Humanity appears to be facing a choice between a version of Pascal's wager by creating and engaging the self-deception and lingering doubt of a new religious myth, or dwelling in a kind of despairing nihilism by "letting technology and science serve us as well as they may in our journey from nothing to nothing" (p. 22). The modern age is consequently one of dissatisfaction, disquiet, protest, and craving as people seek their pleasure in the desperations of time. "Somehow we must grab what we can while we can, and drown out the realization that the whole thing is futile and meaningless" (p. 21).

BRACKETING THE NATURAL ATTITUDE OF INSECURITY

Bracketing is a key procedural means in transcendental phenomenological inquiry consisting of a thoughtful endeavor to set aside existential beliefs about the character and core of things and events. In so doing, the actuality of the world is not denied but merely situated into a temporary pause. As Idhe (1986) remarked, transcendental phenomenology via its bracketing procedures "necessarily departs from familiar ways of doing things and accepted ways of thinking. It overturns many presuppositions ordinarily taken for granted and seeks to establish a new perspective from which to view things" (p. 17). For his part, Watts (1951b) alerted readers that they will frequently find themselves "in a topsy-turvy world in which the normal order of things seems to be completely reversed, and common sense is turned inside out and upside down" (p. 9). This course of action by way of bracketing makes the intentionality of experiencing into the fundamental issue for phenomenological consideration. Watts began his bracketing of the natural attitude of insecurity by conceding all the skepticism of science:

> We may admit frankly that we have no scientific grounds for belief in God, in personal immortality, or in any absolutes. We may refrain altogether from trying to believe, taking life as it is, and no more. From this *point of departure* there is yet another way of life that requires neither myth nor despair. But it requires a complete revolution in our ordinary, habitual ways of thinking and feeling. (pp. 22–23)

THE INTENTIONALITY OF INSECURITY

Applying a bracketing procedure allowed Watts (1951b) to treat insecurity as an intentional act of consciousness, and he subsequently identified four intentional ways of experiencing the world as an insecure place: By (a) an act of temporal consciousness emphasizing anticipation (dread) or retrospection (regret) to the detriment of the present moment; (b) believing ourselves as separated into a fixed, cognizant identity and an inconstant bodily process resulting "in a war between consciousness and nature, between desire for permanence and the fact of flux" (pp. 42–43); (c) confusing linguistic representation with the actuality of lived experience. People are accordingly "dumbfounded" when language does not jive with the experience of living; and (d) the "rationalization of life," where logical thinking is allowed to expand and dictate our lives all out of proportion to "instinctual wisdom." The experiential upshot is that we are at war within ourselves where (a) the rational mind is requiring things that the body does not desire, (b) the body is desiring conditions to which the mind does not consent, (c) the mind is presenting commands with which the body will not adhere, and (d) the body is emitting inclinations that the mind fails to comprehend.

THE SECOND BRACKETING PROCEDURE

Through a process of examining several examples for each of the four intentional acts of insecurity, a task that phenomenologists call *imaginative (or free) variation,* Watts (1951b) identified an essential constituent common to all of them and described it as follows: "the desire for security and the experience of insecurity are the same thing" (pp. 77–78). He was pointing to these acts of insecurity as seeking to isolate and protect the person from the ongoing flux of life that, paradoxically, generates a greater sense of anxiety. How are we, therefore, to find refuge and tranquility? Watts intuited the paradoxical intention of eliminating insecurity by relinquishing one's resistances to change and thoroughly engaging the flow of life: "Can we . . . approach our experience—our sensations, feelings, and thoughts—quite simply, as if we had never known them before, and without prejudice, look at what is going on" (p. 81)? This letting go of noetic prejudices provides for a dissolution of the problem of insecurity and (possibly) transforms the experience of living. Said Watts:

> We are concerned here with understanding something which *is*—the present moment . . . It is simply being aware of this present experience, and realizing that you can neither define it nor divide yourself from it. There is no rule but Look! (p. 99)[2]

For Watts (1951b), the mystery of living was a reality for experience rather than a problem needing solution, and his application of the second bracketing procedure created an opening to experience "whose name is . . . wonder" (p. 150). Here we may be reminded of Spiegelberg's (1982) characterization of phenomenology "as a philosophy which has learned to wonder again and to respect wonders for what they are in themselves" (p. 81). Husserl, moreover, asserted that "the wonder of all wonders is the pure ego and pure subjectivity (cited in Spiegelberg, 1982, p. 151). Watts' (1951b) bracketing process removed prejudices and presumptions of insecurity toward affording a more pure experience of the world. Said Watts: "The mind becomes aware that to *be* at this moment is pure miracle" (p. 150).[3]

HERMENEUTICS AND *THE BOOK*

Hermeneutics is an approach to interpretation and understanding of texts. The term has a Greek philosophical etymology with apparent reference to Hermes who functioned as a communicative intermediary between the gods and humans. Consistent with this etymological basis, an early and common variation of hermeneutics concerns the interpretation of religious and sacred scriptural texts, especially Biblical literature, and Watts (1966/1989) apparently was offering a playful reference to this mode of hermeneutic inquiry when labeling his manuscript as *"The Book."* A twentieth-century strand of hermeneutics emerged in the phenomenological school of thought via the works of Heidegger, Gadamer, and Ricoeur that involved what Gadamer (1975) termed a *fusion of horizons* that, in a general sense, is a move toward understanding with emphasis on the interpretation of one arrangement of meaning in light of another seemingly dissimilar or contradictory signification. The hermeneutic method, as described by Arons (a protégé of Paul Ricoeur), begins with an initial identification of two or more networks of meaning related to a topic of interest. This first step is referred to as establishing the "multidimensional significance" of the phenomenon. Second, these various networks of meaning are elaborated and detailed in a process called "differentiation." Third, the differentiated meaning networks are engaged in a "dialectical process" of comparison and contrast toward identifying similarities and differences. Fourth, the dialectical process arrives at greater depth and breadth of comprehension called "intuitive understanding" (Barrell, Aanstoos, Richards, & Arons, 1987).

Alan Watts seems to have used a hermeneutic phenomenological strategy in composing *The Book* (1966/1989). This text was an exploration of identity written in the middle 1960s when the "baby-boom generation" in the United States was reaching adolescence and young adulthood. The question of identity is central to adolescent development, and Watts described his work as a "lowdown on life and existence" (p. 1) which parents might discretely offer to their sons and daughters on the verge of maturity. In *The Book*, Alan Watts introduced a multidimensional consideration of identity, differentiated two distinct networks of meaning vis-à-vis identity, engaged these horizons of meaning in a dialectical process, and fused these horizons of identity toward greater intuitive comprehension. What follows is a brief explication of Watts' hermeneutic method.

THE MULTIDIMENSIONAL SIGNIFICANCE OF IDENTITY

Watts (1966/1989) recognized two apparently dichotomous notions of identity. One sense of identity is the experience of a disconnected ego in a foreign world. As Watts described it:

Most of us have the sensation that "I myself" is a separate center of feeling and action, living inside and bounded by the physical body—a center which "confronts" an "external" world of people and things, making contact through the senses with a universe both alien and strange. (p. 8)

The other sense of identity is more expansive and inclusive. "I" resides:

in the whole surge of energy which ranges from the galaxies to the nuclear fields in my body. At this level of existence, "I" am immeasurably old; my forms are infinite and their comings and goings are simply the pulses or vibrations of a single and eternal flow of energy. (p. 13)

THE DIFFERENTIATION OF IDENTITY

In a chapter entitled "The Game of Black-and-White," Watts (1966/1989, pp. 25–52) elaborated the more expansive and profound sense of identity as the "Self of the World" by referencing Tillich's "Ground of Being," and hyphens were used in the chapter title to indicate the basic unity between self and other, individual and universe. As Watts described it, however, "the essential trick of the Game of Black-and-White is a most tacit conspiracy for the partners to conceal their unity, and to look as different as possible" (p. 51). Watts sought to recover, explicate, and restore the larger sense of identity that is usually obscured in the practicalities of everyday life. He employed the German term, *hintergedanke*, in reference to the hidden sense of identity and defined it as "an apprehension lying tacitly in the back of our minds which we cannot easily admit to, even to ourselves" (p. 12). Ricoeur (1970) described this process of recovering or recollecting distant yet profound existential meanings as a *hermeneutics of faith*.

By contrast, in a chapter entitled "How To Be A Genuine Fake," Watts (1966/1989, pp. 53–86) described the usual and more limited sensation of an individualized self as a "hoax" and a transitory persona that people are swindled into exhibiting with their own silent compliance. *The Book* is therefore subtitled *On the Taboo Against Knowing Who You Are* and thereby reflects what Ricoeur (1970) called a *hermeneutics of suspicion* because Watts sought to lay bare how a deceptive awareness of identity as an isolated ego becomes manifest in experience and obstructs consciousness of the larger sense of Self. Here also is an implicit consistency with Heidegger's hermeneutics of Being as described by Caputo (1970):

Being conducts a "masquerade" with man, concealing itself in its truth and hiding that very concealment. Being on this account is quite

literally "il-lusive" (*il-ludens*). It plays with man by showing a masked
face, an "il-lusion" which represents a withdrawal of its origin-al truth. ·
In such a view Being carries on a pretense which it is the role of man
to unmask. (p. 38)

Compared with a transcendental phenomenology that offers the reader a
set of concrete directions about the noetic act of consciousness, hermeneutic
phenomenology sees that inherent tendencies, suppositions, and prejudgments
that may be set in one's biological nature or historical situation cannot be suf-
ficiently bracketed but instead need to be recognized and rendered with clarity.[4]
Thus it is not surprising that Watts (1966/1989) suggested the experience of
an isolated ego, considered as illusory, "has its history in ways of thinking—in
the images, models, myths, and language systems which we have used for
thousands of years to make sense of the world" (p. 57). These "ways of thinking" affect our everyday perceptions of reality. Here it is worth mentioning
that Watts' (1966/1989) chapter titles, such as "The Game of Black-and-White"
and "How To Be A Genuine Fake," are not merely incidental labels because
hermeneutic phenomenology looks to afford comprehension and revelation of
experience by way of language, and, on occasion, it may be poetic language
that makes available the lone sufficient mode of portraying human meaning and
permitting the appreciation of a phenomenon with greater clarity and insight
(Hein & Austin, 2001). In his autobiography, Watts (1973b) wrote that "much
of my work is poetry disguised as prose. . . . I am trying to get *thinking* people
to be aware of the actual vibrations of life as they would listen to music" (p. 5,
emphasis added). In *The Book*, Watts (1966/1989) was speaking via "myth" and
"special metaphors, analogies, and images" (p. 13) because, he suggested, the
foundations or "ground" of existence cannot be grasped by conceptual thinking. Instead, he sought a radical shift in his readers' perceptual experience by
using figures of speech. As Idhe (1986) pointed out:

> Story tellers, myth makers, novelists, artists and poets have all used
> similar means to let something be seen. . . . Within the context set
> by the story, experience takes shape. . . . There is a gestalt-event. All
> at once, the desired effect is achieved; one sees it in an instant. (p. 88)

The story devices and figurative expressions engaged by Watts (1966/1989)
were used to create conditions that immediately situate readers' perceptual possibilities thus allowing something to be seen and experienced. The experiences
of the readers take shape within the context set by these figures of speech.
Additionally, Watts used story devices and figurative expressions, particularly
"play" and "game" metaphors, that were intended to be commensurate with,
and accessible to, the sensibilities of an adolescent audience. These figurative
expressions consequently may appear as rather sophomoric, or even puerile, to

a more erudite readership. A Hindu creation myth, for example, is described as God playing a game of hide-and-seek with itself. A second example is the previously mentioned "game of black-and-white" metaphor intended to describe basic unities between apparently dichotomous categories such as self and other or person and world. Yet Caputo (1970, 1978) pointed out that Heidegger's concept of "Being at play" was itself founded on the paradigmatic example of childhood playfulness. Watts, in fact, used many "game" and "play" metaphors such that it may be worth remembering Heidegger's (1971) observation that hermeneutic processes achieve understanding "by a playful thinking that is more persuasive than the rigors of science" (p. 29). More to the point, perhaps, is Gadamer's (1975) notion of "play as the clue to ontological explanation" (p. 75) because the structure of play engrosses the players into the event and thereby transfiguring the participants in the process.

The Dialectic of Identity

The dialectic process in hermeneutical analysis seeks to compare and contrast dichotomous horizons of meaning toward fusing perspectives into a more expansive vision. In the chapter entitled "The World Is Your Body," Watts (1966/1989) moved in the direction of Merleau-Ponty's (1962) *Phenomenology of Perception* by insisting on the primacy of consciousness as a double-edged, embodied process that simultaneously reveals and conceals any sense of identity. On one hand Watts said:

> Our knowledge of the world is, in one sense, self-knowledge. For knowing is a translation of external events into bodily processes, and especially into states of the nervous system and the brain; we know the world *in terms* of the body, and in accordance with its structure. (p. 100)

Yet for Watts, as for Merleau-Ponty, this embodied self-knowledge is equivocal or ambiguous because it is an ongoing affair that concurrently references a world beyond itself toward which it is always reaching but never completely grasps in its entirety. "The total environment (or situation) is both spatial and temporal—both larger and longer than the organisms contained in its field" (Watts, 1966/1989, p. 104). Therefore, in Watts' phrasing, "The fact that every organism evokes its own environment must be corrected with the polar or opposite fact that the total environment evokes the organism (p. 104).[5]

Intuitive Understanding of Identity

Watts (1966/1989) sought to fuse the smaller and larger meaning systems of identity into a *"correlative vision"* in which "all explicit opposites are implicit allies" (p. 148); "the 'dimension' in which explicit differences have implicit unity" (p. 149). Nonetheless, Watts asked in his fifth chapter (pp. 109–138), "So What?" Hermeneutical analysis is a circular process, or "double-take" to use Watts' own terminology, in which comprehension of a text as an entirety is recognized through allusion to its particulars while the understanding of the parts is achieved by reference to the whole. This type of part–whole investigation indicates that neither the entire text nor any single portion of it can be comprehended or understood without mutual consideration. As Watts suggested, "what we mean by 'understanding' or 'comprehension' is seeing how parts fit into a whole, and then realizing they don't compose the whole . . . but that the whole is a pattern" (p. 97). The result is a hermeneutic circle of continuously arising data and elucidation the upshot of which is an always expanding discernment of the text. Shaffer (1978) described the hermeneutic circle in Watts' overall body of work as:

> A mutually interacting and interpenetrating polarity; in this more cosmic view, man is but an interconnecting unit within a larger patterned whole, and it is not altogether clear that a person's consciousness cannot, should it become increasingly liberated, grasp this more universal design. (p. 155)

In light of this hermeneutic circle, a return to Watts' (1966/1989) "hoax" allusion regarding the "Self of the World" as God playing hide-and-seek affords a recognition of the punch line to this cosmic joke as being "You're IT!" (pp. 139–159). This "IT" is simultaneously the seeker, that which is hiding, the process of playing, all of it and/or none of it at all. Thus we can hermeneutically circle back to the chapter on "How To Be A Genuine Fake" and understand the phrase "genuine fake" as embodying a variety of meanings, including (a) an experience and belief in the veracity of one's separate and isolated ego, (b) a double-bind of dichotomous and contradictory identities, or perhaps (c) a reference to a real *fakir* with a depth of insight into the mysteries of existence for, as Watts concluded *The Book*, "when IT plays, it plays at being everything else" (p. 159).

WHY DID ALAN WATTS COME FROM THE WEST?

Alan Watts was not a self-declared phenomenologist. He once described himself as having a "lone-wolf inclination to find my own way" (Watts, 1973b, pp. 163–164) and never overtly expressed his belonging to the phenomenological movement in philosophy or psychology. He is usually considered as a philosopher of Asian mysticism so it may therefore be inaccurate, or perhaps gratuitous, to simply project him into the movement as an actual member. Spiegelberg

(1982), however, considered "phenomenology in the widest sense" to include scholars who satisfy methodological criteria without identifying themselves subjectively with the phenomenological movement. Moreover, given the transcendental phenomenology that is evident in *The Wisdom of Insecurity*, Watts (1951b) fulfilled Spiegelberg's (1982) requisites for the "strictest sense" of phenomenology by using bracketing procedures that afford "special attention to the way in which the appearances of an object are constituted in and by an act of consciousness" (p. 6). *The Book* (Watts, 1966/1989), on the other hand, may not be phenomenology in the strictest sense but definitely represents a turn toward hermeneutic phenomenology in the general direction of Heidegger, Gadamer, and Ricoeur. Thus how are we to understand Watts as a philosopher of Asian mysticism in light of his appropriation of apparently Western phenomenological philosophical strategies?

Watts (1951b) wrote *The Wisdom of Insecurity* at a time when his philosophical sensibilities were consonant with the notion of a *philosophia perennis*. The idea of a perennial philosophy concerns the possibility of a universally recognized spiritual experience transcending the definitions of history, context, and culture (Watts, 1973b). Likewise, Husserl's transcendental phenomenology sought to afford the universal foundations of philosophy (Kockelmans, 1994). Additionally, Watts was informed by the negative metaphysic of the East (Watts, 1951a) and the apophatic theology of St. Dionysius (Watts, 1944) from the Catholic tradition that he considered as the Christian equivalent of the Asian approach, particularly the works of Nagarjuna (Watts, 1947/1971). The aim of both Western apophatic theology and Asian negative metaphysics is to remove obstacles to the direct experiencing of what may be called Ultimate Realty. As Watts (1951b) said, "truth is revealed by removing things that stand in its light" (p. 6), and it appears that he employed bracketing procedures resembling transcendental phenomenology toward this end. Although Watts (1951b) claimed to be writing "in the spirit of the Chinese Lao-Tzu, that master of the law of reversed effort, who declared . . . that to know truth one must get rid of knowledge" (p. 10), comparative studies of Husserl's bracketing procedures and Lao-Tzu's negative strategy showed similar methodological approaches (Woo, 1984, 1994). According to Woo (1994):

> Husserl's "consciousness" and Lao-Tzu's "Wu" are two central concepts in which the ancient and archetypal philosophical problems are discussed and resolved. Both "consciousness" and "Wu" are the cosmic center, which is like a source of light radiating in all directions and creating heaven and earth and Ten-thousand-things. This ontological result is based on an epistemological approach both in Husserl's phenomenology and in Lao-Tzu's Tao-te-king; both use the same method of bracketing. (Comparison section, p. 128)[6]

In his preface to *The Book* (1966/1989), Watts claimed to be drawing "on the insights of Vedanta, stating them, however, in a completely modern and Western style" (p. x), and this style appears to be hermeneutic phenomenology. In contrast to *The Wisdom of Insecurity* in which Watts (1951b) employed an implicit transcendental phenomenological strategy consistent with a perennial philosophy, *The Book* (1966/1989) was written after Watts, in *Beyond Theology* (1964/1973a), loosened his hold on *philosophia perennis* as a starting point for philosophical analysis. Watts (1964/1973a) recognized that perennial philosophy may be an untenable point of departure due to the Christian advocacy for "the unique and supreme position of the historical Jesus" and its implications for the meaning of personal identity by virtue of the "absolute distinction between Creator and the creature" (p. xii). This issue of relations between "Creator" and "creature" became the question of dichotomized identity in *The Book* (Watts, 1966/1989).

In *Beyond Theology* (Watts, 1964/1973a), moreover, the dichotomy between perennial philosophy and Christian exclusivity became the point of departure for philosophical analysis where Watts articulated three basic methodological rules with an unmistakable hermeneutic tenor. First, religion is to be taken as a process of living one's life; as a basic way of existing. Thus religion is not merely a reference to life or an explanation of life but rather is "an involvement, a participation" (p. 26) that renders religious practice and spiritual experience as localized narratives. Second, given that religious practices were considered as contextual data, they could be subject to a process "whereby we illuminate one theological system . . . by looking at it and seeing what happens to it in the context of another" (p. 26). This is Watts' variation on the "fusion" of dichotomous meanings and shows itself in *The Book* (Watts, 1966/1989) via consideration of the Western individual ego in relation to Vedanta. Third, Watts (1964/1973a) considered religion at the figurative and metaphorical level as a way of avoiding reification of abstract religious concepts. He wanted to move beyond "theological ideas and symbols" toward "direct, non-conceptual touch with a level of being which is simultaneously one's own and the being of all others" (p. 217). In *The Book*, Watts (1966/1989) said: "The fact is that because no one thing or feature of this universe is separable from the whole, the only real You, or Self, is the whole. The rest of this book will attempt to make this so clear that you will not only understand the words but *feel* the fact" (p. 53). Watts (1966/1989) thus used myth, metaphor, and other figurative expressions and story devices toward noematically structuring the perceptual experience of his readers.[7]

Another issue emerging out of *Beyond Theology* (Watts, 1964/1973a), which influenced the form and substance of *The Book* (Watts, 1966/1989), was Watts' reconsideration of the role and impact of scientific knowledge for understanding mysticism. Whereas the portrayal of science in *The Wisdom of Insecurity* (Watts, 1951b) alluded to its part in alienating humanity from spiritual and religious experience, Watts (1964/1973a) identified three main trends in the scientific thinking of his time which are "three ways of describing the identity of things or events as the mystic feels them" (p. 218). These scientific trends included (a) the mounting appreciation that cause-connected events are not discrete happenings, but facets of a singular process, (b) the emphasis on field theory in the natural and social sciences, and (c) an emphasis on holism and part–whole relationships. Thus said Watts (1966/1989), *The Book* is "a cross-fertilization of Western science with an Eastern intuition" (p. x), and he emphasized Gestalt perceptual theory, cybernetics, and quantum physics in this regard.[8]

HUMANISTIC AND TRANSPERSONAL PSYCHOLOGY

How may the phenomenological exegeses in *The Wisdom of Insecurity* (Watts, 1951b) and *The Book* (Watts, 1966/1989) inform an understanding of Watts' relevance for humanistic psychology in its historical version from the 1960s and contemporary forms in the new millennium? One way to answer this question is by pointing directly at the methodology itself. European phenomenology and Asian mystical traditions are two key influences on the historical emergence and contemporary development of humanistic psychology and its offshoot, transpersonal psychology. Watts is commonly referenced as belonging to the camp of scholars advocating traditional Asian ways of studying psychological life (Daniels, 2005; Rowan, 2001). Klee (1970) described Watts as contributing significantly to the emergence of the humanistic psychology movement in the 1960s due to his skillful advocacy for Zen and Daoism. Watts promoted Daoism and Zen Buddhism in an extraordinary fashion owing to the convincing manner of his writing style. The basic lucidity inherent to Watts' scholarship made traditional Asian philosophies resonate with readers of his texts. "Watts broke the ice, thawed our frozen aesthetic sensibilities and released our reactions to the message. Indeed, for many of us Watts made it our medium" (Klee, 1970, pp. 6–7).

In addition, Klee described the humanistic psychology of his day as offering very few, if any, viable research methods but he acknowledged the phenomenological bracketing intrinsic to the Gestalt works of Kurt Lewin and Kurt Koffka that helped humanistic psychologists transcend the inflated stress on the dichotomy of subject and object so prevalent in the natural science methods of mainstream psychology. Similarly, it can heretofore be suggested that Watts' (1951b) implicit use of phenomenological strategies was a singular methodological contribution to the early development of the humanistic psychology movement prior to the more widespread application of these methods by psychologists in later years. In particular, Watts anticipated phenomenological interrogations of Eastern practices in Western contexts (e.g., Columbus & Rice, 1991, 1998) and recognized the "transpersonal potential" of Husserl's transcendental phenomenological method explicated by Hanna (1993) many years later.

Moreover, the hermeneutical analyses inherent to *The Book* (Watts, 1966/1989) prefigured the increasing overt concern with relations between hermeneutics and psychology (e.g., Crownfield, 1979; Homans, 1975) and the eventual development of explicit hermeneutic–phenomenological strategies for psychological research (e.g., Packer, 1985). The contemporary relevance of Watts' (1951b, 1966/1989) phenomenological strategies lies in the fact that research methods informed by phenomenology remain only partially integrated with humanistic psychology (Rennie, 2007). Consideration of Watts' texts as phenomenological projects may add to this process of incorporation, especially in research concerning transpersonal experience where there is burgeoning interest in phenomenological methods of inquiry (e.g., Barnes, 2003; Miller, 2007; Taylor, 2009b; Valle, 1998).

A second way of considering Watts' relevance for humanistic psychology is in terms of content or subject matter. Watts offered works addressing many issues relevant to humanistic psychology including sexuality (Watts, 1958) and altered states of consciousness (Watts, 1962), but his most salient contribution to a content area concerns applications of Buddhism and Daoism to the theory and practice of psychotherapy (Watts, 1961). *The Wisdom of Insecurity* (Watts, 1951b) as a consideration of anxiety is another of these works. Now there is not an intractable conceptual jump from scholars of Asian mysticism such as Alan Watts to European philosophers of existentialism like Kierkegaard, and it is tempting to locate Watts' (1951b) take on modern angst as an existential piece of work. Some writers would argue, however, that placing *The Wisdom of Insecurity* within a Western existential trajectory is problematic. Shaffer (1978), for example, situated Watts within the humanistic tradition but placed him at a distance from the faction of humanistic psychology that is based in European existentialism due to their stress on an ontological isolation and an unavoidable trepidation of death that Watts ultimately rejected in *The Wisdom of Insecurity* as being artifacts of Western modes of thinking.

Additionally, it may be difficult to consider *The Wisdom of Insecurity* as a neo- or post-Kierkegaardian take on anxiety because Watts emphasized the sense of immediacy in lived experience at the expense of what Kierkegaard considered as a more sophisticated and higher order mode of self-reflection that constitutes an uneasy cognizance of one's failure to actualize a full potential and that results in an understanding of one's identity as separate from and contingent on God (Pattison, 2002). Nevertheless, what is quite notable about Watts' (1951b) application of transcendental phenomenology to the study of insecurity is that it preceded and conceivably augured the appearance of empirical phenomenological studies on the experience of anxiety in the 1960s and 1970s (e.g., Fischer, 1969, 1971). The most obvious contemporary relevance of Watts' (1951b) take on insecurity is that it concerns how people engage, experience, transcend, and transform the world as an unsafe place, an issue of figural significance in a post-September 11, 2001 existence that appears to be imbued with fears of terrorism and a sense of ongoing threat (Marshall et al., 2007; Smith, 2005).

In *The Book*, Watts (1966/1989) addressed the question of identity to adolescent readers by articulating Vedanta philosophy partly in terms of modern Western science. This strategy seems to be founded implicitly on two key observations about Western adolescent development offered by Erikson (1959, 1968). First, adolescents in the twentieth-century West commonly explored their emerging identities by looking toward cultures other than their own. Second, familiarity with contemporary scientific and technological sensibilities renders Western adolescents more adaptable in their own culture. Watts (1966/1989) can therefore be seen as a forerunner to later works that consider Erikson's developmental psychology in relation to Heidegger's phenomenological hermeneutics (Knowles, 1986) and Advaita Vedanta (Paranjpe, 1998). *The Book*, moreover, contains an articulated theme of self-transformation that is emergent in contemporary views of transpersonal experience (Sinnott, 2006; Sleeth, 2006; Taylor, 2009a; Todres, 2000). For example, a meta-analysis of seven research studies on transpersonal dimensions of experience concluded: "The breaking down and reforming of existing patterns of who we think we are is at the heart of spiritual development as a living process" (Valle & Mohs, 1998, p.111).

The notion of "approach" constitutes a third mode for exploring meaningful relations between Watts' (1951b, 1966/1989) phenomenology and humanistic psychology. The concept of approach refers to the ways that scholars orient themselves toward defining their problems for study and choosing appropriate methods for researching their topics of interest (Giorgi, 1970). The question of approach is fueling the forward motion of the humanistic movement in psychology (Aanstoos, 2003). Embedded in the humanistic approach is a recognition of "the double problem of knowledge," meaning that psychologists must deal with conceptual data typically relevant to academic scholarship while also transacting with pre-reflective, lived experience; the process of being present to the immediacy of ongoing life (Klee, 1970). Klee noted that early humanistic psychologists emphasized the latter issue while developing and congealing as a movement at the innovative margins of fields like mental health, business, and education where individuals could not wait for the statistical certainties of mainstream psychological science before facing the necessities of action in real-world situations. Here one is reminded of Wheelwright's (1953) description of Watts (1951b):

> The Wisdom of Insecurity is not a way of evasion, but of carrying on wherever we may happen to be stationed—carrying on, however, without imagining that the burden of the world, or even of the next moment, is ours. It is a philosophy not of nihilism but of the reality

of the present—always remembering that to be of the present is to be, and candidly know ourselves to be, on the crest of a breaking wave. (p. 500)

Here again Watts prefigured contemporary trends in humanistic and transpersonal psychology as exemplified by Gordon's (2003) contention that "psychology must inevitably be transpersonal because an unpredictable universe transcends the merely unknown and raises the issue of the unknowable" (p. 96). Gordon envisions "the possibility for a psychology in which uncertainty is regarded not as a limit but as an expression of the boundless creativity inherent in the universe" (p. 96).

It is established that humanistic psychology historically considered the quandary of double knowledge through a holistic approach that overcame dualistic visions of the world in favor of perspectives that emphasized the interconnectedness of all things (Aanstoos, 2003). Aanstoos, moreover, viewed this holistic approach, which he suggested continues to foment through "a complex stew" of "variegated sources" from East and West, as most favorable for addressing the dilemmas of disaffection that seem endemic to issues such as globalization, ecology, health, and spirituality that will be vital contents for contemporary and future generations of humanistic psychologists. In this regard, Capra (2004) wrote:

During the 1960s I realized that the numerous crises we were facing (and are still facing today)—the environmental crisis, the economic crisis, the nuclear weapons crisis, etc—were all different facets of one and the same crisis, which is ultimately a crisis of perception. The book that first triggered this insight was The Book by Alan Watts, published in 1966. (p. 61)

In light of this "crisis of perception" it should be noted, therefore, that Watts' general approach to his subject matter is imbued with what Brannigan (1977) called a "Gestaltian denominator," which is extraordinarily consonant with the holistic vision of humanistic psychology that Aanstoos (2003) projected as the future of the movement. As Brannigan described it, Watts' approach embodied a "psycho-philosophical Gestaltian vision" whereby form and backdrop are seen as a single integrated totality. Although not denying an experience of difference, "there is the absence of dichotomy between subject and object, knower and known, figure and ground" (p. 342) in the philosophy of Alan Watts, and thus his philosophical attitude can be considered as an endeavor to overcome the contemporary predicament of personal and collective estrangement by sensing the implicit oneness permeating our overtly disparate experiences.[9]

CONCLUSION

Explicating the phenomenological strategies that are inherent to *The Wisdom of Insecurity* (Watts, 1951b) and *The Book* (Watts, 1966/1989) reveals some "intertextualities" in Watts' writings that have yet to be recognized in contemporary and historical considerations of his scholarship. Intertextuality is a semiotic notion referring to the ways that prior and contemporary scholarship influence the writing and reading of texts. An intertextual analysis seeks to understand how the meanings afforded by a text via the writer or reader emerge and are transformed by other past and present texts (Kristeva, 1980). The intertextual findings of this chapter, such as Watts' implicit appropriation of transcendental phenomenology and his subsequent transition to hermeneutics, run counter to a common critical appraisal of Watts that was articulated most clearly by Ballantyne (1989): "He ran short of creative insights early on in life, for the most part limiting himself to the refinement of a stockpile of ideas he had learned as a young man" (p. 441). As pointed out elsewhere (Columbus, 1985), such appraisals mistakenly harden Watts' writings into a single philosophical statement while failing to recognize the temporal evolution of his insights and the resulting changes in his philosophical approach.

Further intertextual considerations of Alan Watts' texts seem warranted. One reason is that Watts' style of writing, especially in many of his later works, exuded a sense of brevity that bypassed what he considered as the overly nuanced, highly conditional, and excessively delimited nature of academic scholarship. Watts' economy of style resulted in his branding as either an unoriginal popularizer or as misconstruing preexistent domains of knowledge. In his autobiography, Watts (1973b) said he was "well aware" of the omitted nuances in his works and was ready to "refer those who want the fine points to the proper sources, and can, furthermore, produce the necessary scholarly evidence for my conclusions if asked" (p. 302). Watts (1967), for example, identified a text by Alexandra David-Neel and Lama Yongden as his "I-told-you-so-book" in response to assertions that "I have invented my explanations of Buddhism out of thin air, thus falsifying its authentic teachings." Now at a point many years beyond his death, a revisiting of Watts' writings in light of their intertextuality may reveal him as having greater cognizance of his subject matter than he was chartering to the readers of his books and papers.[10]

There is another reason that Watts' brevity of style calls for further intertextual analyses identifying various forces of intellectual sway on his scholarship: The overidentification of Watts as an original thinker liberated from alternative sources of influence. In *The Wisdom of Insecurity*, for example, Watts (1951b) was seeking to afford in his readers an experience of awakening in and to the present moment. He did not burden them with the technicalities or details of a transcendental phenomenological methodology or a negative metaphysic. "To ask how to do this, what is the technique or method, what are the steps or rules, is to miss the point utterly" (p. 99). One biographer seems to have misunderstood the meaning of this brevity as Watts' virtual independence from textual sources:

> The Wisdom of Insecurity was a different kind of book than anything Alan Watts had done before. Previous works had been stuffed with literary and religious allusions and studded with footnotes, most of them learned citations of other works. Wisdom had only seven foot-notes and no bibliography at all. . . . This was Alan Watts being Alan Watts, an important thinker in his own right. (Stuart, 1983, p. 131)

A third mode of advocacy for intertextual reflection concerns the intellectual heritage and continuing sway of the 1960s counterculture vis-à-vis the present age. Indeed, as phenomenologists are mindful of pointing out, the past is what was before as it is experienced in the present moment. Furlong (2001) stated the issue most succinctly with respect to Alan Watts: "the legacy of the counterculture has increased rather than diminished . . . it is more important than ever to examine the lives of people who, like Alan Watts, are counted as the movement's movers and shakers" (p. ix). The idea of intertextuality refers not only to writers, but to readers of texts as well. So how is contemporary discourse beyond psychology under the influence of "Wattsian" texts? One pre-liminary answer is Prosser's (2004) assertion that Watts' *The Way of Zen* (1957) was a substantive influence on Roland Barthes' post-structural writings toward the end of his life, especially *Camera Lucida*. Finally, phenomenologists see the future as what sits ahead when viewed in the now, so perhaps various histori-cal and contemporary structurings and interpretive codes can be brought to readings of Alan Watts' texts toward informing and facilitating personal growth and collective survival in the twenty-first century.

NOTES

1. See James (2007) and Sokolowski (2000) for introductions to Husserl's phe-nomenology. Spiegelberg (1982) offers a substantive historical consideration of the phenomenological movement.

2. As Idhe (1986) pointed out, "if one knows enough about the structures of perception, . . . One may guide viewing from the knowledge of its structural possibili-ties" (pp. 89–90). Through a phenomenological method, Watts (1951b) was assisting his readers in transcending the prejudices of their insecure gaze on the world toward a psychospiritual seeing with greater clarity and insight.

3. Husserl (1936/1970) described his transcendental phenomenological method as affording "a complete personal transformation, comparable in the beginning to a religious conversion, which then, over and above this, bears within itself the significance of the greatest existential transformation which is assigned as the task of mankind as such" (p. 137).

4. See Laverty (2003) for a comparison of Husserl's phenomenology and hermeneutic phenomenology.

5. This reciprocal implication of organism and environment has been thematic in Western hermeneutics as far back as "Goethe's research on organisms whose parts cohere within a living whole" which influenced the philosophical hermeneutics of Friedrich Schleiermacher in the early 1800s (Rajan, 2004, p. 487).

6. In a footnote to his chapter 5, "On Being Aware," Watts (1951b, p. 76) acknowledged the influence of Krishnamurti on his understanding of consciousness. The projects of Krishnamurti and Husserl are similar in spirit because they both seek to examine the essential structures of consciousness while pointing toward a state of awareness without presupposition. See Gunturu (1998) for a consideration of Krishnamurti in light of Husserl's phenomenology. Also, Butcher (1986) has considered Krishnamurti's work as a generic phenomenology. Moreover, given a perennialist approach, when Watts (1951b, p. 99) called his readers to "Look!," reference can be made to Eckhart saying "the Now-moment in which God made the first man and the Now-moment in which the last man will disappear, and the Now-moment in which I am speaking are all one in God, in whom there is only one Now. Look!" (cited in Watts, 1951b, p. 144) *and* to a saying of ancient Zen master, Lin-ji (Rinzai): "On your lump of red flesh is a true man without rank who is always going in and out of the face of everyone of you. Those who have not yet proved it, look, look!" (Sasaki, 2009, p. 4).

7. Watts (1966/1989) was using cataphatic language with a caveat: "My problem as a writer, using words, is to dispel the illusions of language while employing one of the languages that generates them. I can succeed only on the principle of 'a hair of the dog that bit you' . . ." (p. 57). This seems reminiscent of the *Sandokai*, a Zen Buddhist scripture by Sekito Kisen (A.D. 700–790). An English translation entitled *The Identity of Relative and Absolute* says "The absolute works together with the relative like two arrows meeting in midair. Reading words you should grasp the great reality" (Scott & Doubleday, 1992, p. 120). Quinney (1988) referred to this process as going "beyond the interpretive" to "the way of awareness." The interpretive hermeneutic circle is not broken but rather transcended with a mindful nonattachment. Kripal (2001) has described this kind of realization as "hermeneutical mysticism" where readers "do not so much process religious data as unite with sacred realities" (p. 5). Elsewhere, Kripal (2007) described hermeneutical mysticism as "a disciplined practice of reading, writing, and interpreting through which intellectuals actually come to experience the religious dimensions of the texts they study" (p. 61).

8. Watts (1966/1989) pointed directly at Bohm's (1958) *Quantum Theory* and Schrodinger's (1964) *My View of the World*. Although Watts was not the first to elucidate the consonance between contemporary physics and Eastern philosophies, we can see a burgeoning post-Watts trend beginning with Capra's (1975) *Tao of Physics* and extending up to the present time, for example, Wallace (2007).

9. In a paper entitled "A Challenge to Humanistic Psychology in the 21st Century," Criswell (2003) suggested that "individual tendencies of humanistic psychology need to blend with a more collaborative model" (p. 42; See also, Ferrer, 2002; Ferrer & Sherman, 2008).

10. I have in mind here works along the lines of *Heidegger's Hidden Sources: East Asian Influences on His Work* (May, 1996).

REFERENCES

Aanstoos, C. M. (2003). The relevance of humanistic psychology. *Journal of Humanistic Psychology, 43*(3), 121–132.

Barnes, J. (2003). Phenomenological intentionality meets an egoless state. *Indo-Pacific Journal of Phenomenology, 3*(1). Retrieved from www.ipjp.org.

Barrell, J. J., Aanstoos, C., Richards, A. C., & Arons, M. (1987). Human science research methods. *Journal of Humanistic Psychology, 27*(4), 424–457.

Ballantyne, E. (1989). Alan Watts. In C. H. Lippy (Ed.), *Twentieth-century shapers of American popular religion* (pp. 436–445). Westport, CT: Greenwood Press.

Bohm, D. (1958). *Quantum theory.* Englewood Cliffs, NJ: Prentice-Hall.

Brannigan, M. C. (1977). Alan Watts' metaphysical language: Positivity in negative concepts. *Orientalia Lovaniensia Periodica, 8,* 341–350.

Butcher, P. (1986). The phenomenological psychology of J. Krishnamurti. *Journal of Transpersonal Psychology, 18*(1), 35–50.

Capra, F. (1975). *The tao of physics: An exploration of the parallels between modern physics and eastern mysticism.* New York: Random House.

Capra, F. (2004). My five most influential books. *Ecologist, 34*(1), 61.

Caputo, J. D. (1970). Being, ground, and play in Heidegger. *Man and World, 3*(1), 26–48.

Caputo, J. D. (1978). *The mystical element in Heidegger's thought.* Athens: Ohio University Press.

Columbus, P. J. (1985). A response to Nordstrom and Pilgrim's critique of Alan Watts' mysticism. *The Humanistic Psychologist, 13*(1), 28–34.

Columbus, P. J., & Rice, D. L. (1991). Psychological research on the martial arts: An addendum to Fuller's review. *British Journal of Medical Psychology, 64,* 127–135.

Columbus, P. J., & Rice, D. L. (1998). Phenomenological meanings of martial arts.participation. *Journal of Sport Behavior, 21*(1), 16–29.

Criswell, E. (2003). A challenge to humanistic psychology in the 21st century. *Journal of Humanistic Psychology, 43*(3), 42–52.

Crownfield, D. R. (1979). The self beyond itself: Hermeneutics and transpersonal experience. *Journal of the American Academy of Religion, 47*(2), 245–267.

Daniels, M. (2005). *Shadow, self, spirit: Essays in transpersonal psychology.* Charlottesville, VA: Imprint Academic.

Erikson, E. (1959). *Identity and the lifecycle.* New York: International University Press.

Erikson, E. (1968). *Identity: Youth and crisis.* New York: Norton.

Ferrer, J. N. (2002). *Revisioning transpersonal theory: A participatory vision of human spirituality.* Albany: State University of New York Press.

Ferrer, J. N., & Sherman, J. H. (Eds.). (2008). *The participatory turn: Spirituality, mysticism, religious studies.* Albany: State University of New York Press.

Fischer, W. F. (1969). Towards a phenomenology of anxiety. In B. P. O'Rourke (Ed.), *Explorations in the psychology of stress and anxiety* (pp. 105–115). Don Mills, Ontario: Longman.

Fischer, W. F. (1971). Faces of anxiety. *Journal of Phenomenological Psychology, 1,* 31–49.

Furlong, M. (2001). *Zen effects: The life of Alan Watts*. Woodstock, VT: Skylight Paths.

Gadamer, H. (1975). *Truth and method*. New York: Crossroads.

Giorgi, A. (1970). *Psychology as a human science*. New York: Harper & Row.

Gordon, K. (2003). The impermanence of being: Toward a psychology of uncertainty. *Journal of Humanistic Psychology, 43*(2), 96–117.

Gunturu, V. (1998). *Jiddhu Krishnamurtis gedanken aus der phanomenologischen perspective Husserls* [Jiddhu Krishnamurti's thought from the phenomenological perspective of Edmund Husserl]. Frankfurt: Peter Lang.

Hanna, F. (1993). The transpersonal consequences of Husserl's phenomenological method. *The Humanistic Psychologist, 21*, 41–56.

Heidegger, M. (1971). *On the way to language*. New York: Harper & Row.

Hein, S. F., & Austin, W. J. (2001). Empirical and hermeneutic approaches to phenomenological research in psychology: A comparison. *Psychological Methods, 6*(1), 3–17.

Homans, P. (1975). Psychology and hermeneutics: An exploration of basic issues and resources. *The Journal of Religion, 55*(3), 327–347.

Husserl, E. (1962). *Ideas: General introduction to pure phenomenology* (W. R. B. Gibson, Trans.). New York: Collier McMillan. (Original work published 1913)

Husserl, E. (1970). *The crisis of European sciences and transcendental phenomenology*. Evanston, IL: Northwestern University Press. (Original work published 1936)

Idhe, D. (1986). *Experimental phenomenology: An introduction*. Albany: State University of New York Press.

James, J. L. (2007). *Transcendental phenomenological psychology: Introduction to Husserl's psychology of human consciousness*. Oxford: Trafford Publishing.

Klee, J. B. (1970, September). *The humanist perspective*. Paper presented to the American Psychological Association, Miami Beach, FL. (Reprinted in *Humanistic psychology: A source book*, pp. 1–12, by I. D. Welch, G. A. Tate, & F. Richards, Eds., 1978, Buffalo, NY: Prometheus Books)

Knowles, R.T. (1986). *Human development and human possibility: Erikson in the light of Heidegger*. Lanham, MD: University Press of America.

Kockelmans, J. J. (1994). *Edmund Husserl's phenomenology* (2nd ed.). West Lafayette, IN: Purdue University Press.

Kripal, J. J. (2001). *Roads of excess, palaces of wisdom: Eroticism and reflexivity in the study of mysticism*. Chicago: University of Chicago Press.

Kripal, J. J. (2007). *Esalen: America and the religion of no religion*. Chicago: University of Chicago Press.

Kristeva, J. (1980). *Desire in language: A semiotic approach to literature and art*. New York: Columbia University Press.

Laverty, S. M. (2003). Hermeneutic phenomenology and phenomenology: A comparison of historical and methodological considerations. *International Journal of Qualitative Methods, 2*(3). Article 3. Retrieved from http://ualberta.ca/~iiqm/backissues/2_3final/html/laverty.html.

Marshall, R. D., Bryant, R. A., Amsel, L., Suh, E. J., Cook, J. M., & Neria, Y. (2007). The psychology of ongoing threat: Relative risk appraisal, the September 11 attacks, and terrorism-related fears. *American Psychologist, 62*(4), 304–316.

May, R. (1996). *Heidegger's hidden sources: East Asian influences on his work* (G. Parkes, Trans.). New York: Routledge.

Merleau-Ponty, M. (1962). *Phenomenology of perception*. New York: Humanities Press.

Miller, A. L. (2007). The transpersonal psycho-phenomenology of self and soul: Meditators and multiples speak. *Annalecta Husserliana, 94*, 103–124.

Nordstrom, L., & Pilgrim, R. (1980). The wayward mysticism of Alan Watts. *Philosophy East and West, 30*(3), 381–401.

Packer, M. (1985). Hermeneutic inquiry in the study of human conduct. *American Psychologist, 40*, 1081–1093.

Paranjpe, A. C. (1998). *Self and identity in modern psychology and Indian thought*. New York: Plenum.

Pattison, G. (2002). *Kierkegaard's up-building discourses*. New York: Routledge.

Prosser, J. (2004). Buddha Barthes: What Barthes saw in photography (that he didn't in literature). *Literature and Theology, 18*(2), 211–222.

Quinney, R. (1988). Beyond the interpretive: The way of awareness. *Sociological Inquiry, 58*(1), 101–116.

Rajan, T. (2004). Hermeneutics: Nineteenth century. In M. Groden, M. Kreiswirth, & I. Szeman (Eds.), *The Johns Hopkins guide to literary theory and criticism* (2nd ed., pp. 486–489). Baltimore, MD: The Johns Hopkins University Press.

Rennie, D. L. (2007). Methodical hermeneutics and humanistic psychology. *The Humanistic Psychologist, 35*(1), 1–14.

Ricoeur, P. (1970). *Freud and philosophy: An essay on interpretation*. New Haven, CT: Yale University Press.

Rowan, J. (2001). *Ordinary ecstasy: The dialectics of humanistic psychology* (3rd ed.). East Sussex, UK: Brunner-Routledge.

Sasaki, R. F. (Trans.). (2009). *The record Linji* (T. Y. Kirchner, Ed.). Honolulu: University of Hawaii Press.

Schrodinger, E. (1964). *My view of the world*. Cambridge, UK: Cambridge University Press.

Scott, D., & Doubleday, T. (1992). *The elements of Zen*. Rockport, MA: Element.

Shaffer, J. B. P. (1978). *Humanistic psychology*. Englewood Cliffs, NJ: Prentice-Hall.

Sinnott, J. (2006). Spirituality as "feeling connected with the transcendent:" Outline of a transpersonal psychology of adult development. In R. L. Piedmont (Ed.), *Research in the social scientific study of religion* (Vol. 16, pp. 287–308). Leiden, The Netherlands: Brill.

Sleeth, D. B. (2006). The self and the integral interface: Toward a new understanding of the whole person. *The Humanistic Psychologist, 34*(3), 243–261.

Smith, E. M. (2005). Collective security: Changing conceptions and institutional adaptations. In W. A. Knight (Ed.), *Adapting the United Nations to a postmodern era: Lessons learned* (2nd ed., pp. 41–51). New York: Palgrave Macmillan.

Sokolowski, R. (2000). *Introduction to phenomenology*. Cambridge, UK: Cambridge University Press.

Spiegelberg, H. (1982). *The phenomenological movement: A historical introduction* (3rd ed.). The Hague: Martinus Nijhoff.

Stuart, D. (1983). *Alan Watts*. New York: Stein & Day.

Taylor, E. (2009a). *The mystery of personality: A history of psychodynamic theories.* New York: Springer.

Taylor, E. (2009b). The Zen doctrine of "no-method." *The Humanistic Psychologist, 37*(4), 395–306.

Todres, L. A. (2000). Embracing ambiguity: Transpersonal development and the phenomenological tradition. *Journal of Religion and Health, 39*(3), 227–237.

Valle, R. (1998). Transpersonal awareness: Implications for phenomenological thought in psychology. In R. Valle (Ed.), *Phenomenological inquiry: Existential and transpersonal dimensions* (pp. 273–279). New York: Plenum Press.

Valle, R., & Mohs, M. (1998). Transpersonal awareness in phenomenological inquiry: Philosophy, reflections, and recent research. In W. Braud & R. Anderson (Eds.), *Transpersonal research methods for the social sciences: Honoring human experience* (pp. 95–113). London: Sage.

Wallace, A. B. (2007). *Hidden dimensions: The unification of physics and consciousness.* New York: Columbia University Press.

Watts, A. W. (Trans.). (1944). *The theologia mystica of Saint Dionysious.* West Park, NY: Holy Cross Press.

Watts, A. W. (1951a). The negative way. In C. Isherwood (Ed.), *Vedanta for modern man* (pp. 20–24). Hollywood, CA: Vedanta Press.

Watts, A. W. (1951b). *The wisdom of insecurity: A message for an age of anxiety.* New York: Pantheon.

Watts, A. W. (1953a). On philosophical synthesis. *Philosophy East and West, 3,* 99–100.

Watts, A. W. (1953b). The language of metaphysical experience: The sense of non-sense. *Journal of Religious Thought, 10*(2), 132–143.

Watts, A. W. (1958). *Nature, man and woman.* New York: Pantheon.

Watts, A. W. (1961). *Psychotherapy East and West.* New York: Pantheon.

Watts, A. W. (1962). *The joyous cosmology: Adventures in the chemistry of consciousness.* New York: Pantheon.

Watts, A. W. (1967). Foreword. In A. David-Neel & L. Yongden, *The secret oral teachings of Tibetan Buddhist sects.* San Francisco: City Lights Books.

Watts, A. W. (1971). *Behold the spirit: A study in the necessity of mystical religion.* New York: Vintage. (Original work published 1947)

Watts, A. W. (1973a). *Beyond theology: The art of Godmanship.* New York: Vintage. (Original work published 1964)

Watts, A. W. (1973b). *In my own way: An autobiography.* New York: Vintage.

Watts, A. W. (1975). Philosophy beyond words. In C. J. Bontempo & S. J. Odell (Eds.), *The owl of Minerva: Philosophers on philosophy* (pp. 191–200). New York: McGraw-Hill.

Watts, A. W. (1989). *The book: On the taboo against knowing who you are.* New York: Pantheon. (Original work published 1966)

Wheelwright, P. (1953). The philosophy of Alan Watts. *The Sewanee Review, 61,* 493–500.

Woo, P. K. (1984). A comparative study of Lao-Tzu and Husserl: A methodological approach. In A. Tymieniencka (Ed.), *Phenomenology of life in a dialogue between Chinese and Occidental philosophy* (pp. 65–73). Boston: D. Reidel.

Woo, P. K. (1994). Lao-Tzu and Husserl: A comparative study of Lao-Tzu's method of negation and Husserl's epoche. In V. Shen, R. Knowles, & T. Van Doan (Eds.), *Psychology, phenomenology, and Chinese philosophy* (pp. 115–130). Washington, DC: The Council for Research in Values and Philosophy. Retrieved from http//www.crvp.org/book/Series03/lll-6/chapter_vi.htm.

CHAPTER FOUR

The Psychedelic Adventures of Alan Watts

Stanley Krippner

In 1963, I presented an extremely controversial paper at an international conference on general semantics at New York University. The presentation concerned LSD-type substances and how, if administered properly, they could help a person reestablish contact with what general semanticists call the "extensional world:" those aspects of nature that each culture filters and constructs through its own lenses and vocabularies.

Immediately after my talk, I noticed a tall woman wearing a large green hat with a floppy brim supported by a white cane, limping rapidly down the aisle. She wore a necklace of potbellied Buddhas, and earrings decorated with the same. Her first questions to me were, "Do you know Tim Leary? Do you know Alan Watts?" I acknowledged that I knew them both, having attended a reception for Watts when I was a volunteer participant in Leary's Harvard University psilocybin research project.

This colorful woman's name was Virginia Glenn, and I discovered that she had been in the crowded room at the 1961 convention of the American Psychological Association when I first heard Leary discuss psychedelics. After attending the symposium, I had written Leary a letter volunteering my services as a research participant in his study. It was pure serendipity that I arrived the weekend of Watts' reception and Leary graciously invited me to the event. At the sit-down pot-luck dinner Watts entertained the group by answering questions and giving short monologues on a variety of topics ranging from education in England (the land of his birth) to Eastern philosophy.

Watts was a key figure in the life of Virginia Glenn. Upon discovering that she had acute diabetes, she decided to commit suicide but changed her mind after hearing a taped lecture by Watts. In the early 1950s, she traveled between Chicago, Cleveland, New York City, and Washington, DC, playing her collection of Alan Watts' tapes for anyone interested in hearing them. She first met Watts in 1957 while working as a waitress in New York City. By then her diabetes was critical, sending her into frequent comas, and resulting in an incurable infection in her right foot. Despite her suffering, Virginia never complained about her condition. She began to schedule talks and seminars for Watts who looked upon her as a *Bodhisattva*—a living Buddha. I was living in New York City at the time and helped Virginia arrange Watts' lectures, an essential task because she was legally blind.

On July 3, 1970, Virginia and I had dinner in Greenwich Village; she had just returned from Boston where the physicians had examined her thoroughly and, as she put it, had "readjusted my chemicals." She reached into her ever-present carrying bag to pull out a number of articles and announcements she knew would interest me. The next day, Virginia went into a coma, was rushed to a hospital, and died. Alan Watts was in Europe at the time, but on his return he wrote:

> What always interested me was her discrimination and good taste in a dimension thronged with charlatans. . . . Above all, Virginia's genius was to bring together people who . . . would fertilize each other's insight and imagination. She must have been the catalyst of hundreds of friendships. (Watts, 1970, pp. 1–2)

The lasting fruits of my relationship with Alan Watts are a testament to Virginia's divine gift. Her talent of introduction would prove to be a lifelong benefit and the reason I can now write about Alan Watts with such personal perspective.

In this chapter, I suggest that Watts' integrated outlook on individual and transpersonal identity, cultivated through his peculiar upbringing, his interest in Anglican Catholicism and various Asian philosophies, and the randomized series of personal collisions that marked his life, laid a sturdy groundwork for his exploration of psychedelic matters. Undoubtedly, his overweening attachment to material and scientific explanations was counterpart to his experiences of mysticism, but he levied novel and profound attacks on accepted wisdom that served as a prologue to later developments. Although rife with contradiction, the complex intervention of his life in his work and vice versa, was partially responsible for the fertility of his thought.

THE ADVENTURES BEGIN

In 1958, after returning to the United States from lecturing at the C. G. Jung Institute in Zurich, Alan was conversing with Aldous Huxley and Gerald Heard. Alan's two companions were exuding greater tranquility and compassion than in previous meetings which they attributed to their ingestion of mescaline and LSD. Shortly thereafter, Watts was invited to take part in an experiment involving the ingestion of LSD under the direction of Dr. Keith Ditman, then in charge of LSD research at the Department of Neuropsychiatry at UCLA. A goal of the research was to see if ingestion of LSD would invoke mystical experiences in the participants.

Watts considered himself as adventurous with respect to mysticism and open to trying virtually any set of procedures used to unlock such types of awareness, but he initially thought it highly improbable that chemical substances could induce anything resembling an authentic mystical experience. He subsequently described his first LSD experience as aesthetically entertaining, but not spiritual in character. What he did experience, however, was a heightened perceptual awareness, especially of nature, with profuse and vivid colors in leaves and flowers, elaborate patterns of grass on the lawn, trees luminous in a radiant sun, and a sky reflecting the primordial essence of blue (Watts, 1973). Alan explained this experience as a temporary interruption of the usual tendencies toward selective attention in everyday life perception (Watts, 1960a).

Alan once told me that his mother introduced him to the world of color, flowers, and design. In his autobiography, he wrote that she inhabited a "magical world of beauty" despite the "wretched fundamentalist Protestantism she had half-heartedly inherited from her parents" (Watts, 1973, p. 8). Watts' father has been described as a gentle, tolerant, and humorous man (Furlong, 2001). The couple remained devoted to each other all their lives, settling in a cottage surrounded by a large garden. The garden's flora and fauna were allowed to grow wild into "an almost tropical swamp" rather than being tamed and manicured, as were other gardens of that era (Watts, 1973, p. 17). Watts wrote:

> My mother and father brought me up in a garden flutant with the song of birds. They decided, however, that I should be educated as . . . an intellectual, directed toward the priestly, legal or literary professions. As soon as I was exposed . . . to these disciplines, which were studious and bookish, I lost interest and energy for the work of the garden, though I remained enchanted with the flowers and the fruit. (p. 24)

Perhaps the interruption of selective attention during Watts' initial exposure to LSD brought forth, and allowed him to reconnect with, his childhood experiences of the natural world.

Watts experienced his first LSD experiment in the office of the supervising psychiatrist, Keith Ditman, whom Alan trusted and described as having good professional judgment. Watts would eventually point out that the most important quality of an individual leading a drug session is a feeling of assurance in the circumstances that can be recognized by people in the heightened condition of awareness that the psychedelics encourage. He argued, however, that psychedelic experimentation should be done in a supportive and homey atmosphere rather than in a sterile clinic or regimented laboratory situation that may leave the participants feeling they are located in insecure or unfriendly confines thus leading to problematic or negative experiences (Watts, 1965).

THE NEW ALCHEMY

During the ensuing year after his first psychedelic experience, Watts experimented with the drug again, a half dozen times, at the invitation of two psychiatrists, Michael Argon and Sterling Bunnell, at the Langley-Porter Clinic in San Francisco. In light of these subsequent experiences, he was "reluctantly compelled to admit that—at least in my own case—LSD had brought me into an undeniably mystical state of consciousness" (Watts, 1973, p. 399). As described in his essay, "The New Alchemy" (Watts, 1960a), the most extraordinary aspect regarding experiences on psychedelics is that various domains of consciousness, usually seen as fundamentally irreconcilable in everyday awareness, such as thinking and feeling, practicality and mysticism, reason and poetics, appear rather to harmonize and enrich one another, thus pointing to a way of living in which humanity "is no longer an embodied paradox of angel and animal, or reason fighting against instinct, but a marvelous coincidence in whom Eros and Logos are one" (p. 153). The beauty, the visions, the sense of mystical unity made him conclude that such chemicals were to be approached with much care and on the order of a religious sacrament.

Alan was already well schooled in the sacred rituals of the Anglican church. As an altar boy he carried the train of the Archbishop of Canterbury during his enthronement. As a priest he served as a liturgy master at a "pontifical Solemn High Mass" at Canterbury Cathedral. Watts was an expert on Anglican sacramental procedures, having perfected his liturgy skills at Seabury-Western Theological Seminary and through subsequent Episcopal ministry at Canterbury House on the campus of Northwestern University. During these years, he wrote a substantive monograph on *The Meaning of Priesthood* (1946), and composed a cutting edge book on *Myth and Ritual in Christianity* (1953) after leaving the Episcopal church. Despite resigning from the church, Watts maintained a lifelong commitment to a spiritual vocation, once writing to Episcopal Canon, Bernard Iddings Bell, in October 1950: "I know that I am a priest forever and have no thought whatever of going back to a former state" (Watts, 1973, p. 246). Alan, incidentally, officiated a strikingly beautiful wedding ceremony for my wife and me at Spencer Memorial Presbyterian Church in Brooklyn, New York, in 1966.

I remember Timothy Leary cautioning during a weekend retreat at his Millbrook commune in summer 1965, saying that "an LSD trip is a frightening experience. If you're not ready to look at yourself and your ambitions, your lusts, desires, and pride through a clear amplifying lens, stay away from psychedelic experience" (cited in Krippner, 1975, p. 38). In his autobiography, Watts (1973) mentioned that his religious training and spiritual formation guided him during his more treacherous and untoward psychedelic journeys. Elsewhere, he recollected an LSD experience of looking at "surely one of the most horrendous products of human imagination," the painting of *The Last Judgment* by Van Eyck. Under ordinary circumstances, Van Eyck's depiction is gruesome and terrifying, and is exponentially more so in the sway of LSD. Yet Watts (1960a) knew that "union with the Good that is beyond good and evil" leaves one "no longer moved by the terror of hell" (pp. 148–149). On another occasion, Easter Sunday at Timothy Leary's home in the early 1960s, Alan Watts led an LSD session in the form of an Anglican liturgy replete with New Testament readings and communion supper, including sacramental bread and wine. Leary (1998) subsequently described Alan's guidance as "High Church psychedelic":

> Alan Watts is highest Anglican. Precise, ceremonial, serene, aesthetic, classic, aristocratic with a wink. The ancient rituals executed perfectly with a quiet twinkle in the eye. My understanding of marijuana and LSD is mainly due to my listening to and watching Alan. (p. 105)

In addition to his renown with Eastern philosophies, Alan's wisdom with psychedelics was deeply informed by his Anglican training.

THE TRIP TO HARVARD

When I arrived in Cambridge in April 1962, for my first psilocybin experience as a participant in Leary's psychedelic research at Harvard University, Alan generously shared the insights he had acquired through his psychedelic sittings when "the veil is lifted." He warned of the need for looking at these new perceptions afterward with temperance. Although some remarkable insights may linger, he pointed out, other experiences may appear as completely unintelligible. Watts' accounts of his experiences with LSD and his thoughts about its possibilities, as well as its potential misuse, were often cited in his books, essays, tapes, and lectures. His central text on psychedelic experience, *The Joyous Cosmology*, was first published in 1962 (with a foreword by Leary and Richard Alpert). It remains one of the most vivid phenomenological accounts of psychedelic experience in print. In this book, Watts identified a pattern to his psychedelic experiences consisting of undulations of personality ranging from a sense of individual identity, to an expanded unity with a primordial Self, and back again. This "play of life" unfolds first as a cynical game of self/other one-upmanship that transforms into a situation where "humor gets the better of cynicism" and "finally, rapacious and all-embracing cosmic selfishness turns out to be a disguise for the unmotivated play of love" (Watts, 1965, p. 89).

Contemporaneous with the publication of *The Joyous Cosmology*, Watts received a two-year travel and study fellowship from the Department of Social Relations at Harvard University where he was already involved with Leary's psychedelic research. One of Alan's main projects during this fellowship at Harvard was his book, *The Two Hands of God* (Watts, 1963b). This text was an exposition of the "Myths of Polarity," the symbolic representations of dualities (e.g., good–evil, light–dark, self–other) and their underlying unity found in various cultural narratives and stories. *The Two Hands of God* reads like an unfolding psychedelic adventure. It begins with myths and images dealing with the inner unity of opposites, moving on to myths reflecting the "cosmic dance" of good and evil, followed by the disappearance of inner unity in the mythologies of absolute dualism, and concluding with myths that reconnect and restore the experience of inner union.

Watts (1963b) described *The Two Hands of God* as emerging from many years of interest in the relations between opposites. Indeed, in 1939, Alan presented a paper on the reconciliation of opposites in Asian philosophy and Jungian analytical thought entitled "The Psychology of Acceptance." During that time in his life, Alan also was fascinated by the seeming conflict in Mahayana Buddhism regarding the relative merits of effort versus faith in spiritual practice. He published his solution to this problem in the *Review of Religion* in 1941. This paper had a tremendous personal impact on Watts as he came to recognize parallel issues in Christianity. This insight inspired him to attend seminary and study for ordination as a priest in the Episcopal church (Watts, 1973), a vocation that would substantively inform his understanding of psychedelics many years later.

While at Harvard, Watts inevitably ran into B. F. Skinner, the noted behaviorist. Watts often spoke of "the skin encapsulated ego" that is transcended during mystical experience, drug induced or not. He saw, moreover, the sense of unity that is heightened by psychedelics "carries Gestalt psychology, which insists on the interdependence of figure and background, to its logical conclusion in every aspect of life and thought" (Watts, 1973, p. 399). This perspective allowed him to discover what he felt was "the flaw" in Skinner's behaviorist system. Watts observed in his autobiography:

> I saw that his [Skinner's] reasoning was still haunted by the ghost of man as a something—presumably a conscious ego—determined by environmental and other forces, for it makes no sense to speak of a determinism unless there is some passive object which is determined. But his own reasoning made it clear, not so much that human behavior was determined by other forces, but rather that it could not be described apart from those forces and was, indeed, inseparable from them. It did not seem to have occurred to him that "cause" and "effect" are simply two phases of, or two ways of looking at, one and the same event. It is not, then, that effects (in this case human behaviors) are determined by their causes. The point is that when events are fully and properly described they will be found to involve and contain processes

which were at first thought separate from them, and were thus called causes as distinct from effects. Taken to this logical conclusion, Skinner is not saying that man is determined *by* nature, as something external to him; he is actually saying that man *is* nature, and is describing a process which is neither determined nor determining. He simply provides reason for the essentially mystical view that man and universe are inseparable. (Watts, 1973, pp. 404–405)

He explained his insights during a lecture to the Social Relations Colloquium at Harvard on April 12, 1963, where he identified certain passages from Skinner's writings that were "the purest mysticism, which might have come straight from Mahayana Buddhism" (Watts, 1963a, p. 63). Skinner did not attend this lecture and I doubt he wanted to be seen as a mystic, but Watts nevertheless offered profound and innovative insights into Skinner's behaviorist approach to psychological life. (For a brief discussion of Skinner vis-à-vis Watts, see Claxton, 1981, pp. 131–139.)

MUTUAL CONCERNS

Because I had met Watts through Leary (but owed our friendship to the ministrations of Virginia Glenn), we discussed Leary's projects on several occasions. We both began to be concerned at the direction of what Watts (1973) called Leary's "enthusiasm" for altered states of consciousness. Psychedelics radically lift one out of a taken-for-granted sense of the world such that the usual and mundane affairs of life can seem ridiculous and absurd. Watts pointed out that psychedelic substances can induce an acute reaction to "pomposity." People chatting "memorandumese," or engaging political, scientific, or religious jargon sound so preposterous that it is easy to break out in laughter. This phenomenon, in fact, emerged during my first psychedelic session when we decided to study the impact of psilocybin on intellectual performance. I tried giving a test of mental ability to one of my co-participants but, after 30 minutes, my assessment questions evoked strong laughter from each of us and we subsequently abandoned the project. Likewise, Alan and I saw that Timothy was losing interest in constructively addressing criticisms of his work. His passion for psychedelics was compromising the scientific integrity of the research, rendering him more and more distant from the expected academic standards and practices at Harvard University.

Watts' (1973) autobiography reveals a similar kind of incident from his own childhood. As a youth of thirteen, Alan accompanied the family of a boyhood friend on an extended summer vacation to France. "The very moment we stepped off the boat," Alan said, "I felt a vivacious, sunny human atmosphere that was quite new to me and luminously exhilarating" (Watts, 1973, p. 81). During this journey, Alan experienced a novel culture, cuisine, and lifestyle that liberated him from what he considered as a staid English provincialism. Upon returning from this trip, "the curriculum, the sports, and the ideals of King's School, Canterbury, seemed, with some few exceptions, to be futile, infantile, and irrelevant" (p. 81).

Leary eventually became a charismatic religious leader to his own circle of friends and students. Although Leary was well trained in psychology, he knew very little about the possible snares of religious studies and mystical practices. As Watts (1973) pointed out:

> The uninstructed adventurer with psychedelics, as with Zen or yoga or any other mystical discipline, is an easy victim of what Jung calls "inflation," of the messianic megalomania that comes from misunderstanding the experience of union with God. It leads to the initial mistake of casting pearls before swine, and, as time went on, I was dismayed to see Timothy converting himself into a popular store-front messiah with his name in lights, advocating psychedelic experience as a new world-religion. (p. 407)

Gary Fisher (2005) recounted the story about Watts and Leary on their way to the Civic Auditorium in Santa Monica, California, for a large psychedelic gathering, and musing about what the placards for the event should say: "Alan Watts said, 'Oh Tim, Just say it like it is—Timothy Leary: The Second Coming' . . ." (p. 109).

Watts (1973) clearly saw that Leary "was moving to a head-on collision with the established religions of biblical theocracy and scientific mechanism, and simply asking for martyrdom" (p. 408). Alan could easily have recognized this kind of trajectory from his own life experience. During his adolescence, Watts arrived at a turning point as he was on the academic track to Oxford from King's School in Canterbury. His veritable passion for Zen Buddhism combined with misgivings about the Western view of reality inspired a rapidly developing boredom with the established academic curriculum. After reading *Zarathustra*, he composed essays in the voice of Nietzsche on a university scholarship examination judged by the graders as nonsensical. Watts had foreclosed on an opportunity for advancement to an undergraduate university degree (Watts, 1973).

Life with Leary, as we both saw it in his Newton Center and Millbrook communes was by no means lackluster, even though, as Watts (1973) noted, it was difficult to comprehend how individuals, having seen the magnificence of psychedelic revelation, could be so oblivious to the displeasure of incessant messiness, with dilapidated furniture, dirty floors, and disheveled beds. I recall having dinner at Millbrook when half a dozen dogs rushed into the room. Instead of shooing them away, our hosts simply held the food above their heads, commenting, "They have as much right to this space as we do." Yet, I agreed with Watts, "through all this, Timothy himself remained an essentially humorous, kindly, lovable, and (in some directions) intellectually brilliant person" (p. 408).

THE ONTOLOGICAL STATUS OF PSYCHEDELIC EXPERIENCE

Alan Watts was one of the primary theoreticians of the psychedelic era. Indeed, he published one of the most important and influential books of his career, *Psychotherapy East and West,* in 1961. It introduced the postwar generation of clinicians to a completely new dimension of the therapeutic process—the appeal to spiritual experience as the crux of personality change. Modern scientific psychotherapy could now be informed by Asian religious disciplines, with potential results on consciousness dramatically different than that produced by orthodox psychoanalysis and behaviorism. Watts lectured on this and other topics at Columbia, Yale, Cornell, Chicago, and elsewhere around the world. These travels brought Alan into public and private discussion with many leading members of the psychiatric profession, and he found himself astounded by what appeared to be their real fear of altered modes of awareness. Watts (1973) had assumed that psychiatric professionals would possess a familiarity with otherwise uncharted regions of the mind, but his review of the scientific literature revealed "only maps of the soul as primitive as ancient maps of the world . . . accompanied with little more solid information than 'Here be dragons' . . ." (p. 413).

The prevailing psychoanalytic and behaviorist theories of that era were unequipped to deal with psychedelic experience. In fact, there was a fundamental lack of regard for the whole issue of consciousness. Behaviorists insisted that "consciousness" and "mind" were beyond the bounds of science, and neo-behaviorists showed virtually no interest in human subjective experience. These psychologists saw the individual as a sort of computer with stimulus inputs and behavioral outputs. They could only note that LSD and similar substances made behavior seem unpredictable by creating a short-circuit in the computer. On the other hand, psychoanalysts, influenced by a Freudian worldview, played down the impact of conscious processes on human action. Psychedelic chemicals were seen as provoking "toxic schizophrenic reactions." The role of psychedelic substances was not readily understandable in the language of the Freudian paradigm informed by an outdated mechanistic physics of the nineteenth century. A large number of psychoanalysts thought of the human psyche as a "hydraulic pump" in which libido (sexual energy) that is inhibited in one part of the mind eventually erupts in an alternative part of psychological life. The psychoanalyst functioned as a kind of plumbing engineer by routing the flow of libidinal energy toward socially appropriate outlets. The ebb and flow of perceptual experiences and cognitive insights that distinguish the psychedelic journey were hard to situate on the hydraulic pump designs and so were considered by the psychiatric community as resembling psychotic symptoms (Krippner, 1967).

Additionally, many psychiatrists and psychologists, as individuals and scientific professionals, considered themselves as separate and detached observers in their field of study and in everyday life. Their outlook of separateness lagged far behind the insights of twentieth-century sciences informed by quantum physics and field theory. These perspectives implied that every human being, and every facet of human existence, is an integral aspect of the world. Watts (1964a) therefore asked: "How is twentieth-century man to gain a feeling of his existence that is consistent with twentieth-century knowledge?" (p. 128). His answer was that psychedelic substances may facilitate the elicitation of an alternative feeling of self, affording the initial heightening of awareness to lift an individual out of the ordinary confining of "I" to a hazy location inside and bounded by the skin of the body.

Watts combined his insights about psychedelics with the sophisticated models of consciousness described in Buddhist and Hindu texts; models that encompassed altered states of consciousness in a more optimistic and comprehensive fashion than allowed by the psychiatric jargon of his time. He often said that his own psychedelic experiences, where a sense of individual identity expands to a cosmic-consciousness, had the flavor of Hindu mythology. Hinduism regards the universe as an immense drama in which a Single Player enacts all the roles. Each role is a particular persona or mask. The sensation of being only this one particular self/role is due to the Player's complete assimilation in the "cosmic drama" and in each and every role (Watts, 1974). Alan recognized that psychedelic substances can expand awareness beyond the usual limited sense of identity toward an immediate feeling of connectedness and "play" of the larger process. Alan saw, moreover, that this overall connectedness and inclusiveness was consistent with the newer twentieth-century "field theories" in the natural and social sciences: "The mystic's subjective experience of his identity with 'the All' is the scientists objective description of ecological relationship, of the organism/environment as a unified field" (Watts, 1964a, p. 129).

In the twenty-first century, thanks in part to Watts' pioneering triangulation of Eastern thought, modern science, and psychedelic experience, the fields of psychology and psychiatry have been opened up to a panoply of spectrums (Krippner & Welch, 1992; Wilber, 1977), models (Kokoszka, 2007; Lancaster, 2004), and typologies (Cardena, Lynn, & Krippner, 2000; Metzner, 1998) of consciousness—something virtually absent in the 1960s. Even contemporary behavior analysts are opening up to the study of mystical experience (Hayes, 1997). Watts' insights, moreover, continue to resonate with postmodern approaches to consciousness studies because "postmodernity requests that scientists question their own assumptions, and learn from non-Western perspectives, alternative conscious states, and narratives of exceptional human experience" (Krippner

& Winkler, 1995, p. 255; Krippner, 2000), all of which are thematic issues in Alan's writings. Such an approach allows us to break the traditional (objectivist) natural science taboos against studying human subjectivity in order to establish a fresh and innovative science of consciousness (e.g., Wallace, 2000).

THE PROBLEM OF NEUROPOLITICS

The decade of the 1960s began as a promising time for psychedelic research. Eventually, however, there was mounting governmental regulation and prohibition of substances that afford altered states of consciousness on the grounds that psychedelics are dangerous to those who use them. The irony, as Watts (1973) pointed out in his autobiography, was that legal prohibition created its own self-fulfilling prophecy by instigating fears of criminal prosecution manifesting as intense feelings of paranoia while under the influence of psychedelics. Watts was deeply worried, and rightly so, that prohibited access to LSD and similar substances would inspire the manufacture of the psychedelic counterpart of bootlegged liquor. These chemicals, sans appropriate content and dosage, could be fabricated for use in unsuitable settings devoid of any expert guidance.

The common explanation for prohibition of psychedelics is that concerns about the medical safety of these substances, rather than social or political reasons, prompted the government crackdown (Novak, 1997). An alternative interpretation is that psychedelics were outlawed because they radicalized individuals using them (Dyck, 2005). As I suggested elsewhere (Krippner, 2006a), the contributions of LSD and comparable substances in generating social and cultural transformation in the United States and around the world has been underrated, particularly in connection with fostering innovative approaches to protesting the Vietnam War, advocating the civil rights of racial minorities and women, liberating gay and lesbian lifestyles, and enlivening the deep-ecology movement. Every one of these issues reflects a transformation of awareness, a novel and innovative way of thinking, feeling, and behaving that emerged in the psychedelic 1960s. Reverberations of this new consciousness and its influences can be seen in the present calls in the United States to end the war in Iraq, to save and protect threatened species and their habitats, to alleviate global climate change, to make medical marijuana available to patients in need, and to undo the draconian drug laws that choke the American prison system and side track law enforcement from channeling its labors in opposition to grave criminal and terrorist acts that jeopardize public safety.

In a rather prescient essay entitled "Who Will Run Your Nervous System?" Watts (1964b) elaborated the problem of *neuropolitics*, an issue anticipated by Leary, Litwin, Hollingshead, Weil, and Alpert (1962) and now resonating at the contemporary intersection of neuroscience, religion and political discourse (e.g., Connolly, 2002; Leary, 2006; Moosa, 2007; White, 1982). Watts recognized the emerging capacity to effectively mold and shape human personality and emotion through chemical means. Alan confronted the issue of just what kinds of feelings or human character should be cultivated, and who among the many invested parties gets to decide such questions. Although he saw that governments would undoubtedly seek to regulate the use of psychedelics, and that psychiatry was the profession usually mandated to prescribe and dispense these substances, Watts argued that it would likely have to be acknowledged that transfiguring awareness and identity, whether it be through prayer, Yoga, meditation, or psychedelic substances, is primarily a religious problem and is entitled the same legal protection as the right to worship.

In April 1966, however, government authorities led by G. Gordon Liddy raided Leary's Millbrook commune. They searched the premises, confiscated property, and arrested Leary and three others on charges of marijuana possession. A few months later, LSD was made illegal by government legislation. In 1968, responding to the legislative prohibition of LSD, Watts wrote an article on "Psychedelics and Religious Experience" for the *California Law Review* that was reprinted in a compilation of his essays (Watts, 1971). Watts concluded:

> To the extent that mystical experience conforms with the tradition of genuine religious involvement, and to the extent that psychedelics induce that experience, users are entitled to some constitutional protection. Also, to the extent that research in the psychology of religion can utilize such drugs, students of the human mind must be free to use them. (p. 95)

Forty years later, we are seeing the fruits of advocacy by Watts and others as peyote, psilocybin mushrooms, and ayahuasca are currently used as sacraments in both old and new religious institutions (Roberts, 2001), while legally sanctioned psychedelic research has finally resumed in the United States and elsewhere around the world (Friedman, 2006; Krippner & Sulla, 2000).

Friedman suggests this renaissance of research activity "could herald the singularly greatest change in modern psychology's future" (p. 54) due, in part, to the capacity for psychedelics to evoke spiritual and transpersonal experiences in certain settings. Similarly, Richards (2005) sees the resurgence of interest in psychedelics as a "frontier in the psychology of religious experience that could prove to have profound implications for advancing our understanding of spiritual dimensions of consciousness" (p. 377). However, I offer the following caveat: I often use the term *potential entheogen* rather than *entheogen* in reference to psychedelics in order to acknowledge that ingesting the substances will not always evoke a spiritual or mystical experience. The term *entheogen* implies "bringing forth the God within" but the factors of personal mind-set and socio-environmental setting have a complexity greater than the substances themselves such that calling them *entheogen* seems to guarantee something that may not necessarily be delivered, especially to the naive or misguided user (Krippner, 2006b; see also, Krippner, 1968; Richards, 2008).

LIFE ON THE S. S. VALLEJO

When I moved from New York City to San Francisco in the early 1970s, I maintained my relationship with Watts, attending parties and assisting at his seminars on the Sausalito houseboat known as the *S. S. Vallejo*. Alan and his third wife, Mary Jane ("Jano"), had been sharing the vessel with the lively and eccentric collage artist, Jean Varda, since 1961. (Varda died in 1971.) The S. S. Vallejo is where Watts and a nexus of friends originated the Society for Comparative Philosophy from whom I was able to secure, with the assistance of Virginia Glenn, a grant for my dream research at Maimonides Medical Center (Krippner, 1993; Ullman, Krippner, & Vaughn, 1973). In February 1967, the Vallejo was the site of the legendary countercultural discussion between Watts, Allen Ginsberg, Leary, and Gary Snyder that came to be known as the "Houseboat Summit." As I remember it, the conversation centered around the question of whether individuals should "drop out" and join the counterculture or should the counterculture just go ahead and take over society at large.

Through my visits, I deepened my friendship with Alan and Jano, but developed a growing concern about their incredible consumption of alcohol. On one occasion, Watts greeted me at his houseboat with the news, "Jano and I have given up booze, but come in and have some sparkling cider with us." I was delighted with the news and told them how much I enjoyed their newly discovered beverage. However, on my next visit, the apple concoction had disappeared and the "demon rum" had triumphed once again.

I remember attending an elegant social gathering with Watts shortly after his relapse. His hostess was a society matron in Sausalito, and he had fortified himself for the event with at least two bottles of wine. When we arrived at her door, I had to support Watts because he was completely unable to stand upright. I guided him to the nearest chair where he sat, resplendent in an Oriental gown, affecting an enigmatic smile that passed for deep wisdom. People asked him questions and he gave short answers, few of them to the point of the query. But the questioners would often remark, "I have never heard such wise comments put in so few words." I refrained from telling them that those few words were all that Watts was capable of delivering in his condition. Perhaps, as Richard Price commented, "Alan could always play Alan, drunk or sober" (cited in Anderson, 1983, p. 273).

Alan once suggested that a consequence of seeing through the illusion of the ego "may not be behavior along the lines of *conventional* morality. It may well be as the squares said of Jesus, 'Look at him! A glutton and a drinker, a friend of . . . sinners!' . . ." (Watts, 1966/1989, p. 21). For me, it was ironic that he would enjoy a lunch replete with healthy fruits, fish, and vegetables, and then negate much of the nutritional benefit with copious amounts of alcohol while chain-smoking cigarettes. Once I dared to ask him about these addictions and he blithely replied, "Well, I'm a very oral being—I like to drink, smoke, talk, and kiss." I suggested that he might emphasize the talking and kissing. After laughing at the suggestion, he commented that those two pastimes required a partner or audience while smoking and drinking did not. Here I am reminded of a dream involving Alan and his houseboat that was reported elsewhere in detail (Krippner, 1975). The dream occurred after reading a section of *The Odyssey* and listening to a musical based on the story:

> I was . . . on the ocean. . . . The craft was Alan Watts's boat, the S.S. Vallejo, and it held, as well as myself and Watts, Virginia Glenn and the Grateful Dead. Watts was steering the barge and it was approaching a large, dangerous rock. And on that rock were sitting two beautiful Sirens with banners draped across their bosoms just as if they were contestants in a bathing beauty contest. They were singing, "We can tell you anything, anything at all. We will give you everything, come on and have a ball!" . . . The Sirens' banners had letters printed on them. . . . Virginia was too blind to read those letters, the Dead were too stoned, and Watts was too drunk. I told them all what was in store for us if we headed toward the Sirens and warned them of the impending tragedy. Nevertheless, Watts kept steering his boat straight toward the rocks. I screamed, "Can't you see what's happening? The barge is heading for disaster! We're done for, doomed, finished!!!" . . . Watts replied, "But the girls are so lovely and their music is so beautiful." Then pulling himself together for a moment, Watts mimicked a gruff sea captain, saying, "If we really are going to crash, I will consider it an honor and a duty to go down with my ship!" He laughed loudly, took another belt of booze, and passed out. (pp. 94–95)

A biographer described life on the S. S. Vallejo as "Alan Watts' bohemia, a rich compendium of sights and smells and women and ideas, and liquor and LSD and pot and irreverent people who were all doing their thing" (Stuart, 1983, p. 205). This imagery is also reminiscent of Watts' lifestyle during his young adulthood in London where he was affiliated with a cadre of intellectual seekers known as the "Wild Woodbines," with philosopher, Dmitrije Mitrinovic, at the social center of the group. Although this network focused primarily on a live-for-the-moment revelry, it was Mitrinovic who one evening offered a discourse on "the mutual interdependence of all things," an idea that proved to be influential in Alan's writings on Asian philosophy and psychedelics in later years (Watts, 1973).

There are, in addition, events from childhood that seem to foreshadow the intertwining of alcohol (and tobacco) and Eastern philosophy in Alan Watts' life and work. Francis Croshaw, the patriarch of the family with whom Watts vacationed in France as a thirteen-year-old, bought Alan his first alcoholic drink on that excursion. Croshaw, moreover, whom Watts (1973) described as a smoker of large Burmese cigars, had an extensive library and recognizing Alan's interest in Asian philosophy, especially Buddhism, started lending him texts and engaging lengthy conversations accentuated with red wine and stogies.

In his adolescence, Alan would eventually surprise his parents and classmates by rejecting Christianity and declaring himself a Buddhist. He saw the Christian God of his youth as seeking to undercut life's *gaiete d'esprit* with overbearing authority. It was, therefore, a tremendous liberation for him to identify with people outside of the Christian tradition who did not have that particular sense of deity. Reminiscing on those early years, Watts (1973) wryly commented (in a colloquial tone that now seems anachronistic): "I knew that the Buddha had taken a dim view of wenching and boozing, but he never called it a *sin*—a damnable offense against ultimate reality. It was just one's own way of delaying *nirvana*—if that was what you wanted to do" (p. 93).

In Mahayana Buddhism, one who delays their ascendance to nirvana in order to continue benefiting the welfare of others is called a *Bodhisattva*. I would not be the first to suggest that, in light of Alan's life and work in the fields of psychology, philosophy, and religion, he was indeed a Bodhisattva for the West (Foster, 1986). Virginia Glenn would surely concur with this sentiment, but Alan once cautioned his readers not to confuse the "philosopher as artist" with the preacher. The role of the philosopher as artist, which he considered himself to be, "is to reveal and celebrate the eternal and purposeless background of human life. Out of simple exuberance or wonder he wants to tell others of the point of view from which the world is unimaginably good as it is, with people just as they are" (Watts, 1960b, p. 33). When the philosopher is forced into the role of preacher and viewed as a moralist or reformer, "the truth of what he says is tested by his character and his morals . . . whether he depends upon 'material crutches' such as wine or tobacco . . . or falls in love when he shouldn't, or sometimes looks a bit tired and frayed at the edges" (p. 31). Alan was not a preacher.

IN RETROSPECT

Watts contrasted his use of alcohol and psychedelics, saying, "personally, I am no example of phenomenal will power, but I find that I have no inclination to use LSD in the same way as tobacco or wines and liquors. On the contrary, the experience is always so fruitful that I must digest it for some months before entering into it again" (Watts, 1960a, p. 153). Alan described in his autobiography the end of his psychedelic adventures with these words:

In sum I would say that LSD, and such other psychedelic substances as mescaline, psilocybin, and hashish, confer polar vision; by which I mean that the basic pairs of opposites, the positive and the negative, are seen as the different poles of a single magnet or circuit . . . so that the voluntary and the involuntary, knowing and the known, birth and decay, good and evil, outline and inline, self and other, solid and space, motion and rest, light and darkness, are seen as aspects of a single and completely perfect process. The implication of this may be that there is nothing in life to be gained or attained that is not already here and now. . . . Polar vision is thus undoubtedly dangerous—but so is electricity, so are knives, and so is language. (Watts, 1973, pp. 399–400)

It is impossible to fully discern whether the sense of divination, polarity, and contradiction that governed Watts' life from childhood is the result of reminiscence or that which makes it important, but Watts (1973) himself wrote the following:

I carry over from childhood the vague but persistent impression of being exposed to hints of an archaic and underground culture whose values were lost to the Protestant religion and the industrial bourgeoisie, indeed to the modern West in general. This may be nothing but fantasy, but I seem to have been in touch with lingering links to a world both magical and mystical that was still understood among birds, trees, and flowers and was known—just a little—to my mother and perhaps to one or two of my nursemaids. (p. 37)

In 1973, I had a telephone call from Joan Tabernik, Watts' daughter. She wanted to discuss alternatives to stimulant drugs as a treatment for children with learning disabilities, an area in which I had worked for many years. We made an appointment to see each other on November 16 at Sonoma State University where I was scheduled to give a colloquium. Tabernik was unable to keep our appointment; her father died in his sleep the previous night. It was my sad duty to tell the university community of Watts' death before I began the seminar.

Watts' final European lecture and seminar tour apparently exhausted him, and he died on his return to California. But disturbing news reached me from one of the seminar participants. "Alan was drunk most of the time, and both during the seminar and at meals made lewd comments about the women in the group. Some women were flattered, but others were disgusted." I knew that Watts was quite aware of his alcoholism. By the late 1960s he was living with an enlarged liver and was hospitalized while suffering from delirium tremens (Furlong, 2001). Two decades earlier he had written the following in

The Wisdom of Insecurity:

> One of the worst vicious circles is the problem of the alcoholic. In very many cases he knows quite clearly that he is destroying himself, that for him, liquor is poison, that he actually hates being drunk, and even dislikes the taste of liquor. And yet he drinks. For dislike it as he may, the experience of not being drunk is worse. It gives him the "horrors" for he stands face to face with the unveiled, basic insecurity of the world. (Watts, 1951, pp. 79–80)

After his death I was told by a mutual acquaintance that Watts had registered for the experimental LSD psychotherapy program at Spring Grove Hospital in Maryland, a program known to have helped many alcoholics initiate their recovery. But his request came too late, an unfortunate circumstance because LSD psychotherapy was an intervention that he could have appreciated and accepted.

Michael Murphy, co-founder of Esalen Institute, offered an appropriate eulogy for Alan. He said:

> If you wanted a marriage performed, a building or a bathtub blessed, a Mass celebrated (in the High Episcopalian manner, with Roman and Orthodox touches added), a Buddhist prayer invoked for the New Year, or a grace said at meals, he was usually the first person we asked. Sometimes when he came to lead a seminar, we would find him in the kitchen, preparing one of his well-known dishes or admiring the latest vegetables from the Big Sur garden or letting us know that the cooking wasn't up to our usual standards.
>
>   So he taught us by who he was. We learned from his infectious, outrageous laughter, from his virtues and his faults, from his sense of play and his eye for the binds we would get ourselves into. He was our gentlest and most joyous teacher. (cited in Krippner, 1975, p. 196)

I deeply value my relationship with Alan Watts, and learned a great deal from his seminars, his writings, and our conversations. He often described himself as "an entertainer" and predicted "fifty years after I am dead, nobody will remember me." But Saybrook Graduate School has established an Alan Watts professorship (that I currently hold), awarded several Alan Watts scholarships to students, and offers a course on his life and work. I was one of several speakers at two memorial celebrations of Watts' life and work arranged in San Francisco by our mutual friend, Robert Shapiro, who was instrumental in establishing the Alan Watts professorship at Saybrook. At one of these events I described Watts' personality typology: people are either "prickles" or "goos."

However, most people were either "prickly goos" or "gooey prickles." I also noted that the God that made most sense to Watts was a "two-handed God," a "hide-and-seek God," a deity that I described as a "now you see Her, now you don't" God. "God" may be a word we use to describe transcendent trickery, the ultimate deconstructing of boundaries, and paradoxically the unifying of all divisions. This is the God of fluidity, of change, of transcendence—the very Dao itself (Krippner, 2002).

Watts once translated "Tao" as "not forcing," and this statement characterized his life. Others may disagree, but I doubt that Watts had a rigorous, well-developed meditative regimen that he practiced faithfully. Indeed, in our discussions it seemed to me that he had gained much of his knowledge of meditation though extensive reading and informal conversations with such spiritual teachers as Christmas Humphreys and D. T. Suzuki rather than through long-term instruction. Nonetheless, perhaps more than any other writer, Watts brought the spiritual wisdom of the East to the United States and other Western countries. Watts' books, tapes, articles, and lectures initiated both scholarly dialogue and personal transformation that affected hundreds of thousands of men and women, including me and my circle of friends. Leary (1999) called Alan "the smiling scholar of the acid age. . . . Cool, gracious, never ruffled, chuckling to share with us his amused wonder at God's plans for the planet and, with quizzical eye, glancing to see if we will catch on" (p. 100). Like all of us, he had his shortcomings, inconsistencies, and personal demons, but what he accomplished is an admirable record for one lifetime and, in one form or another, his legacy continues.

REFERENCES

Anderson, W. T. (1983). *The upstart spring: Esalen and the American awakening.* Reading, MA: Addison-Wesley.

Cardena, E., Lynn, S. J., & Krippner, S. (Eds.). (2000). *Varieties of anomalous experience.* Washington, DC: American Psychological Association.

Claxton, G. (1981). *Wholly human: Western and Eastern visions of the self and its perfection.* London: Routledge & Kegan Paul.

Connolly, W. E. (2002). *Neuropolitics: Thinking, culture, speed.* Minneapolis: University of Minnesota Press.

Dyck, E. (2005). Flashback: Psychiatric experimentation with LSD in historic perspective. *Canadian Journal of Psychiatry, 50*(7), 381–388.

Fisher, G. (2005). Treating the untreatable. In R. N. Walsh & C. S. Grob (Eds.), *Higher wisdom: Eminent elders explore the continuing impact of psychedelics.* Albany: State University of New York Press.

Foster, M. (1986). A Western Bodhisattva. In R. Miller & J. Kenny (Eds.), *Fireball and the lotus: Emerging spirituality from ancient roots* (pp. 135–149). Sante Fe, NM: Bear and Co.

Friedman, H. (2006). The renewal of psychedelic research: Implications for humanistic psychology. *The Humanistic Psychologist, 34*(1), 39–58.

Furlong, M. (2001). *Zen effects: The life of Alan Watts.* Woodstock, VT: Skylight Paths.

Hayes, L. J. (1997). Understanding mysticism. *The Psychological Record, 47,* 57–596.

Kokoszka, A. (2007). *States of consciousness: Models for psychology and psychotherapy.* New York: Springer.

Krippner, S. (1963, August). *Consciousness expansion and the extensional world.* Paper presented to the International Society for General Semantics, New York.

Krippner, S. (1967). Afterword. In P. G. Stafford & B. H. Golightly, *LSD: The problem-solving psychedelic.* New York: Award Books.

Krippner, S. (1968). Of hell and heavenly blue. In R. Metzner (Ed.), *The ecstatic adventure* (pp. 46–54). New York: Macmillan.

Krippner, S. (1975). *Song of the siren: A parapsychological odyssey.* New York: Harper & Row.

Krippner, S. (1993). The Maimonides ESP-dream studies. *Journal of Parapsychology, 57,* 39–54.

Krippner, S. (2000). Research methodology in humanistic psychology in the light of postmodernity. In K. J. Schneider, J. F. T. Bugental, & J. F. Pearson (Eds.), *The handbook of humanistic psychology* (pp. 259–304). Thousand Oaks, CA: Sage.

Krippner, S. (2002). Dancing with the trickster: Notes for a transpersonal autobiography. *International Journal of Transpersonal Studies, 21,* 1–18.

Krippner, S. (2006a, January). *Consciousness and the mythologies of society.* Paper presented at LSD: Problem Child and Wonder Drug, An International Symposium on the Occasion of the 100th Birthday of Albert Hoffman, Basel, Switzerland.

Krippner, S. (2006b, January). *The future of religion.* Paper presented at LSD: Problem Child and Wonder Drug, An International Symposium on the Occasion of the 100th Birthday of Albert Hoffman, Basel, Switzerland.

Krippner, S., & Sulla, J. (2000). Identifying spiritual content in reports from ayahuasca sessions. *International Journal of Transpersonal Studies, 19,* 59–76.

Krippner, S., & Welch, P. (1992). *The spiritual dimensions of healing: From tribal shamanism to contemporary health care.* New York: Irvington Press.

Krippner, S., & Winkler, M. (1995). Postmodernity and consciousness studies. *Journal of Mind and Behavior, 16*(3), 255–280.

Lancaster, B. L. (2004). *Approaches to consciousness: The marriage of science and mysticism.* New York: Palgrave Macmillan.

Leary, T. F. (1998). *Politics of ecstasy.* Berkeley, CA: Ronin. (Original work published 1968)

Leary, T. F. (1999). *Turn on, tune it, drop out.* Berkeley, CA: Ronin.

Leary, T. F. (2006). *Neuropolitique.* Tempe, AZ: New Falcon.

Leary, T., Litwin, G., Hollingshead, M., Weil, G., & Alpert, R. (1962). The politics of the nervous system. *Bulletin of the Atomic Scientists, 18*(5), 26–27.

Metzner, R. (1998). *The unfolding self: Varieties of transformative experience.* Novato, CA: Origin Press.

Moosa, E. (2007). Neuropolitics and the body. In G. ter Haar & Y. Tsuruoka (Eds.), *Religion and society: An agenda for the 21st century* (pp. 47–60). Leiden, The Netherlands: Brill.

Novak, S. J. (1997). LSD before Leary: Sidney Cohen's critique of 1950's psychedelic drug research. *Isis, 88*(1), 87–110.

Richards, W. A. (2005). Entheogens in the study of religious experience: Current status. *Journal of Religion and Health, 44*(4), 377–389.

Richards, W. A. (2008). The phenomenology and potential religious import of states of consciousness facilitated by psilocybin. *Archives for the Psychology of Religion*, 30(1), 189–199.

Roberts, T. B. (Ed.). (2001). *Psychoactive sacramentals: Essays on entheogens and religion.* San Francisco: Council on Spiritual Practices.

Stuart, D. (1983). *Alan Watts.* Briarcliff Manor, NY: Stein & Day.

Ullman, M., Krippner, S., & Vaughn, A. (1973). *Dream telepathy: Experiments in nocturnal ESP.* New York: Penguin.

Wallace, A. B. (2000). *The taboo of subjectivity: Towards a new science of consciousness.* New York: Oxford University Press.

Watts, A. W. (1939). *The psychology of acceptance.* New York: Analytic Book Club.

Watts, A. W. (1941). The problem of faith and works in Buddhism. *Review of Religion*, 5(4), 385–402.

Watts, A. W. (1946). The meaning of priesthood. *Advent Papers*, No. 7. Boston: Church of the Advent.

Watts, A. W. (1951). *The wisdom of insecurity.* New York: Pantheon.

Watts, A. W. (1953). *Myth and ritual in Christianity.* New York: Vanguard Press.

Watts, A. W. (1960a). The new alchemy. In *This is IT; and other essays on Zen and spiritual experience* (pp. 125–153). New York: Pantheon.

Watts, A. W. (1960b). This is IT. In *This is IT; and other essays on Zen and spiritual experience* (pp. 15–39). New York: Pantheon.

Watts, A. W. (1961). *Psychotherapy East and West.* New York: Pantheon.

Watts, A. W. (1963a). The individual as man/world. *The Psychedelic Review*, 1(1), 55–65. (Paper presented to the Social Relations Colloquium, Harvard University, April 12, 1963)

Watts, A. W.(1963b). *The two hands of God: The myths of polarity.* New York: George Brazilier.

Watts, A. W. (1964a). A psychedelic experience: Fact or fantasy. In D. Solomon (Ed.), *LSD: The consciousness-expanding drug* (pp. 119–131). New York: Putnam.

Watts, A. W. (1964b). Who will run your nervous system? *The New Republic*, 150(22), 15–16.

Watts, A. W. (1965). *The joyous cosmology: Adventures in the chemistry of consciousness.* New York: Vintage Books.

Watts, A. W. (1970, November). Virginia Glenn—1931–1970. *Bulletin of the Society for Comparative Philosophy*, pp. 1–2.

Watts, A. W. (1971). Psychedelics and religious experience. In *Does it matter? Essays on man's relation to materiality* (pp. 78–95). New York: Vintage.

Watts, A. W. (1973). *In my own way: An autobiography.* New York: Vintage.

Watts, A. W. (1974). The cosmic drama. In *The essence of Alan Watts* (M. J. Watts, Ed., pp. 173–193). Millbrae, CA: Celestial Arts.

Watts, A. W. (1989). *The Book: On the taboo against knowing who you are.* New York: Vintage. (Original work published 1966)

White, E. (1982). Brain science and the emergence of neuropolitics. *Politics and the Life Sciences*, 2(1), 47–60.

Wilber, K. (1977). *The spectrum of consciousness.* Wheaton, IL: Theosophical Publishing House.

CHAPTER FIVE

From the Joyous Cosmology to the Watercourse Way: An Appreciation of Alan Watts

Ralph Metzner

My first encounters with Alan Watts occurred via the Psychedelic Research Project under the direction of Timothy Leary at Harvard University. The research program originated when Leary happened upon psychedelics while vacationing in Mexico during summer 1960. He tried "sacred mushrooms" at the suggestion of psychologist Frank Barron and had a profoundly moving mystical experience. Leary returned to Harvard with the determination to commit significant time to researching psychedelic substances. On the whole, a set of ground-breaking explorations unfolded where researchers and study participants, informed by Leary's (1960) existential-transactional approach, experienced LSD, mescaline, and psilocybin beyond the standard scientific laboratory settings of the traditional medical model. The substances were ingested in an ambiance of "esthetic precision, philosophic inquiry, inner search, self-confident dignity, intellectual openness, philosophic courage, and high humor" (Leary, 2000, p. 4; see also, Riedlinger, 1993).

Leary often asserted that the intellectual sway of the early psychedelic researchers at Harvard and elsewhere had yet to be fully appreciated in the academic literature. In the twenty-first century, however, there is renewed enthusiasm for psychedelic research after many years of prohibition and disinterest (Metzner, 2005, 2008; Roberts, 2006). The pioneers of psychedelic exploration now constitute a unique source of wisdom for new research agendas moving forward in time. These "eminent elders" have a depth of insight to offer contemporary explorers as they embark on new psychedelic journeys (Walsh & Grob, 2005, 2006). In 2004, one of our most distinguished elders, Huston Smith, offered his retrospective reflection on psychedelics and religion (Smith et al., 2004). In 2010, Ram Dass and I published conversations about the Harvard experiments and Leary's Millbrook commune (Dass, Metzner, & Bravo, 2010). In this volume, writings are devoted to Alan Watts, a preeminent member of our research group at Harvard University. My goals for this chapter are threefold. First, some recollections of my early Harvard years are correlated with those of Watts and Leary as described in their autobiographical writings. Second, the experiential riches contained in Watts' (1965) classic text, *The Joyous Cosmology*, are detailed, and his ambivalence about sharing this information is juxtaposed against the institutional resistances to Leary's psychedelic works at Harvard. Finally, Watts' transition out of his psychedelic phase toward renewed focus on Chinese Daoism is elaborated and followed by a final appreciation for the profound impact of Alan's mentoring on the trajectory of my professional life.

SET AND SETTING

By the time Alan Watts came into contact with psychedelics in 1958, he was enthusiastically engaged in a midlife process of separating from the conventional forms of his early life. From a boyhood in strict English boarding schools, he had been an Anglican priest, college professor, author of a dozen books on Eastern philosophy and the arts, and dutiful husband and father. He had migrated first to New York and Chicago, and then to California, where "at the age of forty-five I broke out of this wall-to-wall trap, though it was a hard shock to myself . . . I discovered who were my real friends and became closer to them and indeed to friends in general, than had hitherto been possible for me" (Watts, 1973c, pp. 352–353). Alan had met the woman, Jano, who was to be his constant companion for the rest of his life. He found himself in the midst of the cultural flowering associated with the San Francisco Beat poets, the humanistic and Gestalt psychotherapy movements, the Esalen Institute with its personal growth seminars, and the beginnings of what later became known as the New Age. In his autobiography, Watts (1973c) speaks with fondness of his newfound friendship with "people who were not embarrassed to express their feelings, who were not ashamed to show warmth, exuberance, and earthy *joie de vivre*" (p. 353).

Alan was told of Leary's research program by Aldous Huxley, and from the academic and aloof tenor of Huxley's version of the project, Watts (1973c) was expecting Timothy to be "a formidable pandit" but instead found "an extremely charming Irishman who wore a hearing-aid as stylishly as if it had been a monocle (p. 403). Watts eventually secured a two-year fellowship at Harvard through the Department of Social Relations chaired by the renowned psychologist Henry Murray. This fellowship gave Alan time to work on two of his major publications, *The Two Hands of God* (1963b) and *Beyond Theology* (1964), in addition to participating in the drug studies. Years later, Watts (1973c) offered a flattering reminiscence, saying that whenever he was in the vicinity of Cambridge, he would keep close contact with Leary "and his associates Richard Alpert and Ralph Metzner, for—quite aside from the particular fascinations of chemical mysticism—these were the most lively and imaginative people in the department other than Murray himself" (p. 404).

My association with Watts and Leary developed during my doctoral and postdoctoral studies at Harvard. I became involved with Leary's research as a third-year psychology graduate student after hearing about my fellow classmates' experiences with psilocybin (the active compound of the sacred mushroom of pre-conquest Mexican culture). Their descriptions were animated with astonishment as they communicated insights about love and death, sharing and identity, unity and ecstasy, topics not usually considered as central issues to students of psychology in the early 1960s. A greater inspiration came from Leary himself. We initially met during my second year of graduate study. He came to Harvard after serving as research director of the Kaiser Foundation Hospital in Oakland. There he had written the very influential *Interpersonal Diagnosis of Personality* (Leary, 1957), earning a Book of the Year award from the American Psychological Association. Timothy had developed a reputation in his pre-psychedelic days as one of a minority of faculty members conveying a particular kind of ethical sensibility toward people and the study of psychology. Contrary to the prevailing mode of professional conduct in the field of psychology at that time, Leary refused to take the objective stance of the natural sciences that obscures the subjectivity (and humanity) of research participants and reduces them to mere combinations of symptoms. The abbreviated version of a longer story is simply this: "He had dropped out and was ready to turn on. I saw American psychology as a cynically professionalized pseudo-science, and was ready to turn on too" (Metzner, 1968a, p. 8).

After hearing about my classmates' psychedelic experiences, I approached Leary vis-à-vis his research concerning the behavioral impact of psilocybin on maximum security inmates at the Massachusetts Correctional Institute at Concord. Apparently, a certain kind of character impression preceded my visit with Timothy as he remembered our meeting this way:

> I was in my office when a knock came on the door, and I was visited by a graduate student named Ralph Metzner. Metzner had a reputation for being one of the smartest students in the department. He was a graduate of Oxford, an experimentalist, a precise, objective, and apparently very academic young man. He said he heard about the prison project and wanted to work with me on it. (Leary, 1968/1995, p. 181)

Leary also recollected his initial sense that I might not be the right person for the job, saying, in his own inimitable way, "Metzner was too academic, too dainty-British, too bookish, too ivory tower to walk into a prison, roll up his sleeves and take drugs that would put him out of his mind, with rough and tumble prisoners" (p. 181). Nevertheless, I expressed my willingness to learn and my readiness to try psychedelics, and soon I was part of a six-person pre-paratory meeting intended to initiate and explore the psilocybin experience in a supportive environment.

The session was conducted at Timothy's home in Newton, Massachusetts. His notes for that evening indicate "each member of this six-person group reported a deep, ecstatic, educational experience" (Leary, 1968/1995, p. 181). The impact of this session on my life was beyond measure. The experience was thoroughly and completely unlike anything I had encountered before, feeling nearer to my "true self" and lucidly attuned to my deepest thoughts and feel-ings (Metzner, 1999b). In his autobiography, Leary (1983) said this introductory session revealed me as "a natural inner explorer" (p. 85). A few days after the preliminary meeting, we conducted the first of our psychedelic encounters at the prison. These prison encounters evoked a full range of experience, from stark terror to ecstatic joy, but I remember vividly during one session with the inmates, the sensation of having 360-degree vision and a boundless freedom of human spirit unaffected by the walls, bars, and locks of the jail. A report on the methods and findings of our prison study can be found in the journal, *Psychotherapy: Theory, Research, and Practice* (Leary et al., 1965; see also, Doblin, 1998; Leary & Metzner, 1968; Metzner, 1998).

As a participant in the Harvard University-sponsored research project on psilocybin, I felt delighted and inspired when Alan Watts joined our venture as a consultant and participant-observer. We had found the existing paradigms of psychoanalysis and behaviorism woefully inadequate for describing the profound expansions of consciousness triggered by psychedelics, and were searching for more comprehensive theories of consciousness. Our research group held a series of monthly meetings involving psychologists, ministers, and theologians where we conjectured that "religious concepts and symbols might prove to express the elusive quality of psychedelic drug experiences more satisfactorily than the stilted language of academic psychology" (Metzner, 1968a, p. 69). Because of his deep knowledge of Zen Buddhism and Eastern philosophy in general, Watts found appreciative audiences among people searching for deeper understanding of the world and its mysteries than could be had from mainstream education. With scintillating eloquence and joyous humor he exposed the shortcomings of dualistic Western thinking, with its separation of body and mind, spirit and matter, and the self-imposed isolation of a "skin-encapsulated ego."

Aldous Huxley had, with his books *The Doors of Perception* (1954) and *Heav-en and Hell* (1956) published a few years before, introduced the world to the mystic visionary potential of mescaline experiences. Huxley used the language of the perennial philosophy and the concept of "Mind-at-Large" on which the personal human mind operates with a kind of "reducing valve." Watts went beyond Huxley with the publication of *The Joyous Cosmology* in 1962. (I am using the 1965 Vintage Books Edition for this chapter.) He applied his pro-found understanding of Eastern philosophy to the deeper psychological and philosophical dimensions of psychedelic experience: "My own main interest in the study of comparative mysticism has been to . . . identify the essential psychological processes underlying those alterations of perception which enable us to see ourselves and the world in their basic unity" (Watts, 1965, p. 11).

Watts immediately recognized and confirmed the basic insight of previous researchers, including Huxley and Leary, that the psychedelic experience is neither hallucinogenic nor narcotic escapist, but involves an enormous heightening of sense perception, and that therefore the content of one's experience is entirely a function of one's mind-set, preparation and social setting:

> Despite the widespread and undiscriminating prejudice against drugs as such, and despite the claims of certain religious disciplines to be the sole means to genuine mystical insight, I can find no essential difference between the experiences induced, *under favorable conditions*, by these chemicals and the states of "cosmic consciousness" recorded by R.M. Bucke, William James . . . and other investigators of mysticism. (Watts, 1965, p. 17, emphasis added)

The issues of mind-set, preparation, and social setting are pivotal for the facilitation of psychedelic experiences. The drug acts as a catalyst between a person's attitudes, intentions, moods, personality, and so forth, and the particular social, interpersonal, or environmental context in which an individual is situated. Given this catalytic effect, the early psilocybin studies of the Harvard Psychedelic Research Project were enacted "without imposing either a medical-therapeutic or a psychological-experimental model on the situation. The purpose: to see if a 'natural,' unforced way of ritualizing psychedelic experiences would develop" (Metzner, 1968a, p. 8; see also, Leary, Litwin, & Metzner, 1963). Eventually, post-Harvard, we developed a model for conducting psychedelic sessions based on the *Tibetan Book of the Dead* (Leary, Metzner, & Alpert, 1964). Incorporated in our "practical recommendations" for "orienting procedures" (sometimes called "priming" in the contemporary parlance of psychological science) was a suggestion to read various writings on mystical experience, including those of Alan Watts.

Alan naturally approached psychedelic experiences as a philosopher interested in a deeper understanding of reality, rather than as a psychotherapist concerned with personal problem solving, or as an artist seeking evocation of fantastic and other-worldly imagery. He described his preferred "set and setting" in *The Joyous Cosmology* as follows:

> I usually start with some such theme as polarity, transformation (as of food into organism), competition for survival, the relation of the abstract to the concrete, or of Logos to Eros, and then allow my heightened perception to elucidate the theme in terms of certain

works of art or music, or some such natural object as a fern, a flower, or a sea shell, of a religious or mythological archetype (it might be the Mass) . . . (Watts, 1965, pp. 27–28)

THE JOYOUS COSMOLOGY

The Joyous Cosmology (Watts, 1965) is a verbal *tour-de-force*. It is a weaving of several psychedelic experiences into a single narrative for "reasons of poetic unity" (p. 89), and is likely the most vibrant qualitative report on psychedelic journeying available in the literature on consciousness. Years ago I described Alan as:

> one of the most gifted word-choreographers writing in the English language. . . . He is not so much a writer as a dancer-with-words. Alan Watts experiences in the transcendental mode and has a neural network so imprinted that he can report the flashing flow of ecstatic visions with an immediate accuracy which is reflex. As others breathe or blink their eyes, as dancers move to the beat, Alan Watts converts into shimmering prose. (Metzner, 1968a, pp. 92–93)

Alan's shimmering prose is nowhere more evident than in *The Joyous Cosmology*. Within this narrative, Watts (1965) described the expanding and deepening layers of associations in listening to a recording of a priest chanting the Mass: At first he hears the priest's voice of "serene authority" and the "innocent devotion" of the nuns response; then, listening deeper, the priest's "inflated . . . unctuous tones," and the nuns "cowed, . . . but playing possum . . . to survive." Deeper again, "I congratulate the priest on his gamesmanship, on the sheer courage of . . . such a performance of authority when he knows precisely nothing. Perhaps there is no other knowing than the mere competence of the act." Below this level, where there is no "real self" and thus "sincerity is simply nerve, . . . the unabashed vigor of the pretense," he hears in the priest's voice "the primordial howl of the beast in the jungle, ..inflected, complicated, refined and textured with centuries of culture." Like Tim Leary describing the evolutionary remembering in his first experience with the Mexican sacred mushroom, Watts now hears "in that one voice the simultaneous presence of all the levels of man's history, as of all the stages of life before man" (p. 45). Then again, the shift to the personal history—"I, as an adult, am also back there alone in the dark, just as the primordial howl is still present beneath the sublime modulations of the chant" (p. 45).

Trying to find the agent behind the act, the motivating force, "I see only an endless ambivalence. Behind the mask of love I find my innate selfishness" (Watts, 1965, p. 45). And yet this posture too has "something phony about every attempt to define myself . . . since I don't know fully what I am"(p. 46). The philosopher's solipsistic conundrum is now resolved in the trickster's joke:

Life seems to resolve itself down to a tiny germ or nipple of sensitivity. I call it the Eenie-Weenie—a squiggling little nucleus that is trying to make love to itself and can never quite get there. The whole fabulous complexity of vegetable and animal life, as of human civilization, is just a colossal elaboration of the Eenie-Weenie trying to make the Eenie-Weenie. (p. 46)

Going deeper still, he finds that every seeming knowing of self is really the knowing of "something other, something strange. The landscape I am watching is also a state of myself . . . and all knowledge of other knowledge of self" (p. 48). Then again, following the chain of personal history, going far beyond childhood,

long before I was an embryo in my mother's womb, there seems the ever-so-familiar stranger, the everything not me, with a joy immeasurably more intense than a meeting of lovers separated by centuries, to be my original self. The good old son-of-a-bitch who got me involved in this whole game. (p. 50)

Now, as he sits in the garden, the erstwhile solipsist revels in the sacredness of the other. He sees his companions as no longer the "harassed little personalities with names . . . the mortals we are all pretending to be, . . . but rather as immortal archetypes of themselves" (p. 50). One could also call this "seeing" the essence behind the personality, and it is a classic psychedelic vision. I remember from my own first experience with psilocybin, when in looking at my companions, I saw them beyond the persona mask in the form of archangels, freed from all pretense and dissimulation. Watts goes on to describe the woman, Ella, his hostess who had planted the garden they were sitting in, as a "beneficent Circe—sorceress, daughter of the moon, familiar of cats and snakes, herbalist and healer—with the youngest old face one has ever seen" (p. 51). This kind of seeing into the mythic archetypes of others, filled with affectionate humor and compassion, is a gift Alan Watts carried with him from his psychedelic explorations. I remember one time I went to visit him when he was living in a house boat in Sausalito, I brought with me a woman I was dating at the time—and he described her, with a friendly chuckle, as an "Irish witch." Immediately I felt I understood something deeper about my friend that lifted me out of a confused tangle of attractions and doubts.

The key philosophical teachings about the interdependent unity of self and world that Watts had already absorbed on the intellectual level from his study of Vedanta and Zen were reinforced, confirmed, and extended in his psychedelic vision:

It is this vivid realization of the reciprocity of will and world, active and passive, inside and outside, self and not-self, which evokes the aspect of these experiences that is most puzzling from the standpoint of ordinary consciousness: the strange and seemingly unholy conviction that "I" am God. In Western culture this sensation is seen as the very signature of insanity. But in India is simply a matter of course that the deepest center of man, *atman*, is the deepest center of the universe, *Brahman*. Why not? Surely a continuous view of the world is more whole, more holy, more healthy, than one in which there is a yawning emptiness between the Cause and its effects. . . . the feeling of self is no longer confined to the inside of the skin. Instead, my individual being seems to grow out from the rest of the universe like a hair from a head or a limb from a body, so that my center is also the center of the whole. (Watts, 1965, pp. 67–69)

Also in the *Joyous Cosmology* experience, Watts returned to philosophical themes he had explored in *Nature, Man and Woman* (1958) and that presaged the Daoist nature mysticism featured prominently in his later years: "A journey into this new mode of consciousness gives one a marvelously enhanced appreciation of patterning in nature, a fascination deeper than ever with the structure of ferns, the formation of crystals, the markings upon sea shells . . ." (Watts, 1965, p. 61). The ordering of nature is an art akin to music, its swirling complexity "like smoke in sunbeams or the rippling networks of sunlight in shallow water. Transforming endlessly into itself, the pattern alone remains" (p. 61).

Pattern perception across sense modalities is known as synesthesia. It is classically characteristic of psychedelic experience. The multisensory pattern perception then also can extend into the cognitive realm, as sight becomes insight and hearing leads to understanding. Listening, eyes closed, to the music of "Bach in his most exultant mood," Watts (1965) writes of his experience that day:

in wave after wave and from all directions of the mind's compass, there has repeatedly come upon me the sense of my original identity as one with the very fountain of the universe. I have seen, too, that the fountain is its own source and motive, and that its spirit is an unbounded playfulness which is the many-dimensioned dance of life. (p. 83)

This is the classic mystic vision of the *Upanishadic* seers: Behind the endless display of forms ceaselessly transforming, disappearing, and appearing—the *maya* magic-show of the phenomenal world—lies no other motive than exuberant play, *lila*, the dance of life.

Triggered by listening to the rhythm chants of Indian musicians, Watts (1965) expounds the key insight of *maya-lila*:

Life. . . . isn't being driven by anything; it just happens freely of itself . . . It isn't *happening* to anyone. . . . It is completely purposeless play—exuberance which is its own end. . . . Time, space, and multiplicity are complications of it. There is no reason whatever to explain it, for explanations are just another form of complexity. . . . Pain and suffering are simply extreme forms of play. . . . there isn't any substantial ego at all. The ego is a kind of flip, a knowing of knowing, a fearing of fearing. It's a curlicue, an extra jazz to experience, a sort of double-take or reverberation, a dithering of consciousness which is the same as anxiety. (p. 78)

Watts' delight in the aesthetic beauty of natural forms and appreciation of the dynamic patterns revealed by music, no doubt already present in his earlier life, was enormously heightened by his psychedelic experiences and he carried this over into his modes of teaching in the later years. When he was living in the houseboat in Sausalito, friends and students would assemble to listen to him philosophize, tell Zen stories, expound on difficult questions of Eastern philosophy and religion, and sometimes laugh uproariously as he delighted in the absurdity of the cosmic game of "hide-and-seek" that we play with ourselves. I was able to bring him a large hemisphere of tempered steel, salvaged by a friend from an industrial junkyard, which had a marvelously long resonant tone when struck. He incorporated this instrument into his meditation sessions, much as resonant brass bowls are found in Buddhist temples throughout Japan. These sessions would contain periods of silent meditation marked by the sound of gongs or bells. But Watts would have no patience with what he called "the aching legs school of Buddhism," whose practitioners were prideful of their long, silent sittings. "When the legs start to ache," he would say slyly, "I prefer to get up and dance."

LIFE IS A GESTURE

In his autobiography, Watts relates how his first experiences with LSD under the auspices of UCLA psychiatrist Keith Ditman and then with Sterling Bunnell at the Langley-Porter clinic in San Francisco,

set me off on a series of experiments which I have recorded in *The Joyous Cosmology,* and in the course of which I was reluctantly compelled to admit that—in my own case—LSD had brought me into an undeniably mystical state of consciousness. But oddly, considering my absorption in Zen at the time, the flavor of these experiences was Hindu rather than Chinese. Somehow the atmosphere of Hindu mythology and imagery slid into them, suggesting. . . . Hindu philosophy was a local form of a sort of undercover wisdom, inconceivably ancient, which everyone knows at the back of his mind but will not admit. This wisdom was simultaneously holy and disreputable, and therefore necessarily esoteric. (Watts, 1973c, p. 399)

In light of the esoteric qualities of his psychedelic experiences, Watts hesitated a long time before writing *The Joyous Cosmology,* "considering the dangers of letting the general public be further aware of this potent alchemy." But because Huxley had already "let the cat out of the bag," and mindful of discussions about the drugs already taking place in psychiatric journals and the press, he wanted "mainly to soothe public alarm and to do what I could to forestall the disasters that would follow from legal repression" (Watts, 1973c, p. 400). He was alarmed by the prospect of prohibitionist policies leading to widespread ingestion of impure bootlegged psychedelics in inappropriate settings without guidance, prospects that turned out to be all too realistic as we now know. During those years, the early 1960s, Watts contributed extensively to the professional, academic, and public discussion, speaking at various conferences and symposia about the significance, potential benefits and cautions around psychedelics. Astonished at the rigid shallowness and "actual terror of unusual states of consciousness" that he found in the professional literature of psychiatry, he wrote and published *Psychotherapy East and West* (1961) to help open the ruling psychological paradigms; much as he would eventually write *Beyond Theology* (1964) to broaden the prevailing paradigms in religious thought.

In autumn 1962, Leary, Alpert, and I were sharing a large house in Newton Center, Massachusetts. Alan and his wife, Jano, were living in Cambridge at this time and would engage evening visits to our home. Alan often shared intriguing stories of the lives and works of legendary mystics, occultists, and spiritual seekers throughout history. More importantly, however, Alan exemplified the epitome of an independent philosopher not beholden to any academy or bureaucratic structure. Situated outside of the traditional academic institution, he had published more influential books on Asian philosophy than any scholar of his generation. Even though, in Leary's view, Alan "could teach rings around any tenured professor," he remained true to his temperament as a traveling mystic. "He was a full-time all-out philosopher in his words and in his actions" (Leary, 1983, p. 149). Watts' example would be auspicious because, as Leary put it, we were being "ambushed by the Harvard squares," those faculty and university administrators who were opposed to our new research paradigm focused on exploring the nature of consciousness through psychedelic means.

In response to the emerging institutional opposition to our psychedelic work, including threats of expulsion to graduate students who dared participate, we held a meeting of the research group at our Newton Center home and formed (subsequently incorporating) the short-lived, and perhaps infamous, International Federation for Internal Freedom (IFIF), designating Leary, Alpert,

Watts, and myself, among others, on the board of directors. The purpose of the IFIF was to further the cause of psychedelic exploration in the face of mounting resistance against it. Watts saw himself as trying to facilitate a rapprochement between the Leary group and the university by articulating an "intellectual structure" for our work with psychedelics that would be amenable to both sides. First he tried to persuade Leary to exude a natural scientific rigor in his research, to express his psychedelic findings "in terms people bending over backwards to be scientific would understand" (Watts, 1973c, p. 405).

Watts also tried persuading university administrators to understand that Leary's existential-transactional approach was consistent with contemporary developments in psychology and other sciences such as quantum physics that are, he suggested, "theoretical descriptions" of what mystics experience in their direct perceptions of the world. Toward this end (but a little too late), Alan gave a lecture to the Social Relations Colloquium at Harvard that eventually appeared with the title "The Individual as Man/World" (Watts, 1963a) in the first issue of *The Psychedelic Review* (of which I was co-editor), a journal that Watts helped to initiate and publish under the auspices of the IFIF. Watts said:

> The problem confronting all sciences of human behavior is that we have the evidence (we are *staring* at it) to give us an entirely different conception of the individual than that which we ordinarily feel and which influences our common sense: a conception of the individual not, on the one hand, as an ego locked in the skin, nor, on the other, as a mere passive part of the machine, but as a reciprocal interaction between everything inside the skin and everything outside it, neither one being prior to the other, but equals, like the front and back of a coin. (p. 65)

He argued that even behaviorist psychology has a tacit "organism-environment field" and was in fact implicitly transcending the dualisms of subject and object, as Eastern philosophy had taught for centuries, and as psychedelic experiences made an obvious fact of commonsense perception.

Detailing the eventual termination of the Psychedelic Research Project at Harvard and subsequent IFIF activities is beyond the scope and trajectory of this paper, and accounts of these events can be found elsewhere (Dass et al., 2010; Downing, 1964/2009; Leary, 1983; Leary, Alpert, & Metzner, 1964/2009; Metzner, 1996, 1999b). However, it is worth mentioning that Alan Watts was present at a dinner gathering where Leary initially granted the request of David McClelland, director of the Center for Personality Research (and the one who originally invited Leary to Harvard), to withdraw psychedelic research from his university activities. Watts strongly disagreed with McClelland's assertion that anyone with a deeply spiritual orientation could not really do substantive research in psychological science, but he appreciated David's suggestion that too much "enthusiasm" can compromise the integrity of scientific work (Watts, 1973c). Another of our IFIF board members, Huston Smith, shared the following anecdote in his classic paper, "Do Drugs Have Religious Import?": "Until six months ago, if I picked up my phone in the Cambridge area and dialed KISS-BIG, a voice would answer, 'if-if.' " Smith went on to say that KISS-BIG, the alphabetic analogy of a telephone number assigned by chance, "caught the euphoric, manic, life-embracing attitude that characterized one of the most publicized of the organizations formed to explore the newly synthesized consciousness-changing substances" (Smith, 1964, p. 517).

In 1968, post-Harvard, I published a collection of psychedelic explorations, self-reports garnered from academics (including theologians, philosophers, scientists) and people from other walks of life (i.e., architects, businessmen, writers, musicians, secretaries). This book, entitled *The Ecstatic Adventure,* supported the view that psychedelic substances offer the opportunity to see beyond the isolated sense of individual identity toward recognizing a connection with the greater cosmic processes at play. In light of this connection, "the real evolutionary challenge" put forward by the existence of psilocybin, LSD, and the like, is whether humanity "can finally learn to become a wholly responsible being (Metzner, 1968a, p. 14; see also, Metzner, 1968b, 1989). Alan Watts graced this book with a foreword proffering that continuing psychedelic experimentation may afford clearer perceptions of the human condition at a key point in history when science and technology, in the name of progress, are effecting sweeping alterations of the natural world, leading to the "fouling of our own nest" and careless misuse of resources. It is very important, wrote Watts, that we begin to recognize ourselves as "integral features of nature, and not as frightened strangers in a hostile, indifferent or alien universe" (Watts, 1968a, p. xiii). Contained in this volume was Alan's own account of a psychedelic experience from several years earlier. Leary had given Watts a bottle of psilocybin in New York City during autumn 1960, and Alan returned a self-report of the experience to Timothy shortly thereafter. Alan wrote:

> I was somehow plunged immediately into the most vivid cosmic-consciousness experience I have ever had. It was so marvelous that I called everyone to come into the room. "I've got to explain this to you," I said, . . ."You're all divine, you're all Buddhas just as you are. . . . The point is that life is a gesture." (Watts, 1968b, p. 94)

In the twenty-first century, a region of interest for humanistic and transpersonal research in psychology concerns what are now called the *entheogenic* or mystical/spiritual qualities of psychedelic experience (Metzner, 1999a, 2004; Richards, 2002; Roberts & Hruby, 2002). Contemporary researchers would do well to revisit the wisdom of Alan Watts.

The Watercourse Way

Watts would not be surprised by present-day research showing how psilocy-bin can promote mystical experiences with lasting spiritual meaning (Griffith, Richards, McCann, & Jesse, 2006, 2008). Alan surmised that psychedelics in the 1960s basically set off a sudden upsurge of curiosity about mysticism already developing via escalating contact with Asian cultures and disillusionment with Western theologies focused on dry concepts instead of living percepts. He witnessed many people who, having experienced worthwhile episodes with psychedelics, moved on to study various spiritual disciplines and meditation practices. Alan contended that numerous individuals may not have had their mystical intuitions illuminated without the "catalytic experience" afforded by psychedelic chemicals (Watts, 1973c). Some people turned to Buddhism and Zen practice (Badiner & Grey, 2002; Stolaroff, 1999). My colleague, Richard Alpert, studied mysticism in India, becoming Baba Ram Dass in the process. I embarked on a decade-long period of concentrated participation with a West-ern school of esoteric yoga and afterward immersed myself in learning and performing shamanic practices. Watts transitioned out of his own psychedelic phase—saying "I think I have learned from it as much as I can" (Watts, 1973c, p. 402)—toward a period in his last years of life that returned to, and exuded, a deeper and richer Daoist sensibility.

The basic spiritual insight of Alan's early life, as conveyed in his autobi-ography, was that in the present moment, needing no contrived motivation or effort, the stream of human existence is "inseparably one with the Tao, the flow of the universe" (1973c, p. 191). He once reported having a near *satori* experience upon hearing his first wife, Eleanor, make the chance remark that "the present is just a constant flow, like the Dao, and there is simply no way of getting out of it." Alan was ebullient during the entire week following his wife's comment and later reflected "when I am in my right mind I still know this is the true way of life, at least for me" (p. 153). Thus it is not surprising that, in what was perhaps one of Alan's final essays on psychedelics, he wrote:

> In my own experience, the most interesting thing seems to happen just at the moment when the effect of the chemical wears off and you "descend" from those exalted and ecstatic experiences into your ordinary state of mind. For here, in the "twinkling of an eye," there is the realization that so-called everyday or ordinary consciousness is the supreme form of awakening. (Watts, 1971a, p. 136)

Like the ancient Chinese hermit sages of lore, Watts found a mountain retreat where he explored and clarified his Daoist intuition. It was a small cottage located just north of San Francisco in the foothills of Mount Tamalpais. There

Watts wrote his aptly named autobiography, *In My Own Way* (1973c), penned a collection of Dao essays entitled *Cloud-hidden, Whereabouts Unknown* (1973a), and prepared Dao-inspired lectures (Watts, 2002) for presentation at Esalen Institute and elsewhere. In one of his essays, he suggested that Dao, which he translated as meaning "the energy of the universe as a way, current, course or flow," has a distinctive vibration resonating in the lifestyles of the old-time poets, artists and sages of China (Watts, 1973b, p. 29). There is, in fact, an exotic archetype of Daoist gatherings where individuals are savoring delectable wines while delighting in creative poetry, music and works of art (Clarke, 2000). As Watts described it, "they relished drinking fine tea on lazy afternoons" (Watts, 1973b, p. 30). Alan, in some ways, exuded this sensual spirit of Daoist elegance when he said: "I am an immoderate lover of the opposite sex, of fine food, wine, and spirituous drink, of smoking, of gardens, forests, and oceans, of jewelry and paintings, and of superbly bound and printed books" (Watts, 1977, p. 18). On the other hand, there is the classic image of the Daoist sage indifferent to convention, in Alan's phrasing, "sometimes amiably drunken, wandering in the mountains, and laughing at falling leaves" (Watts, 1973b, p. 29). Here, too, is Alan's reflection when he wrote: "I am lucky. The wind is bringing a thin mist up the valley. There is no one in sight but an old goat, who comes out of the forest and dances on top of a vast, lonely rock" (Watts, 1973c, p. 351).

Watts (1973c) recognized that Daoist lifestyles may seem frivolous or sentimental in apparent avoidance of the critical problems confronting a world "with drab poverty, with slums, with ghettos, and prisons, with napalmed babies and atomic bombs, and with all those things which now seem far more real than lemons in the sun and aromatic trees" (p. 191). But he considered Daoism as an antidote to what he experienced as rigidity and regimentation in Western life; something that "would counterbalance, out-fox, soften, and allay the martial, mechanically marching, tick-tock and saw-toothed jagged life-rhythm which has been rattling the world at least since the Caesars' legionnaires stamped out of Rome" (p. 306). Indeed, Daoist philosophy radiates the notion of *wu-wei*, which translates roughly as "effortless action" or "non-doing." Daoist philosophers see an organic balance in the natural world that belies the call to force one's will on the universe. Forcing human will on the world often creates its own set of disharmonizing consequences. Watts wrote: "Most of the hell now being raised in the world is well intentioned. We justify our wars and revolutions as unfortunate means for good ends, as a general recently explained that he had destroyed a village in Vietnam for its own safety" (Watts, 1971b, p. 23; see also, Watts, 2006).

Alan Watts' last written work, *Tao—The Watercourse Way* (Watts, 1975), was published posthumously and co-authored with *tai-chi* dance-master, Chungliang Al Huang, who provided ink-brush calligraphy to go with Alan's text. Watts had planned to write two more chapters, so it was incomplete, but Huang completed it and added a tribute and biographical reminiscences of their teaching adventures together. Huang (1975a) writes that, in the final two chapters:

Alan hoped to let it be seen how the ancient, timeless Chinese wisdom was medicine for the ills of the West. Yet, paradoxically, it must not be taken as medicine, an intellectually swallowed "pill," but allowed joyously to infuse our total being and so transform our individual lives and through them our society. (p. x)

Elsa Gidlow, Alan's long-time friend and neighbor, said that in the writing of his final book, the *Way of the Tao* "transformed him as he allowed it to permeate his being, so that the reserved, somewhat uptight young English-man, living overmuch in his head, in his mature years became an outgoing, spontaneously playful, joyous world sage" (cited in Huang, 1975a, p. xi). Not that the joyousness and playfulness came to him without cost and without strain. "But I don't like myself when I am sober," he confessed once to Huang, noting his penchant for drinking too much. Yet as Huang (1975b) wrote in his epilogue, Alan had "a rare and wonderful ability to be both Occidental and Oriental . . . when he allowed it, he could be both at once, easily bridging the gaps within his own learning and experience" (p. 126).

Alan Watts expressed the integration of Eastern and Western worldviews in his writings and embodied their synergy in the transformations of his life. He was "an old-fashioned sage. A lover of wisdom. A hard-working scholar who has mastered complex subject matters. . . . One who can see the wisdom of the ages in the ecstatic flicker of the next moment" (Metzner, 1968a, p. 92). Huang (1975a) called him a "philosophical entertainer . . . [whose] foremost concern was enjoyment for himself and for his audience" (p. xi). I am now reminded of a remark by Lin Yutang: "I call no man wise until he has made the progress from the wisdom of knowledge to the wisdom of foolishness, and become a laughing philosopher" (cited in Huang, 1991, p. 23). Nowadays, I like to think of Alan as the *laughing philosopher*, affirming both the highs and lows of existence, knowing the "wisdom of insecurity" (in one of his most inspired book titles), and like the "true men of old" that Chuang-Tzu (1974), Alan's favorite philosopher, wrote about, "when he entered death, there was no sorrow. Carefree he went. Carefree he came. That was all. He did not forget his beginning and did not seek his end. He accepted what he was given with delight" (p. 114). On the evening of his last day, Alan Watts reportedly was hap-pily playing with balloons, and remarked that the weightless, floating sensation was "like my spirit leaving my body."

A CONCLUDING APPRECIATION

After our initial personal and professional connections in the psychedelic 1960s, I maintained my friendship with Alan through occasional visits to his houseboat and mountain cottage, and then surprisingly reconnected with a leg-acy of his in a different way. In the early 1950s, Alan Watts had, together with

Frederic Spiegelberg, Haridas Chaudhuri, and wealthy supporters, founded the Academy of Asian Studies in San Francisco. The academy was a place where Westerners could study Asian philosophies and cultures with teachers from Japan or India, both intellectually and experientially in meditative disciplines. Studies were organized not by the usual separate academic departments but by the converging interests of teachers and students. Alan eventually became dean of the academy, although he found he had no head or stomach for the administrative and business aspects of running an educational institution. "By the end of 1956 it was becoming clear that I was as much out of place in the groves of academe as in the Church, that I was never, never going to be an organizational man" (Watts, 1973c, pp. 319–320). When Watts resigned from the Academy of Asian Studies, Chaudhuri, together with Spiegelberg as well as Michael Murphy and Richard Price, founders of the Esalen Institute, went on to establish the California Institute of Asian Studies (CIAS), which continued as a kind of "alternative graduate school" at the edge of culture and counterculture—and still continues to this day, with the new name California Institute of Integral Studies (CIIS). This was the place where, in 1975, I started teaching East–West Psychology and Agni Yoga meditation, and, following in Alan's footsteps, eventually became the academic dean for ten years during the 1980s.

After leaving the Academy of Asian Studies in 1957, Alan had completely and finally disengaged from any academic institutions, even countercultural or alternative ones. He was living the life of the independent scholar, philosopher, itinerant teacher, guru to the flower-children, storyteller, and *bon vivant*. Settling with his wife Jano in a houseboat in Sausalito, he entertained, delighted, and taught friends, collaborators, and students from all over the world—with occasional lecture and study tours, including one to Cambridge, Massachusetts in 1961, where he came into contact with our psychedelic research project. So Alan Watts has been my mentor in two different phases of his, and my, life. First, in the psychedelic early 1960s, he offered us his deep knowledge of Asian philosophies as a historical and cultural context for the mystical experiences sometimes induced by these unusual substances. In the 1970s (after Watts' death in 1973), when Leary had become an international countercultural prisoner, fugitive, and exile, and Alpert, as Baba Ram Dass, the devoted follower of an Indian bhakti yogi and folk-guru to millions of hippies, I came across an educational institution that Alan had had a hand in founding two decades earlier that provided me with a framework again focused on the integration of Eastern and Western philosophies and psychologies for my teaching work for the next thirty years. As he and I also shared a certain affinity stemming from the fact that we were both brought up in the peculiarly stifling educational milieu of British boarding schools, I will always be grateful for the light-hearted and clear-sighted life wisdom that he imparted.

REFERENCES

Badiner, A. H., & Grey, A. (Eds.). (2002). *Zig, zag, zen: Buddhism and psychedelics.* San Francisco: Chronicle Books.

Chuang-Tzu. (1974). *Chuang Tsu: The inner chapters* (G. Feng & J. English, Trans.). New York: Random House.

Clarke, J. J. (2000). *The Tao of the West: Western transformations of Taoist thought.* New York: Routledge.

Dass, R., Metzner, R., & Bravo, G. (2010). *Birth of a psychedelic culture: Conversations about Leary, the Harvard experiments, Millbrook, and the sixties.* San Francisco: Synergistic Press.

Doblin, R. (1998). Dr. Leary's Concord prison experiment: A 34-year follow-up. *Journal of Psychoactive Drugs, 30*(4), 427–428.

Downing, J. J. (2009). Zihuatanejo: An experiment in transpersonative living. In R. Blum (Ed.), *Utopiates* (pp. 142–177). Piscataway, NJ: Transactions Publishers. (Original work published 1964)

Griffiths, R. R., Richards, W. A., McCann, U., & Jesse, R. (2006). Psilocybin can occasion mystical-type experiences having substantial and sustained personal meaning and spiritual significance. *Psychopharmacology, 187*(3), 268–283.

Griffiths, R. R., Richards, W. A., McCann, U., & Jesse, R. (2008). Mystical-type experiences occasioned by psilocybin mediate the attribution of personal meaning and spiritual significance 14 months later. *Journal of Psychopharmacology, 22,* 621–632.

Huang, C. (1975a). Foreword. In A.W. Watts, *Tao: The watercourse way* (pp. vii–xiii). New York: Pantheon.

Huang, C. (1975b). Once again: A new beginning. In A.W. Watts, *Tao: The watercourse way* (pp. 123–127). New York: Pantheon.

Huang, C. (1991). *Quantum soup: Fortune cookies in crisis.* Berkeley, CA: Celestial Arts.

Huxley, A. (1954). *Doors of perception.* New York: Harper.

Huxley, A. (1956). *Heaven and hell.* New York: Harper.

Leary, T. (1957). *Interpersonal diagnosis of personality.* New York: Ronald Press.

Leary, T. (1960). *The existential transaction.* Cambridge, MA: Harvard Center for Personality Research.

Leary, T. (1983). *Flashbacks.* Los Angeles: Jeremy P. Tarcher.

Leary, T. (1995). *High priest.* Berkeley, CA: Ronin. (Original work published 1968)

Leary, T. (2000). *Change your brain.* Berkeley, CA: Ronin.

Leary, T., Alpert, R., & Metzner, R. (2009). Rationale of the Mexican psychedelic training center. In R. Blum (Ed.), *Utopiates* (pp. 178–186). Piscataway, NJ: Transactions Publishers. (Original work published 1964)

Leary, T., Litwin, G., & Metzner, R. (1963). Reactions of psilocybin administered in a supportive environment. *Journal of Nervous and Mental Disease, 137*(6), 561–573.

Leary, T., & Metzner, R. (1968). The use of psychedelic drugs in prisoner rehabilitation. *British Journal of Social Psychiatry, 2,* 27–51.

Leary, T., Metzner, R., & Alpert, R. (1964). *The psychedelic experience: A manual based on the Tibetan Book of the Dead.* Secaucus, NJ: The Citadel Press.

Leary, T., Metzner, R., Presnell, M., Weil, G., Schwitzgebel, R., & Kinne, S. (1965). A new behavior change program using psilocybin. *Psychotherapy: Theory, Research, and Practice, 2*(2), 61–72.

Metzner, R. (Ed.). (1968a). *The ecstatic adventure.* New York: Macmillan.

Metzner, R. (1968b). On the evolutionary significance of psychedelics. *Main Currents in Modern Thought, 25*(1), 20–25.

Metzner, R. (1989). Molecular mysticism: The role of psychoactive substances in the transformation of consciousness. In C. Ratsch (Ed.), *The gateway to inner space: Sacred plants, mysticism, and psychotherapy* (pp. 73–88). Dorset, UK: Prism Press.

Metzner, R. (1996). Introduction. In T. Leary, *Psychedelic prayers and other meditations* (pp. 9–21). Berkeley, CA: Ronin.

Metzner, R. (1998). Reflections on the Concord prison project and the follow-up study. *Journal of Psychoactive Drugs, 30*(4), 419–420.

Metzner, R. (Ed.). (1999a). *Ayahuasca: Hallucinogens, consciousness, and the spirit of nature.* New York: Thunder Mouth Press.

Metzner, R. (1999b). From Harvard to Zihuatanejo. In R. Forte (Ed.)., *Timothy Leary: Outside looking in* (pp. 155–196). Rochester, VT: Park Street Press.

Metzner, R. (Ed.). (2004). *Teonanacatl: Sacred mushroom of visions.* El Verano, CA: Four Trees Press.

Metzner, R. (2005). Psychedelic, psychoactive, and addictive drugs and states of consciousness. In M. Erlywine (Ed.), *Mind-altering drugs: The science of subjective experience* (pp. 25–48). New York: Oxford University Press.

Metzner, R. (2008). *The expansion of consciousness.* Berkeley, CA: Regent Press.

Richards, W. A. (2002). Entheogens in the study of mystical and archetypal experiences. In R. C. Piedmont & D. O. Moberg (Eds.), *Research in the social scientific study of religion* (Vol. 13, pp. 143–158). Leiden, The Netherlands: Brill.

Riedlinger, T. J. (1993). Existential transactions at Harvard: Timothy Leary's humanistic psychotherapy. *Journal of Humanistic Psychology, 33*(3), 6–18.

Roberts, T. (2006). *Psychedelic horizons.* Charlottesville, VA: Imprint Academic.

Roberts, T., & Hruby, P. J. (2002). Toward an entheogen research agenda. *Journal of Humanistic Psychology, 42*(1), 71–89.

Smith, H. (1964). Do drugs have religious import? *Journal of Philosophy, 61*(18), 517–530.

Smith, H., Grob, C., Jesse, R., Bravo, G., Agar, A., & Walsh, R. (2004). Do drugs have religious import? A 40-year retrospective. *Journal of Humanistic Psychology, 44*(2), 120–140.

Stolaroff, M. (1999). Are psychedelics useful in the practice of Buddhism? *Journal of Humanistic Psychology, 39,* 60–80.

Walsh, R. N., & Grob, C. S. (Eds.). (2005). *Higher wisdom: Eminent elders explore the continuing impact of psychedelics.* Albany: State University of New York Press.

Walsh, R. N., & Grob, C. S. (2006). Early psychedelic investigators reflect on the psychological and social implications of their research. *Journal of Humanistic Psychology, 46*(4), 432–448.

Watts, A. W. (1958). *Nature, man and woman.* New York: Pantheon.

Watts, A. W. (1961). *Psychotherapy East and West.* New York: Pantheon.

Watts, A. W. (1963a). The individual as man/world. *The Psychedelic Review, 1*(1), 55–65.

Watts, A. W. (1963b). *The two hands of God: Myths of polarity.* New York: Pantheon.

Watts, A. W. (1964). *Beyond theology.* New York: Pantheon.

Watts, A. W. (1965). *The joyous cosmology: Adventures in the chemistry of consciousness.* New York: Vintage Books.

Watts, A. W. (1968a). Foreword. In R. Metzner (Ed.), *The ecstatic adventure* (pp. xi–xiii). New York: Macmillan.

Watts, A. W. (1968b). The point is that life is a gesture. In R. Metzner (Ed.). *The ecstatic adventure* (pp. 92–95). New York: Macmillan.

Watts, A. W. (1971a). Ordinary mind is the way. *The Eastern Buddhist* (New Series), 4(2), 134–137.

Watts, A. W. (1971b). Wealth versus money. In *Does it matter? Essays on man's relation to materiality* (pp. 3–24). New York: Vintage.

Watts, A. W. (1973a). *Cloud-hidden, whereabouts unknown: A mountain journal.* New York: Pantheon.

Watts, A. W. (1973b). Flowing with the Tao. In *Cloud-hidden, whereabouts unknown: A mountain journal* (pp. 25–31). New York: Pantheon.

Watts, A. W. (1973c). *In my own way: An autobiography.* New York: Vintage.

Watts, A. W. (1977). Speaking personally. In *The essential Alan Watts* (M. Watts, Ed., pp. 15–22). Berkeley, CA: Celestial Arts.

Watts, A. W. (2002). *Tao: Way beyond seeking.* Boston: Tuttle Publishing.

Watts, A. W. (2006). Taoist ways. In *Eastern wisdom, modern Life: Collected talks, 1960–1969* (M Watts, Ed., pp. 115–122). Novato, CA: New World Library.

Watts, A. W. (with Al Huang). (1975). *Tao: The watercourse way.* New York: Pantheon.

CHAPTER SIX

Alan Watts and the Neuroscience of Transcendence

Donadrian L. Rice

Among the central aims of neuroscience researchers are (a) to determine what neural activities afford particular behaviors and mental states, and (b) to describe changes in the structure and function of the brain due to experience. Because of advances in brain-imaging techniques and other measurement strategies, neuroscientists are now able to explore in finer detail areas of the brain that might correspond to what has traditionally been considered the domain of psychology (i.e., cognition, memory, emotions, sensation, and perception). Moreover, the elusive question of "what is consciousness and where does it come from?" has now found a comfortable home in neuroscience with the belief that consciousness emerges from the neural activity of the brain. Although there are variations on exactly how this happens—whether due to the brain's computational abilities, specialized neurons, or the particular property of a neural network—leading neuroscientists tend to agree that what is called consciousness is a characteristic of the brain (Albright, Jessell, Kandel, & Posner, 2000; Edelman & Tononi, 2000; Gazzaniga, 2000; Greenfield, 1998). Research studies published in academic journals and reported in the popular media now broach the possibility that a strong connection exists between neural activity and subjective experiences of transcendence.

My intention in this chapter is to position Alan Watts' thinking on the subjective experience of transcendence in the context of contemporary neuroscience research. It should be noted that for the purposes of this writing, I am not making fine distinctions at the outset among terms such as *transcendent, mystical, ecstasy,* and *cosmic consciousness.* One reason is because the researchers in this area vary in the precision of their definitions of these terms, and there is disagreement as to which terms are more or less useful in neuroscientific research. Second, Watts himself found these terms to be rather cumbersome, loaded as they are with religious and philosophical implications beyond the scope of his considerations of transcendent experience-as-experienced. Therefore, the use of the term *transcendent* in the present context is meant to include all altered experiences where one might employ any of the above terms (and others of the kind) in descriptions of that experience. Setting the stage for the present discussion is a brief survey of six contemporary neuroscience approaches to the study of transcendence. This consideration of research programs is followed by an exploration of Watts' writing on the nature of transcendent experience, especially certain of his works from the early 1960s. Finally, I conclude by examining some possible implications of Alan Watts' thinking for a neuroscience of transcendence in the twenty-first century.

TRANSCENDENCE IN THE LABORATORY

What follows is a brief survey of six research programs in neuroscience that claim to address the issue of transcendent experience. This survey is not intended as a thorough exploration but merely serves to exemplify certain trends in the neuroscientific study of transcendence. Moreover, I am not suggesting that only six research approaches are available because others could have been included, for example, Varela's (1996) neurophenomenology. Thus, my goal here is simply to establish a background against which Alan Watts' thinking on transcendent experience can be brought to the fore. For various comprehensive reviews of specific domains in the neuroscience of transcendence, see Cahn and Polich (2006); Chiesa (2009); Lutz, Dunne, and Davidson (2007); Nichols (2004; Nichols & Chemel, 2006); Stoerig (2007); Treadway and Lazar (2008); and Voland and Schiefenhovel (2009). For an accessible text oriented toward a general readership, see Fuller (2008).

The six research approaches considered here that investigate neural activity vis-à-vis transcendent experiences are as follows:

1. electroencephalographic (EEG) studies;

2. d'Aquili and Newberg's neuroimaging studies;

3. Hamer's genetic research;

4. entheogenic drug studies;

5. Michael Persinger's electromagnetic field research; and

6. Richard Davidson's affective neuroscience.

EEG STUDIES

Electroencephalographs measure the electrical activity of the brain via electrodes attached to the scalp. An earlier generation of researchers used EEG technology to investigate neural functioning during meditation by, for example, yogis (Anand, Chhina, & Singh, 1961) and Zen priests (Kasamatsu & Hirai, 1966). These researchers linked alpha brain rhythms with changes in parasympathetic nervous system activity during meditation. Alpha rhythms indicate a state of relaxed yet heightened awareness. These findings suggested that meditation, at the very least, produces physiological relaxation in the body. Contemporary EEG studies on meditative practice employ improved technology, greater sophistication in research designs, and complex quantitative analyses for more elaborate and nuanced results. Present-day EEG research agendas also have an expanded focus on a variety of meditative regimens and participant populations such as practitioners of a yoga breathing exercise called Bhramari Pranajama (Vialette, Bakardjian, Prasad, & Cichocki, 2009), the "triarchic body-pathway relaxation technique" (Chan, Han, & Cheung, 2008), and Vipassana meditation (Cahn, Delorme, & Polich, 2010). Newer research findings support the idea that continued training in a meditative practice affects the neurophysiology underlying changes in EEG patterns (Huang & Po, 2009; Qin, Jin, Lin, & Hermanowicz, 2009), and that certain "neuroplasticity effects of long-term meditation practice, subjectively described as increased awareness and greater detachment, are carried-over to non-meditating states" (Tei et al., 2009, p. 158).

D'AQUILI AND NEWBURG'S NEUROIMAGING STUDIES

Eugene d'Aquili and Andrew B. Newberg (1999; Newberg, d'Aquili, & Rause, 2001) employed single-photon emission computed tomography (SPECT) in developing a substantive model of peak transcendent experience during meditation as it unfolds neurologically in the brain over time. SPECT is a technique of nuclear medicine employing gamma rays in the production of three-dimensional imaging of the brain. SPECT imaging allows researchers to visualize the brain and its activity by measuring cerebral blood flow. The greater the flow of blood to a brain area, the greater its activity. In their model, derived from SPECT studies of Buddhist monks and Catholic nuns during periods of meditation, the intention to meditate stimulates the right hemispheric attention association area of the prefrontal cortex and, thus, begins a cascade of effects that eventually reverberate through the brain. Newberg and Waldman (2009) point out in their studies that prayer, meditation, and other spiritual practices have a profound effect on neurotransmitters in the brain leading to altered states of awareness. They speculate that when one engages in a spiritual discipline (i.e., meditation, yoga, etc.), this causes the neurotransmitter dopamine to be released into the frontal lobes, which leads one to have a spiritual/transcendent like experience.

The conclusions drawn from d'Aquili and Newburg's studies are similar to the earlier speculations of Mandell (1980), who proposed a model suggesting that the experience of transcendence results from an overflow of the neurotransmitter serotonin in the hippocampus, an area of the brain that processes memories. Mandell suggests further that states of prolonged extreme excitability can interfere with the gating of emotional input to the hippocampus, thus resulting in the death of the pyramidal cells, which could lead to permanent personality changes following the experience of transcendence (p. 400). Mandell characterized this experience as "God in the Brain." Recently, Newberg has been even more assertive in advancing the view that certain parts of the brain contain "God circuits." He suggests that the occipital-parietal circuit allows one to "identify God as an object that exists in the world," whereas the parietal-frontal circuit establishes the experience of the relationship that one is in unity with God. Engaging in intense meditation or prayer decreases neural activity in the parietal area, which elicits this feeling of unity (Newberg & Waldman, 2009, p. 43). He suggests further that the thalamus allows one to experience an "emotional meaning" of God, whereas the amygdala is responsible for creating the emotional experience of fearing a "punitive God." Finally, the striatum is believed to "inhibit the activity in the amygdala," thus allowing one to feel comfortable or safe when contemplating one's spiritual object (p. 43).

Hamer's Genetic Research

Geneticist Dean Hamer (2004) examined the possibility of a genetic link to spiritual sensitivity. Hamer's research followed earlier studies on identical and fraternal twins indicating that spirituality and religiousness may be heritable characteristics. Kirk, Eaves, and Martin (1999), for example, found that genes accounted for large proportions of the variance (37% for men; 41% for women) on scores of a "self-transcendence scale" intended as a measure of self-reported spirituality. Likewise, Bouchard, McGue, Lykken, and Tellegen (1999) found that genes accounted for large proportions of the variance in scores on the Intrinsic (43%) and Extrinsic (39%) religiousness scales from the Minnesota Study of Twins Reared Apart. Hamer (2004) subsequently ranked one-thousand research participants from low to high based on their scores from a self-report measure of "self-transcendence" and examined their DNA samples for nine genes known to be involved in the production of monoamines that function as neurotransmitters and are associated with moods and emotions. He found a correlation between the "self-transcendence" ranks and variations in the gene VMAT2. Participants ranking high on "self-transcendence" were found to have the nucleic acid *cytosine* in one specific location on the gene. Participants ranking low on self-transcendence had the nucleic acid *adenine* in that same location on the gene.

Hamer concluded that the *VMAT2* gene might be a genetic basis of spirituality. However, Hamer understands that the single-gene explanation is inevitably incomplete and that cultural memes may also play a significant role in religiosity. Too, it is worth mentioning the sociobiological view that religiosity and spirituality may be the result of a complex process of biocultural selection

(Vass, 2009). Yet Hamer's research is not without controversy. See, for example, Zimmer's (2004) scathing scientific criticisms. Nonetheless, Hamer's so-called "God gene" research exemplifies another way in which neuroscientists claim to account for transcendent experience.

ENTHEOGENIC DRUG STUDIES

The use of entheogens as a means of inducing transcendent-like experiences has been reported in a variety of human cultures throughout recorded history. Examples of this practice are found in the ancient Vedic tradition, the Eleusinian mysteries, pre-Christian Europe, Africa, and in cultures of the early Americas (Forte, 1997a; Hofmann, 1997; Metzner, 1999). This practice continues today in North America in the form of the Native American Church (White, 2000), and among various indigenous cultures in South America who adhere to the Santo Daime religion (Alverga, 1999). The substances employed in these diverse spiritual practices are all chemically related and include the amanita muscaria mushroom, which is thought to be "soma" as mentioned in the ancient Indian scriptures of the *Rg Veda;* the psilocybin mushroom; peyote; ayahuasca; and D-lysergic acid diethylamide (LSD).

Entheogens, which means substances that evoke the Divine, contain chemicals that are structurally similar to neurotransmitters found in the brain and throughout the nervous system. Also referred to as "psychedelics," these drugs have a profound effect on mood, perception, and behavior. Hence, the altered state experienced by participants in an entheogenic ritual is believed to have spiritual and/or transcendent significance. Although the exact mechanisms by which these drugs exert their effects remain unclear, research suggests that they work, at least partially, by temporarily affecting the serotonergic and possibly dopaminergic receptor sites (Nichols & Chemel, 2006; Pellerin, 1998).

The most comprehensive study of the use of an entheogenic substance in religious practice is found in a volume entitled *The Peyote Religion among the Navaho* (Aberle, 1966). The ritualistic use of peyote was formalized in the United States with the establishment of the Native American Church in 1914. For the Navaho, peyote is the central feature of their religion and the primary way they experience unity with God. It is considered also a panacea for various bodily and spiritual ills (p. 3). In 1919, the "Indian Bureau" conducted a formal census of peyote use among the Navaho and found that out of 316,000 surveyed, 13,345 used peyote. Interestingly, the general conclusion of the researchers examining peyote use among the Navaho was that lasting harmful psychological or physical affects were not evident. Too, psychiatrist Stanislav Grof (1975, 2001) is well known for his clinical studies where he administered LSD to thousands of subjects, of whom many reported having spiritual like experiences. The experiences reported have ranged from resembling the tenets of Judeo-Christianity to elements found in the religions of Asia and Native American traditions.

PERSINGER'S ELECTROMAGNETIC FIELD RESEARCH

Michael A. Persinger has a wide-ranging research agenda looking at the effects of electromagnetic energy on the brain and conscious experience, both in the laboratory and in everyday life. In the laboratory, Persinger (1987) has recorded what he identifies as "short-lived theta activity seizures" from the temporal lobes of meditating subjects who reported having spiritual like experiences during the period the seizures were produced. He calls this electrical brain activity a "temporal lobe transient" (TLT), which is similar to brain activity during an epileptic seizure. Persinger also has evoked altered experiences in research subjects by applying electormagnetics to the temporo-parietal region of the brain. One kind of paranormal experience evoked by applications of electromagnetics to the brain is the "sensed presence," an intuition of the proximal company of another sentient being (Cook & Persinger, 1997). This phenomenon is more easily facilitated by electromagnetics in combination with certain visual stimuli (Medi & Persinger, 2009), is more prominent in individuals with elevated scores on inventories measuring right temporal lobe sensitivity (Cook & Persinger, 2001), and variations of its manifestation can be influenced by experimental manipulation of the electromagnetic fields evoking, for example, fears, smells, and auditory phenomena (Persinger & Healy, 2002). The subjective intensity of the sensed presence is correlated with theta activity in right frontal and parietal lobes (Booth, Koren, Persinger, 2008; Booth & Persinger, 2009). Furthermore, Persinger (2001) suggests, the sensed presence might be a "prototype" of "the god experience itself" (p. 517; Cook, Koren, & Persinger, 1999; Persinger, 1987). Outside of the laboratory, Persinger (1988; Booth, Koren, & Persinger, 2005) has studied the influence of geomagnetic fluctuations on subjectivity, suggesting neurological explanations for such phenomena as apparitions and transcendent experiences of people visiting sacred locations.

DAVIDSON'S AFFECTIVE NEUROSCIENCE

Richard Davidson's research seeks to "approach the construct of compassion" in Buddhist meditation "and bring it into the scientific lexicon" (Davidson, 2002, p. 108). Davidson and his research team employ EEG and various neuroimaging strategies such as positron emission tomography (PET), magnetic resonance imaging (MRI), and functional MRI (fMRI) to study activities of the brain during meditation, especially emotional self-regulation and corresponding neural correlates. In a study using EEG measurements, Lutz, Greischar, Rawlings, Ricard, and Davidson (2004) found that expert meditators produced much higher gamma-wave activity than novices when engaged in "loving-kindness" meditation. In another study, Lutz, Brefczynski-Lewis, Johnstone, and Davidson (2008) measured brain activity related to empathic responses of expert and novice meditation practitioners generating "a loving-kindness-compassion meditation state" and while at rest. As measured by fMRI, significant differences in brain activity were found between expert and novice meditators when presented with emotional and neutral sounds. The researchers found that expert meditators showed greater activation of the "amygdala, right temporo-parietal junction(TPJ), and right posterior superior temporal sulcus (pSTS) in response to all sounds" than did novices. Lutz, Brefczynski-Lewis, et al. (2008) concluded that "together these data indicate that the mental expertise to cultivate positive emotion alters the activation of circuitries previously linked to empathy and theory of mind in response to emotional stimuli" (Abstract).

Moreover, Davidson's research team has found evidence suggesting a long-term impact of meditation on the neurophysiology associated with focused attention (Brefczynski-Lewis, Lutz, Schaefer, Levinson, & Davidson, 2007). These researchers found that, when presented with distracter sounds while engaged in a "focused-attention" meditation, expert meditators as compared with novice meditators "had less brain activation in regions related to discursive thoughts and emotions and more activation in regions related to response inhibition and attention." These findings, derived via MRI, correlated with degree of expertise as measured by hours of meditation practice suggesting "possible plasticity in these mechanisms" (p. 11483; see also, Lutz, Slagter, Dunne, & Davidson, 2008; Lutz et al., 2009).

The six research agendas discussed here call to mind Austin's (1998) conjecture that the neuroscience of transcendence would coalesce into a field of study called "experiential neurology." Within the broad scope of this emerging discipline would be "such topics as meditation, preconscious functions, absorptions, and insight-wisdom. Its mission will be to uncover the mechanisms by which each one transforms experience and behavior" (p. 697). Substantive knowledge about the brain anatomy and physiology underlying transcendent experiences, as well as their genetic, neurochemical, and electrophysiological correlates, is becoming readily available. To be sure, neuroscience is in its infancy, and in none of the above research programs is scientific explanation of transcendent experience anywhere near complete or certain. Moreover, the self-correcting nature of natural science research implies that findings and conclusions may be tentative and subject to revision as new data emerge via innovative theory, study design, and analysis. But the exact and complete details of the biology of transcendence are not necessary for the present discussion. Whatever the eventualities, virtually all neuroscience research is pointing to the same conclusion: Transcendent experiences are correlated with biological factors and, in some cases, can be triggered by the manipulation of them and perpetuated via neuroplasticity. It therefore appears that Austin's "experiential neurology" is weighted more toward neurology than to experience. To better understand the germane implications of this research bias, the pressing need is to turn to transcendent experiences-as-experienced. Hence, discussion shifts from neuroscience to Alan Watts.

WATTS AND THE NATURE OF TRANSCENDENT EXPERIENCE

Despite growing interest in the field and its findings, the neuroscience of transcendence is not immune to criticism, controversy, and debate. Indeed, the neuroscience research programs discussed here variously elicit two salient yet opposite critiques, each reflecting one side of what may be called a contemporary Cartesian dualism. On one hand, research results and, in some instances, the conclusions drawn would make it appear that experiences subjectively described as "spiritual," "mystical," "transcendent," and so on, can all be reduced to the electrochemical activity of the brain and nervous system. The interpretation of consciousness (and by extension, transcendent experience) as a mere brain property has been criticized as the continuation of an outdated reductionistic and mechanistic model from which neuroscientists tend to operate. As Wallace (2007) asserts:

> Cognitive scientists commonly gauge the success of their research by the extent to which they are able to identify the "underlying mechanisms" of mental processes. This insistence of finding mechanical explanations was equally common among physicists until the late nineteenth century, when it was discovered that natural phenomena, such as electromagnetism, could not always be understood in terms of "underlying mechanisms." The mature discipline of physics has learned this through hard experience. But younger branches of science, especially the cognitive sciences, whose models of neural function are generally based on nineteenth-century physics, are still captivated by the Cartesian belief that something is truly explained only if its underlying mechanisms have been identified. (p. 39)

On the other hand, many scientists remain uncomfortable and in some cases hostile toward the linking of brain research to mystical and religious experiences. Partially fueling this discomfort is the involvement of prominent religious leaders and other spiritual adepts who are offering themselves as research participants for these neuroscience projects.

When it was announced in 2005 that His Holiness, the Dalai Lama, would give an address to the annual meeting of the Society for Neuroscience, the world's largest organization of neuroscientists, several hundred members of the organization signed petitions in protest of the Dalai Lama's appearance, sending a strong signal that this is not an appropriate area of investigation for the serious scientist ("Against Dalai Lama's Lecture," 2005). The key criticism was that neuroscience research on transcendent experience inappropriately blurs the border between natural science and supernatural religion (see also, Helminiak, 1984, 2010). Compounding the issue is the fact that neuroscientists and psychologists engaging in this research on transcendence occasionally employ language that, like Descartes' conjecture about the pineal gland, implies the possibility of a deity existing somewhere within the brain (Alper, 2008; d'Aquili & Newberg, 1999); or that humans are genetically predisposed to be aware of a deity (Hamer, 2004); or that one might find the source of a deity through the ingestion of mind-altering substances (Forte, 1997b).

In his writings about transcendent experience vis-à-vis science, Alan Watts anticipated these controversies and offered alternative viewpoints suggesting neither reductionism nor supernaturalism. Regarding reductionism in the neuroscience of transcendence, Watts (1960/1973b) wrote the following in his essay on psychedelics as "The New Alchemy:"

> In the last few years modern chemists have prepared one or two substances for which it may be claimed that in some cases they induce states of mind remarkably similar to cosmic consciousness.
>
>   To many people such claims are deeply disturbing. . . . The claim seems to imply that spiritual insight is after all only a matter of body chemistry involving *a total reduction of the spiritual to the material.* (pp.127–128, emphasis added)

Further in the essay, however, Watts argued that employing psychedelic substances does not completely reduce transcendent experience to chemical processes of the body. Rather, it is the overgeneralized use of scientific language that diminishes the subject matter:

> The use of such chemicals does not reduce spiritual insight to a mere matter of body chemistry. . . . When we can describe certain events in terms of chemistry this does not mean that such events are merely chemical. A chemical description of spiritual experience has somewhat the same use and the same limits as the chemical description of a great painting. It is simple enough to make a chemical analysis of the paint, and for the artists and connoisseurs alike there is some point in doing so. It might also be possible to work out a chemical description of all the processes that go on in the artist while he is painting. But it would be incredibly complicated, and in the meantime the same process could be described and communicated more effectively in some other language than the chemical. We should probably say that a process *is* chemical only when chemical language is the most effective means of describing it. (pp. 129–130)[1]

Thus it is not merely that, for example, "mind" and "brain" may be two ways of referring to the same phenomenon, but that the technical language of chemistry, and the languages of the natural sciences in general, do not effectively describe phenomena of experience in the ways they are experienced in everyday life. Indeed, in his essay on "Mythological Motifs in Modern Science," Watts (1995) pointed out that the "image" of the world portrayed by natural science "bears less and less resemblance to any form of sensual imagery" (p. 65). He went on to quote physicist Robert Oppenheimer who said that scientific knowledge "has become the property of specialized communities who pursue their own way with growing intensity further and further from their roots in ordinary life" (p. 65).[2]

Watts contended, moreover, that an overemphasis on reductionism through mechanistic imagery in scientific language obscures the holistic and organismic qualities of humanity, a view consistent with the Gestalt psychology of his day:

> I do not wish to press the analogy between the human mind and servo-mechanisms to the point of saying that the mind-body is "nothing but" an extremely complicated automaton. . . . Mechanism and organism seem to me to be different in principle—that is, in their actual functioning—since the one is made and the other grown. The fact that one can translate some organic processes into mechanical terms no more implies that organism is mechanism than the translation of commerce into arithmetical terms implies that commerce *is* arithmetic. (Watts, 1957, pp. 136–137)

The implication here is that experience and behavior exhibit patterns and relationships, which cannot be reduced to simpler mechanistic components. Stated in its most general form, any physiological or neurological event occurs within the context of the total organism and its environment, and may be viewed in a holistic light. As the Gestaltists were fond of saying, the whole is greater than, or at least different from, the sum of its parts, including the sum total of "underlying neural mechanisms." As Watts (1960/1973b) described it from the subjective first-person perspective, transcendent experiences appear "as a vivid and overwhelming certainty that the universe, precisely as it is at this moment, as a whole and in every one of its parts, is so completely right as to need no explanation or justification beyond what simply is" (pp. 17–18).

Alan Watts made no inference that transcendent experiences imply anything supernatural. Indeed, he (1973a) made it clear that in his own writings that he was offering descriptions of transcendent experiences, "not of formal visions and supernatural beings, but of *reality as seen and felt*" (p. 5, emphasis added). Watts (1960/1973c), elaborating on first-person accounts of transcendent experience, described this perceptual activity in a way suggesting "insight" as understood by Gestalt psychologists. Gestaltists understand insight as a perceptual activity where a sudden reorganization of part–whole relationships results in an immediate realization, often called an "aha!" or "eureka!" experience. Transcendent experience for Watts was an "unmistakable sensation . . . emerging quite suddenly and unexpectedly" (p. 17). Watts suggested that this eureka moment of transcendence, what he called a "this is IT" experience, was the "insight" that "the immediate *now*, whatever its nature, is the goal and fulfillment of all living" (p. 18). Watts described this experience as a transcendence of the ego:

> It is usual for the individual to feel that the whole world has become his own body, and that whatever he is has not only become, but always has been, what everything else is. It is not that he loses his identity to the point that he actually looks out through all other eyes, becoming omniscient, but rather that his individual consciousness and existence is a point of view temporarily adopted by something immeasurably greater than himself. (p. 18)[3]

Once this "astonishing moment" of transcendent insight is achieved, according to Watts, a kind of perceptual constancy develops. Gestalt psychologists describe perceptual constancy as a tendency of perceptual experience to remain stable and unchanging despite changes in sensory stimulation. In transcendent experience as described by Watts, a perceptual insight may remain over time despite an ongoing flux and flow of emotion:

> Surrounding and flowing from this insight is an emotional ecstasy, a sense of intense relief, freedom, and lightness, and often of almost unbearable love for the world, which is, however, secondary. Often the pleasure of the experience is confused with the experience and the insight lost in the ecstasy, so that in trying to retain the secondary effects of the experience the individual misses the point—that the immediate *now* is complete even when it is not ecstatic. For ecstasy is a necessarily impermanent contrast in the constant fluctuations of our feelings. But insight, when clear enough, persists; having once understood a particular skill, the facility tends to remain. (Watts, 1960/1973c, pp. 18–19)

Later in the same essay, Watts reiterated this constancy phenomenon when he wrote: "I have come to realize that how I *feel*, whether the actual sensation of freedom and clarity is present or not, is not the point—for, again, to feel heavy or restricted is also IT" (p. 31).

This *transcendent constancy* reveals the fallacy of separating the spiritual from the material or the wonderful from the ordinary. They are in mundane experience what gestaltists call "characteristics-in-relation" (Kohler, 1947, p. 176). The transcendent insight is the realization that "spiritual," "material," "wonderful," and "ordinary" are one. There is, in other words, unity in difference. To be sure, Watts (1960/1973c) acknowledged that transcendent experiences may be interpreted by individuals through the lens of philosophical and religious ideas in their culture. Yet these differences of interpretation often conceal the basic identity of the experiences across contexts. Thus:

> There is no really satisfactory name for this type of experience. To call it mystical is to confuse it with visions of another world, or of gods and angels. To call it spiritual or metaphysical is to suggest that it is not also extremely concrete and physical, while the term "cosmic consciousness" itself has the unpoetic flavor of occultist jargon. (p. 17)

For Watts, the experience of transcendence does not have the element of ethereal strangeness or other worldliness, and does not imply any supernatural separation between self and world. On the contrary, the transcendent experience is an immersion of the self into the world:

> Transcendence is not separation, and similarly, from the metaphysical standpoint, holiness is not "set-apart-ness" but the wholeness of that which is all-inclusive. It is thus, then, that realization comes through a consciousness and deliberate plunging into life, not in retreat from it; through a generous acceptance of finite experience, not in blotting it out of the mind; through utter willingness to be what one is, not in trying to lift oneself to heaven by one's own boot-straps. (Watts, 1950/1965, p. 187)

Transcendence is the perceptual realization—the Gestalt insight—that "*this*—the immediate, everyday, and present experience—is IT, the entire and ultimate point for the existence of a universe" (Watts, 1960/1973c, p. 11).

The experience of Gestalt insight is a sudden event happening beyond control of an individual's will. Watts (1973a) wrote in his autobiography that transcendent insight "has nothing to do with making an effort or not making an effort." Yet he went on to say that "it is simply a matter of intelligence" (p. 290). Watts' use of the term *intelligence* is unfortunate because it is easily interpreted as meaning "intellectualization" or "analytic thinking." A closer reading, however, reveals that Watts was referring to a kind of perceptual intelligence that is a "more or less intelligent 'happening' which is neither voluntary nor involuntary, subjective nor objective, controlled nor uncontrolled" (p. 289). That Watts is referencing perception rather than analytic thinking is evident from an earlier anecdote:

> One evening, when Eleanor and I were walking home from a meditation session, I began to discuss the method of concentration on the eternal present. Whereupon she said, "why try to concentrate on it? What else is there to be aware of? Your memories are all in the present, just as much as the trees over there. Your thoughts about the

future are also in the present, and anyhow I just love to think about the future. The present is just a constant flow, like the Tao, and there's simply no way of getting out of it." With that remark my whole sense of weight vanished. You could have knocked me down with a feather. I realized that when the Hindus said *Tat tvam asi*, "You are That," they meant just what they said. For a whole week thereafter I simply floated, remembering [Frederic] Spiegelberg's telling me of the Six Precepts of Tilopa:

No thought, no reflection, no analysis,
no cultivation, no intention,
Let it settle itself. (Watts, 1973a, pp. 152–153)

With one comment by his wife, Eleanor, Watts experienced a sudden transcendent insight. Yet he went on to describe the event as a "premature Satori" because, Watts wrote, "I was unable to resist the temptation to write, think, and intellectualize about it." Note, however, that Watts suggested that analytic thinking is also "IT" but always subordinate to larger organismic processes at play: "Conscious thought, reflection, analysis . . . are simply using the mind's radar or scanning beam for purposes which the mind as a whole can do of itself, and on its own, with far more intelligence and less effort" (pp. 152–153).[4]

The "premature" nature of this Satori experience, exemplified by the tendency to intellectualize, hints at what is transcended through transcendent insight. In one of his later essays Watts (1973d) wrote:

To be human is precisely to have that extra circuit of consciousness which enables us to know that we know, and thus to take an attitude towards all that we experience. The mistake which we have made— and this, if anything, *is the fall of man*—is to suppose that that extra circuit, that ability to take an attitude toward the rest of life as a whole, is the same as actually standing aside and being separate from what we see. We seem to feel that the thing which knows that it knows is one's essential self, that—in other words—our personal identity is entirely on the side of the commentator. We forget, because we learn to ignore so subtly, the larger organismic fact that self-consciousness is simply a subordinate part and an instrument of our whole being, a sort of mental counterpart of the finger-thumb opposition in the human hand. Now which is really you, the finger or the thumb?

Observe the stages of this differentiation, the levels of abstraction: First, the organism from its environment, and with this knowledge of the environment. Second, the distinction of knowing knowledge from knowledge itself. But in concrete fact all this, like the finger-thumb opposition, is a *difference which does not divide*. (pp. 8–9)

In short, transcendent experience for Alan Watts was a transcendence of dissociated ego consciousness. It is a vividly clear perception that *"what we are talking about is ourselves,* and ourselves in a sense far more basic and real than that extra circuit which knows knowing" (Watts, 1973d, p. 9).

WATTS AND NEUROSCIENCE IN THE TWENTY-FIRST CENTURY

How is Alan Watts' legacy expressed in the neuroscience of transcendence in the twenty-first century? The first way concerns the relations of mind and body. It is clear from Watts' writings that he is of the perspective that the mind and body are inseparable and that it is folly to think otherwise (Watts, 1958/1970, 1961, 1962). He arrived at this perspective by examining his own and others' first-person experiences of transcendence and through the intersubjectivity afforded by his studies of comparative religion. In the prologue to *The Joyous Cosmology,* Watts (1962) wrote:

> One of the greatest of all superstitions is the separation of the mind from the body. This does not mean that we are being forced to admit that we are only bodies; it means that we are forming an altogether new idea of the body. For the body considered as separate from the mind is one thing—an animated corpse. But the body considered as inseparable from the mind is another, and as yet we have no proper word for a reality which is simultaneously mental and physical. To call it mental-physical will not do at all, for this is the very unsatisfactory joining of two concepts which have both been impoverished by long separation and opposition. (p. 3)

Indeed what to call this relationship remains a semantic conundrum today (Damasio, 2006; LeDoux, 1998; Pert, 1999); and most scientists, researchers, and neurophilosophers opt to settle for the notion that the mind is an emergent property of the brain, and perhaps the mind indirectly participates in controlling the body (P. M. Churchland, 1989; Dennett, 1991; LeDoux, 1998). But as Watts (1962) elaborated further:

> This radical separation of the part controlling from the part controlled changed man from a self-controlling to a self-frustrating organism, to the embodied conflict and self-contradiction that he has been throughout history. Once the split occurred conscious intelligence began to serve its own ends instead of those of the organism that produced it. More exactly, it became the intention of the conscious intelligence to work for its own, dissociated, purposes. But . . . just as the separation of mind from body is an illusion, so also is the subjection of the body to the independent schemes of the mind. (p. 5)

Watts appears to be suggesting that scientific concepts that either reduce the mind to the body, or portray body as controlled by the mind, are off the mark.

A contemporary term reflecting the nondualist sentiments that Watts tried to convey is the unhyphenated *bodymind* initially put forth in the field of alternative medicine (Connelly, 1986) and appropriated into mainstream neuroscience by Pert (1986, 1999, 2008) via her groundbreaking work in neuroendocrinology. Pert's (1999) research attempts to explain how various neuropeptides influencing emotional responses may be part of the key that unifies the mind and body. She writes:

> In the popular lexicon, these kinds of connections between body and brain have long been referred to as "the power of the mind over the body." But in light of my research, that phrase does not describe accurately what is happening. Mind doesn't dominate body, it becomes body—body and mind are one. I see the process of communication we have demonstrated, the flow of information throughout the whole organism, as evidence that the body is the actual outward manifestation, in physical space, of the mind. *Bodymind,* a term first proposed by Dianne Connelly, reflects the understanding, derived from Chinese medicine, that the body is inseparable from the mind. (p. 187)

This notion of "bodymind" reflects neither a hierarchy of body controlling mind, nor mind controlling body, but rather a holistic system of reciprocal expression (De Kooker, 2008; Weller, 2010; see also, Watts, 1958/1970).

The amalgam term, *neuroendocrinology,* as well as the holistic *bodymind,* suggest an emerging trend of interdisciplinary research beyond the traditional discipline-specific approaches in academic fields of study. By the early 1960s, Watts (1958/1970, 1961) was in tune with this budding trend in scientific research. He saw that the insular attitude of discipline-specific approaches to understanding the human organism in the natural and social sciences may be inadequate to the task because each person is "at once universal and unique. He is universal by virtue of his inseparability from the cosmos. He is unique because he is just *this* organism" (Watts, 1961, p. 21). In commenting on a quote from Teilhard de Chardin, where Chardin speaks of the futility of dividing the "stuff" of the universe, Watts (1961) wrote:

> The effect of this upon the study of human behavior is that it becomes impossible to separate psychological patterns from patterns that are sociological, biological, or ecological. Departments of knowledge based upon what now appear to be crude and primitive divisions of nature begin to coalesce into such awkwardly named hybrids as neuro-psychiatry, sociobiology, biophysics, and geopolitics. At a certain level of specialization the divisions of scientific knowledge begin to run

together because they are far enough advanced to see that the world itself runs together, however clear cut its parts may have seemed to be. (p. 18)

The proliferation of "awkwardly named hybrids" continues in the twenty-first century, at least in the effort to describe the mind and body relationship. In addition to psychoneuroimmunology, witness, for example, such designations as "psychoneuroendocrinology," "neuropsychology," "psychoneuropharmacology," and "neurotheology."

What of Watts' Gestalt-like descriptions of transcendent insight? Wolfgang Kohler famously concluded his text on *Gestalt Psychology* (1947) by suggesting that "it seems to be the natural fate of Gestalt Psychology to become Gestalt Biology" (p. 210). Kohler was pointing to an inevitable trend toward the scientific study of isomorphic expression as research technologies advance over time. Gestalt Psychology employs the notion of *psychophysical isomorphism* to denote the neurological expression of holistic perception in subjective experience. Gestalt Psychology has indeed become a cognitive-gestalt neuroscience (King & Wertheimer, 2009). For example, there is now a body of contemporary neuroscience research supporting the idea that the binding of discrete sensory information (e.g., color and shape or figure and ground) into holistic perception is expressed neurologically via oscillations of synchronized gamma wave activity across various regions in the brain (Keil, Muller, Ray, Gruber, & Elbert, 1999; Sokolov, 2000). Concerning transcendent experience, as Richard Davidson's research team (Lutz, et al., 2004) demonstrated, high-amplitude gamma activity and phase-synchrony has been shown to occur in individuals practicing a Tibetan Buddhist form of meditation described as "pure compassion" where "benevolence and compassion pervades the mind as a way of being" (Method section). Note, however, that Watts' transcendent insights were of the "sudden" variety whereas the Lutz et al. data are derived from long-term meditators and attributed to such practices. In 2003, Ragsdale offered a consideration of Gestalt theory in relation to Mahayana Buddhism and demonstrated a consonance of various confluent themes. This confluence, perhaps, may serve as a point of departure for a cognitive-gestalt neuroscience of the Mahayana tradition of Buddhist practice.

A central aspect of Gestalt Psychology is a "field theory" of perceptual experience. The Gestaltists appropriated field theory from research in physics. As Kohler (1940/1973) described it:

A theory of perception must be a *field theory*. By this we mean that the neural functions and processes with which the perceptual facts are associated in each case are located in a continuous medium; and that the events in one part of this medium influence events in other regions in a way that directly depends on the properties of both in relation to each other. This is the conception with which all physicists work. The field theory of perception applies this simple scheme to the brain correlates of perceptual facts. (p. 55)

Watts (1963) extended this "simple scheme" to describe the region of the individual self in relation to all that is beyond itself. "The individual is not a skin-encapsulated ego but an organism-environment field. The organism itself is a point at which the field is 'focused,' so that each individual is a unique expression of the behavior of the whole field, which is ultimately the universe itself" (p. 55). Psychedelic experiences may exemplify this phenomenon: "Psychedelics are very frequently successful in giving the individual a vivid sensation of the mutual interdependence of his own behavior and the behavior of his environment, so that the two seem to become one—the behavior of a unified field" (p. 55). Watts thus pointed out that the mystic's first-person experience of "oneness" accords well with the way in which existence is described from the third-person perspective via field theory in the natural sciences. Watts, moreover, was an early proponent of the integration of physics and psychology—a field now called *Quantum Psychology*. Capra (1989), in fact, cited Watts as a key inspiration of his seminal *Tao of Physics* (1975/2000). Fast-forwarding to the twenty-first century reveals a burgeoning genre of quantum physics applied to psychological life. A prime example is Tuszynski's (2006) edited volume, *The Emerging Physics of Consciousness*, in which is suggested that the unity of conscious experience is expressed neurologically via simultaneous quantum computations at the level of tubulins that are subsidiary units of protein located in microtubuler structures in neurons. McFadden (2006) thus put forth the "conscious electromagnetic information (CEMI) field theory" which states:

Digital information within neurons is pooled and integrated to form an electromagnetic information field. Consciousness is that component of the brain's electromagnetic information field that is downloaded to motor neurons and is thereby capable of communicating its state to the outside world. (pp. 396–397)

Note here I am not suggesting that Watts would endorse this version of field theory but merely identifying one variation of trajectory in contemporary scientific thinking about physics and consciousness.

Hameroff and Penrose (1996; Hameroff, 2006) put forth a quantum psychological model that also draws on computational activity of microtubles in brain neurons. However, the details of the model are not important for the present discussion. Instead I want to point out the initial inspiration for their model: Penrose's (1989) grappling with the conundrum of how mathematic computations are comprehended because they require not just following the rules of mathematical logic but also call for comprehending the meaning of quantitative ideas. Note this is a similar conundrum encountered by philosopher, Edmund Husserl, nearly one hundred years earlier that led to his articulation of phenomenological philosophy (Bernet, Kern, & Marbach, 1999). Husserl's phenomenology sought to describe the constitution of meaning via *intentionality*. The notion of intentionality is that consciousness is an active orientation (*noesis*) toward an object (*noema*). The noematic appearance of an object is contingent upon the noetic activity of consciousness. A salient question here, then, in the context of contemporary neuroscience research, is to what extent can the brain-mind know itself? Stated in terms of phenomenology, to what extent can the noesis render itself as the noema?[5] Will neuroscience research ever provide a complete understanding of consciousness in general and transcendent experience in particular?

There are at least two general modes of response to the above questions. First is the view that neuroscience, though still in its infancy, will eventually explain all psychological behaviors and experiences in terms of physiological and neurological activity (e.g., P. S. Churchland, 1986, 2002) or, at least, make significant strides toward that goal (Albright et al., 2000). Second is a response in the negative. Uttal (2005), for example, argued that a complete knowledge of mind-brain may never be solved because of sheer complexity, an intractable problem regardless of scientific maturity. Schneider (2005), moreover, offered the caveat that subjectivity affords "a sense of magnificence and mystery of living (awe)" (p. 167) that is qualitatively different from phenomena measured and expressed by third-person objective strategies in neuroscience. Watts (1973a) called the question:

> the most delicate epistemological puzzle: how the brain evokes a world which is simultaneously the world which it is in, and to wonder, therefore, whether the brain evokes the brain. Put it in metaphysical terms, psychological terms, or neurological terms: it is always the same. How can we know what we know without knowing knowing?
>
> This question must be answered, if it can ever be answered, before it can make any sense at all to say that reality is material, mental, electrical, spiritual, a fact, a dream, or anything else. (p. 414)

Yet neuroscientists simply attempt to translate, for example, subjective transcendent experiences, into operational definitions of objectively measurable variables such as brain waves or cerebral blood flow.

Watts (1975) observed, "to the degree that you make an object of the subject, the subject becomes objectionable" (p. 200). His point was that:

> the order of the brain is complicated because, and only because, we are trying to translate it into words. If I might invent a verb, the more we try to "precise" the world, to discern its clearly cut structure, the more precise we compel ourselves to be. The world retreats into ever

greater complexity by analogy with the whirlings of a dog chasing its
own tail. (p. 199)

The whirling dog is the analytic ego trying to capture itself through the language of objective measurement that ironically, said Watts, amounts to a kind
of "subjective idealism" expressed in the terms of neurophysiology:

> The structure of the nervous system (which we do not really under-
> stand) determines our view of the world and yet is itself, presumably,
> something in that world. Which comes first, egg or hen? And what
> do I mean by "I" in saying "I do not understand my nervous system,"
> which is presumably what I really and truly am? The limitation . . . is
> that you can't kiss your own lips, which is another way of saying, with
> the *Upanishads*, TAT TVAM ASI, or "You're IT." (p. 199)

Stated in phenomenological terms, the neuroscience enterprise, in Watts
view, cannot completely render the noesis as the noema. Doing so is, in one
sense, to confuse symbol (scientific measurement) with reality (first-person
experience), or in another sense, to mistake the "object for consciousness" for
the "act of being conscious."

Alan Watts was mindful that mystery may be an irreducible constituent
of transcendent experience. In *The Wisdom of Insecurity*, Watts (1951) wrote:
"The fascinating mystery of *what* it is that we mark and measure must in the
end 'tease us out of thought' until the mind forgets to circle and pursue its
own processes, and becomes aware that to *be* at this moment is pure miracle"
(p. 150). This is not to say that Watts was anti-science. On the contrary, by
the 1960s he was centering his interests on the philosophy of science, especially relations between Asian mysticism and the organism–environment field
of the Western scientific approach. Nevertheless, neuroscience research and
transcendent experience may of necessity diverge because researchers, in theory
and practice, are not equipped by science to *wholly* understand the subject.
Davidson, for example, suggests the neuroscience of transcendence is simply
an attempt to study "mental activity that could be understood in secular terms"
(as cited in Gilgoff, 2010; see also, Davidson, 2002). On the other hand, suggested Watts (1975), if scholars (including, presumably, neuroscientists) could
stop verbalizing and quantifying, stop thinking, and simply be present to the
breath, and "genuinely come to the state where verbal thinking has stopped,
and consciousness remains bright and clear," they "would then be practicing
what in Sanskrit is called *dhyana*, in Chinese *ch'an*, and in Japanese *zen*, and
which may approximately be translated as 'idealess contemplation'" (p. 197).[6]

The contemporary predicament faced by neuroscience researchers exploring transcendent experience is perhaps summed up in Watts' 1957 preface to
The Way of Zen:

To write about Zen is, therefore, as problematic for the outside, "objective" observer as for the inside "subjective" disciple. In varying situations I have found myself on both sides of the dilemma. I have associated and studied with the "objective observers" and am convinced that, for all their virtues, they invariably miss the point and *eat the menu* instead of the dinner. I have also been on the inside of a traditional hierarchy—not Zen [but Anglican Catholicism]—and am equally convinced that from this position one does not know what *dinner is being eaten*. In such a position one becomes technically "idiotic," which is to say, out of communication with those who do not belong to the same fold. (p. xiii)

Present-day neuroscience researchers appear to be consuming the menu instead of the dinner, and the more dogmatic researchers among them do not know what dinner is being eaten. However, I can easily imagine Alan Watts laughing and exclaiming *"Tat Tvam asi!"*

NOTES

1. See Rose (2006) for a contemporary look at *The Neurobiology of Painting*.

2. "Mythological Motifs of Modern Science" is an essay published posthumously in a 1995 Watts compilation entitled *Talking Zen*. The essay was estimated as written in the 1940s. However, the quote by Oppenheimer initially appeared in an October 1958 issue of *Harpers* magazine.

3. To be clear, it is not that one is possessed by a supernatural force. Instead, "each one of us . . . is an aperture through which the universe knows itself, but not all of itself, from a particular point of view" (Watts, 1975, p. 196). Watts (1983) suggested that "we are symptomatic of the universe. Just as in the retina there are myriads of little nerve endings, we are the nerve endings of the universe (p. 25).

4. Watts' use of the phrase "premature Satori" is interesting, especially in light of his affiliation with Gestalt psychotherapist, Fritz Perls, at Esalen Institute. Perls coined the phrase "mini-Satori" in reference to sudden insights in Gestalt therapy (Smith, 2000).

5. This question brings to mind Husserl's notion of *transcendental ego* and its subsequent rejection by existential-phenomenologists, all of which is beyond the scope of the present paper. However, see Gallagher and Schmicking (2009) for an extensive consideration of phenomenology in relation to contemporary cognitive science.

6. See Kasulis (1985, pp. 70–77) for a noetic-noematic analysis of Zen experience.

REFERENCES

Aberle, D. F. (1966). *The peyote religion of the Navaho*. Chicago: Aldine.

Against Dalai Lama's Lecture at sfn2005. (2005). Retrieved from http//www.petitiononline. com/sfn2005/

Albright, T. D., Jessell, T. M., Kandel, E. R., & Posner, M. I. (2000). Neural science: A century of progress and the mysteries that remain. *Cell, 100*(suppl), s1–s55.

Alper, M. (2008). *The "God" part of the brain: A scientific investigation of human spirituality and God.* Naperville, IL: Sourcebooks.

Alverga, A. P. (1999). *Forest of visions: Ayahuasca, amazonian spirituality, and the Santo Daimo tradition* (S. Larsen, Ed.). Rochester, VT: Park Street Press.

Anand, B. K., Chhina, G. S., & Singh, B. (1961). Some aspects of electroencephalographic studies in yogis. *Electroencephalographic Clinical Neurophysiology, 13*(3), 452–456.

Austin, J. H. (1998). *Zen and the brain: Toward an understanding of meditation and consciousness.* Cambridge, MA: MIT Press.

Bernet, R., Kern, I., & Marbach, E. (1999). Mathematics, logic, and phenomenology. In R. Bernet, *Introduction to Husserlian phenomenology* (pp. 13–57). Evanston, IL: Northwestern University Press.

Booth, J. N., Koren, S. A., & Persinger, M. A. (2005). Increased feelings of the sensed presence and increased geomagnetic activity at the time of the experience during exposure to transcerebral weak complex magnetic fields. *International Journal of Neuroscience, 115*(7), 1053–1079.

Booth, J. N., Koren, S. A., & Persinger, M. A. (2008). Increased theta activity in quantitative electroencephalographic (QEEG) measurements during exposure to complex weak magnetic fields. *Electromagnetic Biology and Medicine, 27*(4), 426–436.

Booth, J. N., & Persinger, M. A. (2009). Discrete shifts within the theta band between the frontal and parietal regions of the right hemisphere and the experiences of a sensed presence. *The Journal of Neuropsychiatry and Clinical Neurosciences, 21,* 279–283.

Bouchard, T. J. Jr., McGue, M., Lykken, D., & Tellegen, A. (1999). Intrinsic and extrinsic religiousness: Genetics and environmental influences and personality correlates. *Twin Research, 2*(2), 88–98.

Brefczynski-Lewis, J. A., Lutz, A., Schaefer, H. S., Levinson, D. B., & Davidson, R. J. (2007). Neural correlates of attentional expertise in long-term meditation practitioners. *Proceedings of the National Academy of Sciences, 104*(27), 11483–11488.

Cahn, B. R., & Polich, J. (2006). Meditation states and traits: EEG, ERP, and neuroimaging studies. *Psychological Bulletin, 132*(2), 180–211.

Cahn, B. R., Delorme, J., & Polich, J. (2010). Occipital gamma activation during vipassana meditation. *Cognitive Processing, 11*(1), 39–56.

Capra, F. (1989). *Uncommon wisdom: Conversations with remarkable people.* New York: Bantam Books.

Capra, F. (2000). *Tao of physics: An exploration of the parallels between modern physics and eastern mysticism* (4th ed.). Boston: Shambhala. (Original work published 1975)

Chan, A. S., Han, Y. M. Y., & Cheung, M-C. (2008). Electroencephalographic (EEG) measurements of mindfulness-based triarchic body-pathway techniques: A pilot study. *Applied Psychophysiology and Biofeedback, 33*(1), 39–47.

Chiesa, A. (2009). Zen meditation: An integration of current evidence. *The Journal of Alternative and Complementary Medicine, 15*(5), 585–592.

Churchland, P. M. (1989). *A neurocomputational perspective: The nature of mind and the structure of science.* Cambridge, MA: MIT Press.

Churchland, P. S. (1989). *Neurophilosophy: Toward a unified science of the mind/brain.* Cambridge, MA: MIT Press.

Churchland, P. S. (2002). *Brain-wise: Studies in neurophilosophy.* Cambridge, MA: MIT Press.

Connelly, D. (1986). *All sickness is homesickness.* Columbia, MD: Center for Traditional Acupuncture.

Cook, C. M., Koren, S. A., & Persinger, M. A. (1999). Subjective time estimation by humans is increased by counterclockwise but not clockwise circumcerebral rotations of phase-shifting magnetic pulses in the horizontal plane. *Neuroscience Letters, 268,* 61–64.

Cook, C. M., & Persinger, M. A. (1997). Experimental induction of the sensed presence in normal subjects and an exceptional subject. *Perceptual and Motor Skills, 85,* 683–693.

Cook, C. M., & Persinger, M. A. (2001). Geophysical variables and behavior, XCII: Experimental elicitation of the experience of a sentient being by right hemispheric, weak magnetic fields: interaction with temporal lobe sensitivity. *Perceptual and Motor Skills, 92,* 447–448.

Damasio, A. R. (2006). *Descartes' error: Emotion, reason and the human brain* (rev. ed.). New York: Vintage Books.

d'Aquili, E. G., & Newberg, A. B. (1999). *The mystical mind: Probing the biology of religious experience.* Minneapolis: Fortress Press.

Davidson, R. J. (2002). Toward a biology of positive affect and compassion. In R. J. Davidson & A. Harrington (Eds.), *Visions of compassion: Western scientists and Tibetan Buddhists examine human nature* (pp. 107–130). New York: Oxford University Press.

De Kooker, M. (2008). Mind, immunity, and health: The science and clinical application of psychoneuroimmunology. *Continuing Medical Education, 26*(1), 18–20.

Dennett, D. C. (1991). *Consciousness explained.* Boston: Little, Brown.

Edelman, G. M., & Tononi, G. (2000). *A universe of consciousness: How matter becomes imagination.* New York: Basic Books.

Forte, R. (1997a). A conversation with R. Gordon Wasson. In R. Forte (Ed.), *Entheogens and the future of religion* (pp. 67–94). San Francisco: Council on Spiritual Practices.

Forte, R. (1997b). *Entheogens and the future of religion.* San Francisco: Council on Spiritual Practices.

Fuller, R. C. (2008). *Spirituality in the flesh: Bodily sources of religious experiences.* Oxford, UK: Oxford University Press.

Gallagher, S., & Schmicking, D. (2009). *Handbook of phenomenology and cognitive science.* New York: Springer.

Gazzaniga, M. (2000). *The mind's past.* Berkeley: University of California Press.

Gilgoff, D. (2010, October 26). *Can meditation change your brain? Contemplative neuroscientists believe it can.* Retrieved from http://religion.blogs.cnn.com/2010/10/26/can-meditation-change-your-brain-contemplative-neuroscientists-believe-it-can/.

Greenfield, S. (1998). *The human brain.* New York: Basic Books.

Grob, C. S. (1999). The psychology of ayahuasca. In R. Forte (Ed.), *Entheogens and the future of religion* (pp. 214–249). San Francisco: Council on Spiritual Practices.

Grof, S. (1975). *Realms of the human unconscious.* New York: Viking Press.

Grof, S. (2001). *LSD psychotherapy.* Sarasota, FL: MAPS Organization.

Hamer, D. H. (2004). *The God gene: How faith is hardwired into our genes.* New York: Doubleday.

Hameroff, S. R. (2006). Consciousness, neurobiology, and quantum mechanics: The case for a connection. In J. A. Tuszynski (Ed.), *The emerging physics of consciousness* (pp. 193–253). Heidelberg: Springer.

Hameroff, S. R., & Penrose, R. (1996). Conscious events as orchestrated space-time selections. *Journal of Consciousness Studies, 3,* 36–63.

Helminiak, D. A. (1984). Neurology, psychology, and extraordinary religious experiences. *Journal of Religion and Health, 23,* 33–46.

Helminiak, D.A. (2010). *God in the brain: Attentively, intelligently, and reasonably untangling neuroscience, psychology, spirituality, and theology.* Unpublished manuscript.

Hofmann, A. (1997). The message of the Eleusinian Mysteries for today's world. In R. Forte (Ed.), *Entheogens and the future of religion* (pp. 31–39). San Francisco: Council on Spiritual Practices.

Huang, H. Y., & Po, P.-C. (2009). EEG dynamics of experienced Zen meditation practitioners probed by complexity index and spectral measure. *Journal of Medical Engineering and Technology, 33*(4), 314–321.

Kasamatsu, A., & Hirai, T. (1966). An electroencephalographic study of the Zen meditation (zazen). *Folio Psychiatrica et Neurologica Japonica, 20,* 315–336.

Kasulis, T. P. (1985). *Zen action, Zen person.* Honolulu: University of Hawaii Press.

Keil, A., Muller, M. M., Ray, W. J., Gruber, T., & Elbert, T. (1999). Human gamma band activity and perception of a Gestalt. *The Journal of Neuroscience, 19*(16), 7152–7161.

King, D. B., & Wertheimer, M. (2009). The legacy of Max Wertheimer and gestalt psychology. In D. B. King & M. Wertheimer, *Max Wertheimer and gestalt theory* (pp. 367–404). New Brunswick, NJ: Transactions Publishers.

Kirk, K., Eaves, L., & Martin, M. (1999). Self-transcendence as a measure of spirituality in a sample of older Australian twins. *Twin Research, 2*(2), 81–87.

Kohler, W. (1947). *Gestalt psychology: An introduction to new concepts in modern psychology.* New York: Liveright Publishing.

Kohler, W. (1973). *Dynamics in psychology: Vital applications of gestalt psychology.* Liveright Publishing. (Original work published 1940)

LeDoux, J. (1998). *The emotional brain.* New York: Simon & Schuster.

Lutz, A., Brefczynski-Lewis, J., Johnstone, T., & Davidson, R. J. (2008). Regulation of the neural circuitry of emotion by compassion meditation: Effects of meditation experience. *PloS ONE 3*(3): e1897.doi:10.1371/journal.pone.0001897

Lutz, A., Dunne, J. D., Davidson, R. J. (2007). Meditation and the neuroscience of consciousness: An introduction. In P. D. Zelazo, M. Moscovitch, & E. Thompson (Eds.), *The Cambridge handbook of consciousness* (pp. 499–553). New York: Cambridge University Press.

Lutz A., Greischar, L. L., Rawlings, N. B., Ricard, M., & Davidson, R. J. (2004). Long-term meditators self-induce high-amplitude gamma synchrony during mental practice. *Proceedings of the National Academy of Sciences, 101,* 16369–16373.

Lutz, A., Slagter, H. A., Dunne, J. D., & Davidson, R. J. (2008). Attention regulation and monitoring in meditation. *Trends in Cognitive Science, 12*(4), 163–168.

Lutz, A., Slagter, H. A., Rawlings, N, B., Francis, A. D., Greischar, L. L., & Davidson, R. J. (2009). Mental training enhances attentional stability: Neural and behavioral evidence. *The Journal of Neuroscience, 29*(42), 13418–13427.

Mandell A. J. (1980). Toward a psychobiology of transcendence: God in the brain. In J. M. Davidson & R. J. Davidson (Eds.), *The psychobiology of consciousness* (pp. 379–464). New York: Plenum Press.

McFadden, J. (2006). The CEMI field theory: Seven clues to the nature of consciousness. In J. A. Tuszynski (Ed.), *The emerging physics of consciousness* (pp. 387–406). Heidelberg: Springer.

Medi, S. C., & Persinger, M. A. (2009). Red light facilitates the sensed presence elicited by application of weak, burst-firing magnetic fields over the temporal lobes. *International Journal of Neuroscience, 119*(1), 68–75.

Metzner, R. (Ed.). (1999). *Ayahuasca: Human consciousness and the spirits of nature.* New York: Thunder's Mouth Press.

Newberg, A. B., d'Aquili, E. G., & Rause, V. (2001). *Why God won't go away: Brain science and the biology of belief.* New York: Ballantine Books.

Newberg, A., & Waldman, M. R. (2009). *How God changes your brain.* New York: Ballantine Books.

Nichols, D. E. (2004). Hallucinogens. *Pharmacology and Therapeutics, 101*(2), 131–181.

Nichols, D. E., & Chemel, B. R. (2006). The neuropharmacology of religious experience: Hallucinogens and the experience of the divine. In P. McNamara (Ed.), *Where God meets science, Vol. 3: The psychology of religious experience* (pp. 1–34). Westport, CT: Praeger.

Pellerin, C. (1998). *Trips: How hallucinogens work in your brain.* New York: Seven Stories Press.

Penrose, R. (1989). *The emperor's new mind.* Oxford, UK: Oxford University Press.

Persinger, M. A. (1987). *Neurological bases of God beliefs.* New York: Praeger.

Persinger, M. A. (1988). Increased geomagnetic activity and the occurrence of bereavement hallucinations: Evidence for melatonin-mediated microseizuring in the temporal lobe? *Neuroscience Letters, 88,* 271–274.

Persinger, M. A. (2001). The neuropsychiatry of paranormal experiences. *The Journal of Neuropsychiatry and Clinical Neurosciences, 13,* 515–524.

Persinger, M. A., & Healy, F. (2002). Experimental facilitation of the sensed presence: Possible intercalation between the hemispheres induced by complex magnetic fields. *The Journal of Nervous and Mental Disease, 190,* 533–541.

Pert, C. B. (1986). The wisdom of the receptors: Neuropeptides, the emotions, and bodymind. *Advances, 3*(3), 8–16.

Pert, C. B. (1999). *Molecules of emotion.* New York: Simon & Schuster.

Pert, C. B. (with N. Marriott). (2008). The science of emotions of consciousness. In D. Goleman (Ed.), *Measuring the immeasurable: The scientific case for spirituality* (pp. 15–34). Boulder, CO: Sounds True.

Qin, Z., Jin, J., Lin, S., & Hermanowicz, N. S. (2009). A forty-five year follow-up EEG study of Qigong practice. *International Journal of Neuroscience, 119*(4), 538–552.

Ragsdale, E. S. (2003). Value and meaning in gestalt psychology and Mahayana Buddhism. In K. H. Dockett, G. R. Dudley-Grant, & C. P. Bankart (Eds.), *Psychology and Buddhism: From individual to global community* (pp. 71–101). New York: Klewer Academic.

Rose, F. C. (2006). *The Neurobiology of painting*. London: Academic Press.

Schneider, K. J. (2005). Biology and awe: Psychology's critical juncture. *The Humanistic Psychologist, 33*(2), 167–173.

Smith, E. W. L. (2000). *The body in psychotherapy*. Jefferson, NC: McFarland.

Sokolov, E. N. (2000). Neurobiology of gestalts. In R. Miller, A. M. Ivanitsky, & P. M. Balaban (Eds.). *Complex brain functions: Conceptual advances in Russian brain sciences* (pp. 247–263). Amsterdam, The Netherlands: Harwood Academic Publishers.

Stoerig, P. (2007). Hunting the ghost: A neuroscience of consciousness. In P. D. Zelazo, M. Moscovitch, & E. Thompson (Eds.), *The Cambridge handbook of consciousness* (pp. 707–730). New York: Cambridge University Press.

Tei, S., Faber, P. L., Lehamann, D., Tsujiuchi, T., Kumano, H., Pascual-Marqui, R. D., Gianotti, L. R., & Kochi, K. (2009). Meditators and non-meditators: EEG source imaging during resting. *Brain Topography, 22*(3), 158–165.

Treadway, T., & Lazar, S. W. (2008). The neurobiology of mindfulness. In F. Didonna (Ed.), *Clinical handbook of mindfulness* (pp. 45–58). New York: Springer.

Tuszynski, J. A. (Ed.). (2006). *The emerging physics of consciousness*. Heidelberg: Springer.

Uttal, W. R. (2005). *Neural theories of mind. Why the mind–brain problem may never be solved*. Mahwah, NJ: Lawrence Erlbaum.

Vass, R. (2009). Gods, gains, and genes: On the natural origin of religiosity by means of bio-cultural selection. In E. Voland & W. Schiefenhovel, (Eds.), *The biological evolution of religious mind and behavior* (pp. 25–50). Berlin: Springer-Verlag.

Varela, F. J. (1996). Neurophenomenology: A methodological remedy to the hard problem. *Journal of Consciousness Studies, 3*(4), 330–350.

Vialette, F. B., Bakardjian, H., Prasad, R., & Cichocki, A. (2009). EEG paroxysmal gamma waves during Bhramari Pranayama: A yoga breathing technique. *Consciousness and Cognition, 18*(4), 977–988.

Voland, E., & Schiefenhovel, W. (Eds.). (2009). *The biological evolution of religious mind and behavior*. Berlin: Springer-Verlag.

Wallace, B. A. (2007). *Contemplative science: Where Buddhism and neuroscience converge*. New York: Columbia University Press.

Watts, A. W. (1951). *The wisdom of insecurity*. New York: Vintage Books.

Watts, A. W. (1957). *The way of Zen*. New York: Pantheon.

Watts, A. W. (1961). *Psychotherapy, east and west*. New York: Pantheon

Watts, A. W. (1962). *The joyous cosmology: Adventures in the chemistry of consciousness*. New York: Pantheon.

Watts, A. W. (1963). The individual as man/world. *The Psychedelic Review, 1*(1), 55–65.

Watts, A. W. (1965). *The supreme identity. An essay on Oriental metaphysic and Christian religion*. New York: The Noonday Press. (Original work published 1950)

Watts, A. W. (1970). Science and nature. In *Nature, man and woman* (pp. 51–69). New York: Vintage Books. (Original work published 1958)

Watts, A. W. (1973a). *In my own way: An autobiography*. New York: Vintage Books.

Watts, A. W. (1973b). The new alchemy. In *This is IT, and other essays on Zen and spiritual experience* (pp. 125–153). New York: Vintage Books. (Original work published 1960)

Watts, A. W. (1973c). This is It. In *This is IT, and other essays on Zen and spiritual experience* (pp. 15–39). New York: Vintage Books. (Original work published 1960)

Watts, A. W. (1973d). The water. In A. W. Watts, *Cloud-hidden, whereabouts unknown: A mountain journal* (pp. 3–10). New York: Pantheon.

Watts, A. W. (1975). Philosophy beyond words. In C. J. Bontemps & S. J. Odell (Eds.), *The owl of Minerva: Philosophers on philosophy* (pp. 191–200). New York: McGraw-Hill.

Watts, A. W. (1983). Play and survival: Are they in necessary contradiction? In A. W. Watts, *The way of liberation: Essays and lectures on the transformation of the self* (M. Watts & R. Shropshire, Eds., pp. 23–38). New York: Weatherhill.

Watts, A. W. (1995). Mythological motifs in modern science. In *Talking Zen* (M. Watts, Ed., pp. 52–70). New York: Weatherhill.

Weller, P. (2010). *Holistic anatomy and physiology.* Berkeley, CA: North Atlantic Books.

White, P. M. (2000). *Peyotism and the Native American Church.* Westport, CT: Greenwood Press.

Zimmer, C. (2004). Faith-boosting genes: A search for the genetic basis of spirituality. *Scientific American,* October, 110–111.

CHAPTER SEVEN

Listening to the Rain:
Embodied Awareness in Watts

Michael C. Brannigan

In his wonderfully written autobiography, *In My Own Way*, Alan Watts quotes Zen *roshi* Morimoto who says "The sound of rain needs no translation" (Watts, 1972, p. 386).[1] What matters is simply listening—not translating, interpreting, deciphering, not sidetracking attention from an encounter that is bodily and sensual. Listening is a confluence of impressions as when a "soft rain" mixes aural and tactile, and a "sweet rain" blends in taste and smell. Although such expressions are reflective translations, the encounter is pre-reflective. It rests on an implicit bodily awareness, awareness in the most fundamental sense. Listening to the rain reminds us of the elemental truth that we are our bodies.

AWARENESS NAKED AND CLOTHED

As he artfully applies the rich texture of Hindu, Buddhist, and Daoist teachings to highlight the distinction between our pre-reflective experience and our description of that same experience, Watts reminds us of this truth[2]: Bodily awareness is the conduit of our experience. We live in and through our bodies. Bodiliness enables taste, sight, smell, hearing, and touch. To a firm degree, we *are* our bodies. Moreover, by bodiliness, Watts does not confine its meaning to the mere physical, "simply a given chunk of flesh and bones," but views body as dynamic, in the spirit of though not identical to Henri Bergson's *élan vital* or the Daoist *chi*, manifesting "as much a streaming pattern of energy as a flame" (Watts, 1972, p. 201). This pre-reflective bodily awareness is a naked awareness, pure and simple.

There is another level of awareness that supersedes nakedness, an added layer of awareness that naturally follows in the wake of listening, seeing, smelling, tasting, and feeling. It is clear mindfulness of my bodily encounter.[3] It is reflective, focused, and aware of awareness. As such, mindfulness clothes our initial naked awareness.

We can think of these two levels of awareness—its primordial rootedness in the body and mindful attention to this rootedness—as an embodied awareness, a theme that runs throughout Watts' works. Watts did not explore our bodiliness with the same philosophical acumen as we find in Maurice Merleau-Ponty's (1962, 1964) ontology of the body. Still, the undercurrent is there. Both naked and clothed awareness anchor us in the experience. Furthermore, embodied awareness enables us to get to the core of our encounter in the experience through providing the groundwork for cultivating what we may consider the "virtue" of presence. That is, through embodied awareness, in both senses as naked and clothed, we remain *present* to the encounter, and the encounter remains *present* in us.

Here we face a problem, a hurdle of our own making. In embodied awareness, transitioning to mindfulness is extraordinarily difficult. Our reflective natures take over so that our own internal mental commotion impedes mindfulness. We face a perennial snag when we proceed to reflect further in ways that in effect remove us from the experience on which we reflect. There is a deep-seated difference between the world we experience and the world that we conceptualize as a result of reflecting on that experience. The process of reflecting is not in itself the problem. Socrates' prescriptive prompt that "The unexamined life is not worth living" only makes sense because we human creatures naturally think and ponder. Problems arise because we do not acknowledge the above distinction, so that we blur the line between our interpretation of our experience, with its attached concepts, theories, and categories, and the experience itself. In so doing, in becoming less present to the encounter, we have trekked away from embodied awareness, our fundamental awareness on both levels.

This has powerful implications for whether or not we can sustain a more ecological consciousness through recognizing our natural connections with the environment. Watts was discerningly ahead of his time in reminding us of our innate affinity with the natural world. As he puts it in his *Nature, Man and Woman*, "the skin is just as much a joiner as a divider, being, as it were, the bridge whereby the inner organs have contact with air, warmth, and light" (Watts, 1958, p. 55). At the same time, he warns us that our natural propensity to divide our "field of awareness" through deliberate acts of "selective attention" artificially structures that which is inherently vibrant, or nonstructurable, and divides that which is indivisible. Although this tendency is epistemic, dangers creep in when we also bestow on it a metaphysical imprint. Furthermore, this has moral consequences in terms of how we treat or mistreat that which we mistakenly consider to be essentially apart from us, namely, the environment (and, of course, the "other"). Watts foresaw the moral blight of our environmental crises well before environmental ethics became fashionable.

Listening to the rain, therefore, is not as simple as it sounds. No doubt, interpreting rain as "soft," "gentle," and "hard" rests on context. The hapless victims of Hurricane Katrina in August 2005, the six million people in India's Gujarat beaten by a monsoon one year later, and all those who suffered the loss of life, livelihood, home, and property in the June 2008 floods that ravaged parts of the American Midwest have painful cause to consider their rains "merciless" and "destructive." At the same time, sensed reality is distinct from conceived reality. Sensed reality, similar to Merleau-Ponty's "lived world," is an experience uncorrupted by the conceptualization and discourse that follows the encounter. While lying on the beach in Newport, Rhode Island, feeling the sun's heat, hearing the lapping of the waves, smelling the sea, staring mindlessly at the vast blue horizon, I may at any time awake from this reverie and think "How pleasing! How restful!" My thoughts carry me further, "Why can't it always be this way?" My reflecting has pulled me away from my fundamental aware-ness. This is of no consequence as long as I recognize the difference between my experience and my interpretation. The disparity between my unreflective sensual encounter with sand and sea and my conceptualization of it is, as the sea, overpowering. As implied in Tilopa's Six Precepts, awareness, both naked and clothed, remains distinct from any mental imposition.

> No thought, no reflection, no analysis,
> No cultivation, no intention,
> Let it settle itself. (cited in Watts, 1972, p. 133)

Some of us may assert that if we can somehow manage to linger in expe-rience without undue reflection, in an embodied awareness of birds, clouds, the sound of rain, and so on, so much the better. This, of course, depends on what it is we are experiencing. Swimming laps "in the zone" can re-energize us in positive ways. Here, my body is fully attentive, completely awake, free from those recurring mental interruptions that can consume me throughout my day and even in my sleep. At the same time, while swimming in the zone, I am fully alert and I am conscious of my body, my movement, and its surround-ings. As Watts maintains, I *am* my body, this "streaming pattern of energy," so that swimmer and the swimming are not separate but one. Neither is there disengagement between my body and the water. Everything lives, breathes, and moves together as one.

Watts' emphasis on embodied awareness clearly comes across in his prefer-ence for a more active style of Zen in contrast to a formal, rigid approach. For him, Zen comes alive, for example, through walking meditation, calligraphy, archery, cooking, and *cha-no-yu*. These more active manifestations of presence presume both bodiliness and a deliberate, focused awareness.[4] This also clearly comes across in his interest in certain martial arts such as judo, ju-no kata, and kendo. As a long-time student of the martial arts (*butoku no gakusei*), I have learned to be especially attuned to my body and its energy, its life-force, its *chi* (*ki* in Japanese). Even the seemingly military style of Wado-Ryu karate, for example, enables me to live naturally in my body, to be aware of my bodiliness, its motility and its inborn energy, to cultivate embodied awareness, to be present through my body.

DISEMBODIED RELIGION AND SENSUAL MYSTICISM

This notion of embodied awareness, as primal and focused, naked and clothed, is apparent in Watts' critique of conventional forms of religious expression. For him, "in a culture that for more than a thousand years had been smothered in and diseased with religion" (Watts, 1972, p. 46), formalized religions tend to repress bodiliness. To illustrate, mainstream Judaeo-Christianity stifles our natural sensuality as well as our potential for ecstasy. "When Christians go to church, they leave their bodies at the door" (p. 187). An overemphasis on dogma and liturgy generates a dangerous disembodiment. The doctrinaire notion that matters of the flesh (along with will, etc.) are a primal source of sin has a way of suffocating our natural sexuality. In contrast, Watts believes that because we are our bodies and we express who we are through our bodies, we can also manifest spirituality *through* our sexuality. Watts' commentary on the Hindu Temple of Konarak describes how the temple's outer sculpture literally depicts the intimacy of spirituality and sexuality, soul and flesh, the intertwining of male and female (Watts, 1971). Unsurprisingly, Watts' ideas had widespread appeal during the San Francisco Renaissance and countercultures.[5] This integration of body and spirit reflects Watts' sensuous approach to mysticism in which the body is construed, not as the prison of the soul, but as the soul's temple. Is the body my temple or my prison? Whether we consider body as temple or prison signifies a profound difference in how we view sexuality.

Mainstream religion's cerebral character unfolds in liturgies crammed with speech. Furthermore, according to Watts, this prattle conceals hypocrisy.

> . . . impoverished Christians do nothing in their religious observances except chatter. They tell God what he ought and ought not to do, and inform him of things of which he is already aware, such as that they are miserable sinners, and proceed then to admonish one another to feel guilt and regret about abominable behavior which they have not the least intention of changing. (Watts, 1972, p. 49)

Here there is little emphasis on the grandeur of silence.[6] Yet silence is a noble response to mystery. Mystery is the lifeblood of our existence, and, for Watts, conventional forms of worship tend to celebrate in ways devoid of mystery. This does not mean that we should discard vernacular liturgies, although Watts himself prefers the traditional Roman Catholic Latin Mass and regrets that "the Catholic Church has lost its magic by celebrating the mass in the vernacular instead of Latin" (Watts, 1972, p. 48). The point is this: Our religious celebrations cannot afford to ignore our response to life's ultimate mysteries. Watts entreats religion to celebrate the mystery of being (including nonbeing), and the dance of life (including death) in ways that call for an embodied awareness. As an ordained Episcopalian priest (also designated as Anglican in his autobiography) and campus chaplain at Northwestern University, Evanston, Illinois, he devised ways to reintroduce the sense of celebration, mystery, and laughter into his liturgies. In my conversation with Richard Adams, who belonged to Watts' campus community and whom Watts (1972, pp. 189–190) describes as a sort of co-conspirator in ministry (Richard is now a retired Episcopal priest and Professor Emeritus of philosophy at Quinnipiac University in Connecticut), he reminisced about some of these liturgies and their popularity among students, faculty, and community members. Watts actually thought himself more of a shaman than a priest. As he puts it, "Priests follow tradition but shamans originate them, though truly original traditions stem from the origins of nature and thus have much in common" (Watts, 1972, p. 185). A religion that takes itself and its doctrine and rules too seriously becomes far too somber; it spawns gravity and discounts bodiliness. For Watts, religion should celebrate in embodied awareness, be filled with laughter, should sing out loud while also relishing moments of utter silence; "real religion is the transformation of anxiety into laugher" (Watts, 1972, p. 60).

Religion should therefore help break us out of our shells of our ordinary state of semi-awareness. On account of inauthentic ego-consciousness, many if not most of us remain less than fully aware. In order to liberate himself from everyday ego-consciousness, Watts even ventured into psychedelic experiments to test the boundaries of awareness. Indeed, in *Everywhere and Nowhere* I maintain that the fundamental thesis throughout Watts' work lies in his attempt to grasp, describe, develop, and come to terms with this journey from a counterfeit ego-consciousness to an authentic, nondualistic (in the Advaita Vedanta sense) Self-consciousness (Brannigan, 1988).

In addition to his experiments with psychedelic, mind-altering agents, he regularly practiced meditation and yoga (Brannigan, 1988). I remember well a conversation with his widow Jano (Mary Jane died in January 1994) who was then studying at the Green Gulch Zen Center near Mount Tamalpais. My good friend Cliff Muldoon, a fellow musician who also studied with me at the University of Leuven in Belgium and who now teaches religion in a high school in Worcester, Massachusetts, also had an extensive interest in Watts' ideas and accompanied me during these interviews. After rolling a pair of dice (ending with the odd number three, an act that Cliff and I found rather curious, as if she was testing the destiny or compatibility of our conversation), Jano confessed to us that she was convinced that Alan had been practicing *pranayama* yoga that rainy November night he "died."[7] Because it took hours for the ambulance to slog through the muddy roads of Druid Heights before reaching their home, she believed the pronouncement of his death was premature, with his soul since then seeking to reenter his body in its *pranayama* state.[8]

Along these lines, Watts was suspicious of the path taken by a few of his friends and "fellow-seekers" such as Aldous Huxley and the "British Mystical Expatriates" Christopher Isherwood and Gerald Heard and their ties to Swami Prabhavananda's Vedanta Society of Hollywood. With little interest in their brand of asceticism, he mistrusted their quest for a disembodied synthesis of Christian and Asian mysticism, aimed at emancipation from bodily influence. Instead, he makes it clear in his early work *Behold the Spirit*, he preferred a mysticism that was organic, rooted in the corporeal and in nature (Watts, 1947).[9]

WRITING STYLE

As all writers know and experience, there is an entrenched gap between having an idea and conveying it through writing. Nonetheless, embodied awareness comes alive in Watts' writing style. University of Chicago's distinguished Professor of English and Linguistics, Joseph M. Williams (he died in 2008), is noted for his classic text on writing, *Style: Ten Lessons in Clarity and* Grace. In it he cites a passage from Watts as an example of elegant writing (Williams, 2002).[10] Watts' prose is consistently crystal clear and reflects his own directly attentive and mindful awareness. To illustrate, his autobiography describes people, places, events, and things with an embodied flair that appeals to the senses. He sketches his boyhood home in the village of Chislehurst, England:

> Rowan Tree Cottage, our home, is one block east of the Royal Parade, and takes its name from a mountain ash or rowan tree which grew in the front garden behind a hedge of sweetbrier and beside an arbor of jasmine and a magnificent tree of green cooking-apples upon which we used to hand coconuts, sliced open for the delectation of wrens and blue tits. (Watts, 1972, p. 14)

He communicates attentiveness to the slightest of details. In describing some of the odd characters in Chislehurst, his fondness for trapping moths, the undeniable influence of his father who was himself an amateur entomologist, he writes with both intellect and senses. He never abandons his fascination with gardens:

> . . . I remained enchanted with the flowers and fruits of other people's work, so much so that in my old age I shall probably return to the craft of the garden, but of a very small garden, consisting mainly of culinary, medicinal, and psychedelic herbs, with nasturtiums, roses, and sweet peas around the edges. Alongside there will be a large redwood barn where the various herbs will hang from the beams to dry,

where there will be shelves of mysterious jars containing cardamom, ginseng, ginger, marjoram, oregano, mint, thyme, pennyroyal, cannabis, henbane, mandrake, comfrey, mugwort, and witch hazel, and where there will also be a combination of alchemist's laboratory and kitchen. I can smell it coming. (Watts, 1972, p. 21)

The imagery is downright sensual. It clearly shows his talent for being aware and comfortable in his body. He urges us to be likewise, for it is through our bodies that we are rooted in the earth and in this world. Rather than static entities, our bodies are inherently dynamic, "streaming patterns of energy," and that energy is who we are. Moreover, his depictions remind us that we authentically *notice* only through our bodiliness:

Walking down Old Hill to Christ Church one would encounter freaky characters like Miss Frieze and her sister, known as Piggylids and Doffles, faded and overblown brunette beauties under vast black hats, struggling up with their black walking sticks. There were also foppish gentlemen who affected pince-nez spectacles and wore straw hats or boaters attached to their lapels with black silk cords, and with all this straw, string, wire, and tweed—plus their formally jerky manner of hat-doffing, speech, and gait—seemed like mechanisms rather than men. (Watts, 1972, p. 50)

ENTER THE MIND'S ELEPHANT[11]

It is Sunday evening. Brooke and I are having dinner, another one of her exquisite meals, her variation of chicken cordon bleu made *sans* recipe. Like her dad, she has a natural skill for cuisine. As we share a bottle of Santa Barbara Pinto Noir (Sea Smoke), she describes to me her plans this week for work, eager about a particular project though concerned about her presentation to her colleagues. Although she shares her concerns, my thoughts are elsewhere, occasionally switching back to her voice and our meal. My mind wanders off to our staff meeting tomorrow, to my new undertaking to help lead a task force in disaster preparation for hospitals, to a journal article I'm writing, to the next meeting of our ethics committee consortium, and to a long overdue chapter that I'm working on for a book on Alan Watts.

I continue to hear Brooke and nod my head as if responding to her concern. She looks me in the eyes, *sees* me, and knows I'm elsewhere. "Are you listening to me?" Her question jolts me back. "Of course," I lie. I'm hearing, yes, but hardly listening. Instead, my thoughts and feelings about my projects fill my mental space and undeniably affect my body. My eyes give it away.

And so it goes, the week-ahead-Sunday, a considerable part of our personal and relational landscape. Yet, although we often feel as if we cannot help but be steered by our impulses, thoughts, and feelings, Watts (along with an historic contingent of Buddhists, Hindus, Daoists, Confucians, and others) reminds us that we are capable of regaining some respectable level of self-direction. Not only is this possible. It is imperative. We must do so, for the stakes are high. We can do so through embodied, mindful awareness. Mindful awareness provides the ground for the virtue of presence I alluded to earlier. This essentially means being present to where we are, what we are doing, what we are thinking and feeling, and whom we are with. It is my belief that we need to cultivate this virtue of presence more so today than ever.

On Sunday evening, although I appear to be eating and go through the motions, do I truly taste the food and savor the wine? Although I sit at the table with my beautiful wife, am I in fact present with her, for her, and to her? Am I really there with her, or am I living inside my head? Do I feel along with her as she shares her apprehension about her presentation? Do I catch this in her eyes? Am I even looking at her, into her eyes? Do I listen to what is said and, more importantly, to what is not said? Am I able to detect my thoughts going elsewhere? If so, do I struggle against my mental detours, or do I simply accept them, yield to them in the sense of Daoist *wu-wei*, acknowledging what is taking place in order to let go? Can I observe what is happening inside of me and set it free, as a cloud whispers away? Can I refocus on Brooke? Mindful awareness means being attentive to where I am. It means being present where I am when I am there, and especially to whom I am with. With Brooke, having our Sunday evening dinner, the reality is clear: I am there with her and nowhere else. That's where I need *to be*.

Being present sounds ridiculously simply, yet it is profoundly difficult. Mindful awareness requires effort. It requires focus, and focus requires training, training the mind to be aware, to be attentive to what is outside of us as well as what is happening within us. As Buddhist scholar David Loy (2003) puts it, it is entirely up to us to "accept responsibility for liberating our own attention and clarifying our own awareness" (p. 39).[12]

During those immeasurable moments when we are with others, with nature, or alone with ourselves, there are no excuses for lack of awareness and presence other than a wandering mind, which, like an untamed elephant, can wreck havoc and thereby diminish the quality of our encounters.

ARE WE CONNECTING YET?

In an earlier conversation with Peter Columbus, he posed this question to me: What relevance would Alan Watts' ideas have for today? So, given this idea of embodied awareness, how would Watts respond to some aspects of contemporary culture? Without presuming to get inside Watts' head and speak for him, at least from my own imperfect understanding of his writings, here is a start.

An incessant litany in Watts' work has to do with the dissimilarity between the artificial and the real. The distinction seems clear enough. Even so, we habitually confuse the two. In California, Hollywood's oasis and where Watts spent much of his life up until his death in Muir Woods, Mill Valley, artificiality's sway is palpable, and in this sense represents a microcosm of most of the United States. A case in point is the Disney phenomenon: Disneyland, occupying 160 acres in rural Anaheim, and its younger sibling Walt Disney World, with its 25,000 acres just outside of Orlando, Florida, probably the largest and most popular family attraction in the world. The seduction of the Disney spectacle lies not only in its remarkably sophisticated high-tech universe, but in its uncanny talent to seem more real than the realities they represent. The religion of Disney spreads beyond the United States with a 140-acre Disneyland Resort near Paris, a 115-acre complex close to Tokyo, and a sprawling 310 acres in Hong Kong. The allure is a token of our fascination with the artificial as we bestow more metaphysical as well as aesthetic value to what is *lifelike* than to what *is life*. SUVs and other popular vehicles now offer compact TV screens with DVD and even satellite hookup as accessories in the back seats so that passengers, in most cases children who get bored on long trips, can watch their favorite movies.[13] This extension of the living room can enable Power Rangers, Garfield, Nickelodeon, movies galore, and even the Discovery Channel to trump the marvels of Yosemite National Park, Big Sur, Yellowstone, Adirondacks, Grand Teton, Maine coastline, and any other natural wonders and landscapes just outside their windows. Admittedly, there are few natural wonders along the New Jersey turnpike. But even these ugly realities, along with ghettos surrounding our nation's opulent capital, or that vast cemetery off Interstate 95 northbound heading into New York City should not be ignored. Watts reminds us that the beauty of the extraordinary can be found in the ordinary, and ordinary ecstasies simply await our discovery. With all of the quips about Kansas' flatness ("What is the state's official tree? A telephone pole."), its luminous fields of sunflowers are exquisite. And discovery can only come about through an embodied awareness, being attentive and mindful to what we encounter and are encountered by and through our senses.

Communication technologies today are unparalleled. Take cell phones. Ubiquitous, they swarm our social landscape. In a restaurant, you may notice the couple across from you, and the gentleman is on his cell phone throughout much of their time together.[14] We've become accidental voyeurs as eavesdropping is now part of the dining experience. Just after your plane hits the runway, the young lady next to you pulls out her cell phone to let her friend know she's landed. (When I once flew into Kansas City airport, a young lady behind me had her speaker phone on! Nearby passengers endured a conversation that included directions to the baggage claim, so perhaps some of the unavoidable eavesdropping was helpful.) While listening to the lecture on avian flu at your library, cell phones occasionally stir the mood with android tones from Pachelbel to hip-hop to simply weird. Is there any reader among you without a cell phone tale? Though the topic is dead serious, cell phones form a distractive relief within the milieu. While jogging on the tread mill at your local gym, eyes glued on the Patriots' preseason match-up with the champion New York Giants, you can't help but hear the fellow on the treadmill next to you reciting his stock options. Whether we are eating, traveling, learning, exercising, throughout much of our waking day, even in the restroom, cell phones have become a vital bodily organ. They stake a claim in our lives, in our spaces and in our times. Yet despite their obvious benefits, there are major trade-offs. The term *cell* is fitting given its prison connotation.

Consider the most dangerous act most of us do on a daily basis, whereby we pose an unavoidable lethal risk to ourselves and others—driving. There is now a new term called *phoneslaughter*. Phoneslaughter occurs when a vehicle-related fatality is somehow linked with the use of a handheld cell phone. With at least one-thousand cell phone-related vehicular deaths per year in the United States, the presence of cell phones has become authoritative in a way that is perilous (Ackerman & Heinzerling, 2005). Their distractive power over us blunts awareness.

Watts died in 1973, well before cell phones invaded the market. In view of his constant warning about the deep danger of confusing the artificial with the real, one wonders how he may have responded to our dependence on these miniature marvels of communication along with email, BlackBerrys, and other multitasking operating systems purported to have us better "connect." As a digital fan, with numerous recorded lectures, he would in all likelihood see these as invaluable *aids* to communication, as a means to an end—but not to replace the end they serve.[15] I'm convinced he would be entirely skeptical as to whether they do in fact bring us any closer to each other and to ourselves. He would most likely ask, as do I, "Do they enable us to be more present to each other? To connect? Do they help to cultivate presence?" My own verdict is a resounding nay. In fact, we seem less connected, not only with others but with ourselves. Sucked into the seduction that Watts warns us against, we've confused the means with the end. We have sadly mistaken the technique with the goal. How Watts describes our obsession with "new tools" of attention can be aptly applied to our addiction with cell phones and other communicative technologies that help to generate the illusion that we are genuinely connecting:

> There is much to suggest that when human beings acquired the powers of conscious attention and rational thought, they become so fascinated with these new tools that they forgot all else. Like chickens hypnotized with their beaks to a chalk line. Our total sensitivity became identified with these partial functions *so that we lost the ability to feel nature from the inside, and more to feel the seamless unity of ourselves and the world.* (Watts, 1958, p. 7, emphasis added)

The ecological underpinnings are evident. Although we believe we may be connecting, our self-imposed separation from the environment and from all that is "not-I," sadly fosters an alienation from each other and from the natural world. We fail to recognize our fundamental "in-betweenness," or *aidagara* according to the Japanese philosopher Watsuji Tetsuro (Watsuji, 1988, 1996). This means that we are naturally situated in-between others and in-between nature so that we are inherently relational. Moreover, we are becoming increasingly disembodied in that we separate "I" from "me." The "me" represents my bodiliness, the fact that I am part of nature. Watts writes in *Wisdom of Insecurity*:

> It is as if we were divided into two parts. On the one hand there is the conscious "I," at once intrigued and baffled, the creature who is caught in the trap. On the other hand there is "me," and "me" is a part of nature—the wayward flesh with all its concurrently beautiful and frustrating limitations. (Watts, 1951, p. 64)

Health care is another prime example of this disembodiment, where medical technological interventions, whose benefits are both certain and spurious, can sadly displace interpersonal interaction. One downside of U.S. health care is that it embodies what has been termed our culture's *technological imperative*, that is, if we *have* the technology, then we *must* use it. Yet, all too often we realize after the fact and when it is too late that maximal use of medical technologies does not equate with its optimal use. I fear the day will come when hospital beds are equipped with cell phones to make them available for dying patients so that family and friends can call and/or leave text messages. I refuse to be text-messaged on my deathbed, nor will I do the same for a seriously ill patient. Simply put, technological connection is no substitute for interpersonal connection, and the latter requires embodied awareness. Beyond any measure of doubt, sick and dying persons require human presence and human touch.

To conclude, our human plight lies in *not being* where we are and in *not being present* to whom we are with. Watts' challenge—to observe things simply *as they are* without imposing layers of interpretation and judgment, to cultivate an embodied awareness and a persistent mindfulness—is more formidable today than ever. Through embodied awareness, we can learn the secret of listening to the rain rather than to our mental traffic.

NOTES

1. For each of us, our philosophies are biographies. Otherwise, we disconnect matters of mind from flesh and blood. In the same way, the intellectual journey of Alan Watts cannot be separated from his personal journey.

2. His popularity on radio also testified to his flair for speaking. His close friends claimed that, in contrast to the more cerebral task of writing, speaking came more easily to him. Twenty-four radio stations throughout the United States, including Athens, Geor-

gia's WUOG, Santa Barbara's KPFK, Plainfield, Vermont's WGDR, and Tampa, Florida's WMNF, continue to broadcast his talks (see http://www.alanwatts.net/watts.htm).

3. Here, we see the six senses at work. In Hindu Nyaya teachings, and throughout Buddhism, the sixth sense is mind.

4. The art and grace of dancing was a significant lesson he learned from his first wife Eleanor Everett; see Watts (1972, p. 126).

5. Around this same time, Herbert Marcuse's *Eros and Civilization*, published in 1955, was a philosophical manifesto opposing unhealthy forms of sexual repression.

6. Bear in mind, Watts' personal experience with the liturgies in the Catholic Church and the Church of England. He also acknowledges that Protestant church services in African American communities bear witness to a more embodied, living expression of worship.

7. That slightly superstitious part of me was hoping that she did not roll a four, the numerological equivalent for death in Japanese. *Shi* in Japanese means "four," and it can also mean "death."

8. Our interview occurred in the late 1970s, at Green Gulch Farm Zen Center, also called Green Dragon Temple (*Soryu-ji*), located in Marin County, north of Sausalito, California. *Pranayama*, along with correct posture (*asana*), is an important feature in yoga practice. *Prana* means "breath." *Pranayama* is aimed to control the mind (*chitta*) through controlling the breath. Jano was referring to the rather esoteric practice of regulated breathing in order to temporarily release the soul from the body, and she believed that Alan was experimenting along these lines. This is not the typical aim in pranayama yoga.

9. This does not translate into unbridled sensuality, although critics may point out that Watts took his idea of bodiliness to the extreme when measured against conventional social and religious mores. Even though Watts himself does not identify sensuousness and sensuality, it was apparent in my interviews prior to *Everywhere and Nowhere* (Brannigan, 1988) that those close to Watts took issue with his public stance regarding free love and open marriage as well as his own affirmation of this while married.

10. Peter Columbus kindly referred me to this source.

11. The "mind's elephant" is in reference to Chapter XXII in *The Dhammapada* (Babbitt, 1936), verses 326, 327. Our thoughts can become uncontrolled and take us over, like an untamed elephant that can tear down a forest. See p. 49.

12. Loy asserts this within the context of examining Buddhist teachings in view of their relevance to concerns of social justice. His point is well taken. Working toward social justice requires inner transformation.

13. With all of our whining about rising gas prices, there is a silver lining. One potential benefit is less purchase and use of gas guzzling, eco-unfriendly monsters like SUVs, Hummers, and the like. (I doubt that Alan Watts, who lived for some time on the houseboat SS Vallejo in Sausalito, actually an old ferryboat built in 1879 in Portland, Oregon, would cruise around in a Hummer.) Even better, we may actually walk more and exercise those muscles supporting the inner tube we carry with us. (I'm speaking for myself here.) By the way, Ruth Costello, executive secretary of the Society for Comparative Philosophy, moved onto the Vallejo in 1974, after Watts' death. There the society was housed for more than six years. She treated Cliff Muldoon and I to a grand tour and history. Thanks, Ruth, wherever you are.

14. When I last visited Tokyo in 2008, restaurants had generally prohibited the use of cell phones. In a society that manufactures and mass produces cell phones, there are certain rituals that continue to be sacred enough to safeguard, such as the social and familial meaning behind eating. When I rented a cell phone while in Japan, at least five pages—in Japanese and in English—were devoted to cell phone etiquette (prohibited areas, using a quiet voice, respecting those nearby, etc.).

15. His son Mark is currently building the Alan Watts Mountain Center, north of San Francisco. He intends to house a digital archive of his father's recordings to make accessible to the public. It will also be a meeting place for conferences, retreats, workshops, etc. (see http://www.alanwatts.com/center/web).

REFERENCES

Ackerman, F., & Heinzerling, L. (2005). *Priceless: On knowing the price of everything and the value of nothing.* New York: The New Press.

Alan Watts Mountain Center. Retrieved June 13, 2008 from http://www.alanwatts.com/center/web.

Babbitt, I. (Trans.). (1936). *The Dhammapada.* New York: New Directions Books.

Brannigan, M. C. (1988). *Everywhere and nowhere: The path of Alan Watts.* New York: Peter Lang.

Loy, D. (2003). *The great awakening: A Buddhist social theory.* Boston: Wisdom.

Marcuse, H. (1955). *Eros and civilization: A philosophical inquiry into Freud.* New York: Vintage Books.

Merleau-Ponty, M. (1962). *Phenomenology of perception* (C. Smith, Trans.). London: Routledge & Kegan Paul.

Merleau-Ponty, M. (1964). *Le Visible et l'invisible.* Paris: Gallimard.

Radio Broadcasts. Retrieved June 13, 2008 from http://www.alanwatts.net/watts.htm.

Watsuji, T. (1988). *Climate and culture: a philosophical study* (G. Bownas, Trans.). Westport, CT: Greenwood Press.

Watsuji, T. (1996). *Watsuji Tetsuro's Rinrigaku: ethics in Japan* (Y. Seisaku & R. Carter, Trans.). Albany: State University of New York Press.

Watts, A. W. (1947). *Behold the spirit: A study in the necessity of mystical religion.* New York: Vintage Books.

Watts, A. W. (1951). *The wisdom of insecurity.* New York: Vintage Books.

Watts, A. W. (1958). *Nature, man and woman.* New York: Vintage Books.

Watts, A. W. (1971). *The temple of Konarak: erotic spirituality* (E. Elisofon, photog.). London: Thames & Hudson.

Watts, A. W. (1972). *In my own way.* New York: Pantheon.

Williams, J. (2002). *Style: Ten lessons in clarity and grace* (7th ed.). New York: Longman.

CHAPTER EIGHT

Alan Watts on Nature, Gender, and Sexuality: A Contemporary View

Miriam L. Levering

Alan W. Watts, in his best-selling books, radio programs, lectures, and workshops in the 1950s, 1960s and 1970s, had far more influence than any other student of "the East" on American thought about nature, gender, and sexuality. Three points Watts made are particularly interesting because they presaged what later became a popular point of view or started a trend within the counterculture. All three ideas are based on his fundamental proposal that the cosmos is a seamless unity in which all participate. They also relate closely to Watts' insight that one of the important tasks facing Westerners as individuals and Western culture as a whole is to overcome the dualistic views that spirit is opposed to matter, and that a successful human life requires conquering "the natural" in all its forms. All three ideas are found in Watts' 1958 book, *Nature, Man and Woman*, as well as elsewhere in his writings and speeches (e.g., Watts, 1963, 1995). These ideas concern the interrelations of (a) nature and gender, (b) men and women, and (c) sexuality and spirituality. The first part of this chapter is a brief description of Watts' ideas. The second part is a consideration of Watts' views in light of contemporary scholarship.

WATTS' THREE IDEAS

NATURE AND GENDER

Thirty years before Lynn White's (1967) famous critique of Christian attitudes toward nature as a source of our ecological problems, Watts (1937/1997) was already tuned in to the "back to nature movement" in 1930s England and began engaging in a comparative analysis of Eastern and Western views of nature. By the late 1950s, in *Nature, Man and Woman* (1958), well before such ideas became widespread, Watts offered a critique of the symbol systems of the West that enshrine and privilege an anti-nature worldview and "masculine" values. In Watts' view, Western religion and philosophy saw God, man, and reason as all separate from and transcending nature, and properly in control of all things "natural," whereas Eastern thought and culture saw men, women, and their environment, the whole world of phenomena, humans, and deities, as a "seamless unity." Man's feeling that he is an isolated being in an alien environment is a basic illusion that leads to others. The West, victim of this illusion, looks down on all things associated with nature, including all things "feminine." Watts saw in Daoism and Buddhism an understanding of universal connectedness and nonaggressive harmony that contrasts with the values of assertive independence and competitiveness typical of modern Western culture. Watts contrasted the Western outsider's reduction of nature to abstract scientific categories with the Eastern mode of understanding Nature by knowing it from within, which gives prominence to immediate and sensual appreciation of the natural world. Watts (1958) wrote: "Our difficulty is not that we have developed conscious attention but that we have lost the wider style of feeling which should be its background, the feeling which would lets us know what nature is from the inside" (p. 7). Watts saw in this fundamental dichotomy a contrast between "masculine" and "feminine" values and approaches to the world and to experience.

The Western cultural association of certain values with the male, and certain other values with the female were not in itself something Watts challenged. But he often argued that "the feminine" needs to be valued as much as "the masculine." For example, he wrote:

> [In the West] The feminine values are despised, and we find typically among men a strange kind of reluctance to be anything but an all-male man. But there is a tremendous necessity for us to value—along-side, as it were, the aggressive, masculine element symbolized by the sword—the receptive feminine element symbolized, perhaps, by the open flower. After all, our human senses are not knives, they are not hooks; they are the soft veil of the eye, the delicate drum of the ear, the soft skin on the tips of the fingers and on the body. It is through these delicate, receptive things that we receive our knowledge of the world. (Watts, 2000, pp. 90–91)

Watts explicitly made the point that in the West, "spirit" and "matter" or "spirit" and "nature" are seen as divided, as opposites. Men and reason are identified with spirit, whereas women, emotions and the body are identified with "matter" or "nature." Much of Western thinking reflects the Gnostic or Platonic view that Spirit must not be entrapped by matter or nature; it should be liberated from matter and nature. And Watts notes that women and all things labeled "feminine," including sexuality itself, often identified with women, are looked down on. In *Nature, Man and Woman* he writes:

The division of life into the higher and lower categories of spirit and nature usually goes hand in hand with a symbolism in which spirit is male and nature is female. . . . The importance of the correspondence between spirit and man and nature and woman is that it projects upon the world a disposition in which the members of several cultures are still involved. . . . The split between man and nature is related to a problematic attitude to sex. In some unknown way the female sex has become associated with the earthy aspect of human nature and with sexuality as such. . . . The catalog of popular images, figures of speech, and customs which associate spirit with the divine, the good and the male, and nature with the material, evil, sexual and female could go on indefinitely. (Watts, 1958, pp. 139–143)

This of course is a point that has been taken up with great emphasis and effect by the feminist and ecological movements, including the feminist goddess movement and Christian and Jewish feminist theology. It is also a point that has been challenged in recent decades with devastating acumen.

POLARITY OF MEN AND WOMEN

Watts frequently brought up a model provided by the Chinese—in his view, Daoist—yin–yang paradigm. Stressing the pervasiveness of polarities of opposites, and the importance of seeing in the world the "correlation of opposites within a unity," Watts emphasized the ways in which, in the yin–yang model, masculine and feminine gender traits are two poles of the same reality. Seen this way, they can be integrated in a harmonious and balanced relationship. According to Watts (1969):

To say that opposites are *polar* is to say much more than that they are far apart; it is to say that they are related and joined—that they are the terms, ends, or extremities of a single whole. Polar opposites are therefore *inseparable* opposites, like the poles of the earth or of a magnet, or the ends of a stick or the faces of a coin. (p. 45)

Sex offers the best opportunity for a full union between two people, or two poles, that are part of a single whole. We are all one, and through sexual relations we can come to understand that all dualities—man and woman, yin and yang, spirit and nature, even what we think of as good and evil—are opposite sides of a single coin and require each other to exist. As opposite poles, men and women need each other not only to exist, but also to reach completeness. We experience evident dualities in our experience of gender, but are all at the deepest level united. Sexual relations provide a way to experience and to celebrate this unity temporarily, which is the same as the oneness that unites all things (Watts, 1958).

Watts' unitive vision was not a reduction of all particulars to one universal. Rather, as he (1958) wrote:

> The crucial point of the whole unitive philosophy of nature as it is set forth in Taoism and Buddhism, which distinguishes it from a merely monistic pantheism, is that distinct and unique events, whether external objects or the internal subject, are seen to be "one with nature" by virtue of their very distinctness, and not at all by absorption into a featureless uniformity. (p. 94)

But a present-day Watts would be challenged to consider the possibility that the diversity and distinctness of gender displayed in the realms of both "external objects" and "internal subjects" cannot be reduced to two poles of a single polarity.

Spirituality and Sexuality

Finally, in *Nature, Man and Woman* and thereafter, Watts offered a new view of spirituality and sexuality. In contrast with the then still dominant paradigm in the West, sex and spirituality are not in opposition. Watts wrote in *Nature, Man and Woman:*

> If we think of spirituality less in terms of what it avoids and more in terms of what it is positively, and if we may think of it as including an intense awareness of the inner identity of subject and object, man and the universe, there is no reason why it should require the rejection of spirituality. On the contrary, the most intimate of the relationships of the self with another would naturally become one of the chief spheres of spiritual insight and growth. (pp. 146–147)

To be spiritual, one need not abandon the practice of sex, or reject sexual feelings. Watts (1958) wrote that the moment of life's origin contains something mystical or divine:

> It is just at this extreme point that we must find the physical and the spiritual to be one, for otherwise our mysticism is sentimental or sterile-pure and our sexuality just vulgar. Without—in its true sense—the lustiness of sex, religion is joyless and abstract; without the self-abandonment of religion, sex is a mechanical masturbation. (p. 204)

Sexual pleasure, when not grasped at by sexual partners or ruined by fears or expectations, is a gift or grace, offering self-transcendence and a joyous participation in the whole cosmos. The key to experiencing sexuality in its real spiritual character is to give all of one's sexual impulses and feelings one's full unattached, ungrasping attention (which he calls by the Chinese term *kuan*, contemplation) without any intention to experience any particular feeling or outcome. Watts draws on the description of South Asian tantra provided by Dasgupta (1950), Woodroffe (1929), and Coomaraswamy (1957) to fill out his understanding of sexuality as spiritual. He denies, however, that any particular sexual technique is needed; if particular positions or techniques are employed, they are a celebration of the gift already given, not as tools to attain it. Spirituality is on a different plane from sexuality; thus it can be revealed as the true nature of sexuality just as it can be revealed as the true nature of all other things on the plane of mundane activity.

Watts was not the only North American author in the 1950s to urge that spirituality and sexuality are not enemies. For example, Beat writer Jack Kerouac in his novel *The Dharma Bums* published in 1958, showed his fictional hero, a thinly disguised portrait of writer Gary Snyder, engaging in "yab-yum" (understood to be "Tantric sex") with a willing female partner. "Beats," jazz musicians, and other countercultural figures felt that, as Kerouac writes in his book, people to thrive need to be free of all the cultural and religious regulation of sex, to be encouraged to act naturally, free of all the sex-negative thinking that associates sexual pleasure with shame, guilt, and sin. But Watts especially became a major spokesperson for the view that spirituality need not be seen as the opposite of sexuality, or the spiritual path as requiring sexual abstinence.

But where the spiritual (or ritualized) practice of sex that is associated in the Western mind with Tantra is concerned, Watts' introduction of serious Indian and Chinese cultural practices to a wide audience in *Nature, Man and Woman* risks being seen as an insufficiently respectful appropriation of expressions from another culture for purposes for which they were not intended. Although Watts cannot be solely blamed for the spiritual shallowness found in much of the more recent Western "neo-tantra," which often seems to seek "spiritual sex" rather than powerfully sexualized transformative ritual, he did open the door for it.

All three of these themes resonated strongly within the North American counterculture of the 1960s and 1970s, which Watts' important writings on these themes predated and fueled. All three still resonate, and are still an important part of discourses related to gender, nature, theology, and sexuality today. Eco-feminism and the embodied, relational theologies popular among progressive mainstream Protestants are two domains in which Watts' insights have taken root, whereas American Buddhists, unlike most of their Asian counterparts, do not demand celibacy of their most dedicated practitioners. However, looked at in the light of contemporary thinking on gender and sexuality and current knowledge of Chinese religion, aspects of Watts' views on all three themes come into question. The remainder of this chapter offers a critical evaluation of Watts' views.

A CONTEMPORARY VIEW

Eco-Feminism

Watts was an important precursor to the second wave of the feminist critique
of Western culture and Western religion, and an important initiator of and precursor to the full development of the ecological and eco-feminist movements.
As Roderick Frazier Nash (1989) wrote in *The Rights of Nature*:

> Americans began to learn about the connection between environmen-
> talism and feminism in Alan Watts, *Nature, Man and Woman* (1958);
> Herbert Marcuse, *Counterrevolution and Revolt* (Boston: 1972); and
> Theodore Roszak, *Person/Planet: The Creative Disintegration of Industrial
> Society* (New York: 1978). (pp. 252–253)

It strikes one immediately that Watts' book preceded the other two by a
decade and a half or more, and was probably much more widely read. Likewise,
Gottlieb (2004) writes:

> Since the 1960's a worldwide feminist movement has called into ques-
> tion virtually every cherished institution and belief system of patri-
> archal culture. In 1974, French feminist Francoise d'Eaubonne coined
> the term "eco-feminism" to express a theoretical perspective that sees
> critical links between the domination of nature and the exploitation of
> women. Early texts by Carolyn Merchant (*The Death of Nature* [1980])
> and Susan Griffin (*Woman and Nature* [1978]) documented how modern
> Western culture associated women and nature, contrasting both to
> the self-proclaimed rationality, moral superiority, and scientific prow-
> ess of "man."
>   Simultaneously, thinkers like Mary Daly [1968], Rosemary Radford
> Ruether [1975, 1984], Carol Christ [1997; Christ and Plaskow, 1979],
> and Judith Plaskow [1980, 1990] brought feminist claims into the realm
> of established religions. They questioned male power in religious
> institutions, sexist teachings about gender relationships, and exclusively
> male images of divinity. These two tendencies are connected in spiritual
> ecofeminism. (p. 386)

Again we note that Watts' important books predated the books and articles
by important religious feminist and eco-feminist writers by some years.

In feminist parlance, patriarchal religion is the ideology of a society in
which men dominate women and nature. Spiritual eco-feminists see patriarchal
Christian thought as providing a view of humans, nature and the universe
that supports the ascendancy of science, the technical order, and individual-

ism. This worldview emphasizes humanity's dominance over all other beings, which become "objects" in an "objectified" universe. Humanity is separated from nature. Spiritual eco-feminists value those aspects of women's social and natural experience that allow them to be aware of and value their connections to the cycles of nature and the non-human world. Eco-feminist spirituality celebrates the body and the earth. It is highly critical of the familiar hierarchies of Western metaphysics (particularly the Platonic strand), which privilege the eternal, the immaterial and the (supposedly) rational over the changing, the physical body and the realm of emotional response and empathic connection.

Summarizing her own pioneering writings since 1975 and those of others, eminent feminist Christian theologian Rosemary Radford Ruether (1993/2004) wrote of what cultural and spiritual eco-feminists believe needs to happen in our culture.[1] First, we need "a new cultural consciousness that would support relations of mutuality rather than competitive power" (p. 389). Second, "nature" must no longer be defined as "a reality below and separated from 'man,' rather than one nexus in which humanity itself is inseparably embedded" (p. 389). "We need to recognize our utter dependence on the great life-producing matrix of the planet" (p. 396). We need, in our culture and ethic, to replace the "hierarchies of domination as the model of relationship between men and women, between human groups, and between humans and other beings," with "mutual interdependency" (p. 396). Third, we must "reshape our dualistic concept of reality as split between soulless matter and transcendent male consciousness" (p. 396). Fourth, we must revisualize "the relation of mind, or human intelligence, to nature. Mind or consciousness is not something that originates in some transcendent world outside of nature, but is the place where nature itself becomes conscious" (p. 396), as Alan Watts had said. Ruether continued: "We need to think of human consciousness not as separating us as a higher species from the rest of nature, but rather as a gift to enable us to learn how to harmonize our needs with the natural system around us, of which we are a dependent part" (p. 389).

Fifth, and perhaps most centrally, the Christian concept of God must change. About the concept of God in feminist and eco-feminist theology, Ruether (1993/2004) writes:

> Such a reintegration of human consciousness and nature must reshape the concept of God, instead of modeling God after alienated male consciousness, outside of and ruling over nature. God, in ecofeminist spirituality, is the immanent source of life that sustains the whole planetary community. God is neither male nor anthropomorphic. God is the font from which the variety of plants and animals well up in each new generation, the matrix that sustains their life-giving interdependency with one another.[2] In ecofeminist culture and ethic, mutual interdependency replaces the hierarchies of domination as the model

of relationship between men and women, between human groups, and between humans and other beings. All racist, sexist, classist, cultural, and anthropocentric assumptions of the superiority of whites over blacks, males over females, managers over workers, humans over animals and plants, must be discarded. In a real sense, the so-called superior pole in each relation is actually the more dependent side of the relationship. (p. 396)

Protestant eco-feminist theologians argue that for the planet to survive and persons to thrive, there must be a conversion of men to the world of women and nature, or the earth. Such conversions will reshape the symbolic vision of salvation. Ruether (1993/2004) writes:

Instead of salvation sought either in the disembodied soul or the immortalized body, in a flight to heaven or to the end of history, salvation should be seen as continual conversion to the center, to the concrete basis by which we sustain our relation to nature and to one another. In every day and in every new generation, we need to remake our relationship with one another, finding anew the true nexus of relationality that sustains, rather than exploits and destroys, life. (p. 397; see also, Ruether, 1984)

A comparison between Alan Watts' ideas as described in the first part of this chapter and the ideas of the feminist and eco-feminist Christian and Jewish theologians reveals the latter's great debt to Watts, as well as a refusal of the latter to go all the way with Watts to a nondualist view of the world in which humans are in a thoroughgoing way part of nature. When thinkers became aware of the already developing ecological crisis in the 1960s and 1970s, Christian theologians could not work directly from Watts because of his allegedly monistic or pantheistic ontology.

With respect to feminism, Watts made the important contribution of calling to our attention that Western culture looks down on/disregards nature as well as anything labeled feminine, because the feminine is seen as a part of/analogous to Nature. He understood that Westerners accepted human domination of nature as ordained by God. He pointed out that the West did not have, and needed, a view of sexuality and gender that thought about women as equal partners with equal rights and needs. He did not raise the point important to the second wave of feminism and to eco-feminism, a point derived from Marxist analysis, that men, or male-created and male-dominated economic and social institutions, exploit, dominate, and oppress women in the same way that they exploit and dominate Nature. But as Ruether's (1993/2004) list of requirements shows, Alan Watts had already presented in *Nature, Man and Woman* a "theology" that gave these movements a lot of what they would need. Although Watts lacked any ecological concern for real animals and trees, much less ecosystems, did not use the category "oppression of women" (or other groups), and did not have much interest in the underpinnings of the actual economic and social domination of one group by another, Watts' Buddhist- and Daoist-influenced theology offered steps forward toward all the changes in Western religious culture desired by Ruether and other eco-feminists.

But Western philosophers and Christian theologians could not accept Watts' theology as such. Watts' theology at the time seemed not a Christian option, in that it seemed willing to dispense with what Christians considered indispensable doctrines and adopt ones (e.g., pantheism) that Christianity had long since rejected. Western Christian theologians and philosophers have rejected Watts's theology because of its insistence on nondualism. Ruether (1993/2004), for example, uses the words "mutual interdependency" and "true nexus of relationality," reflecting the fact that Western eco-feminists have opted for "relational" ontologies that stress the relations between separate beings, rather than more radically nondualist ontologies like that of Watts. A radical nondualist approach to the relation between humans and nature is today philo-sophically suspect, particularly one that, like Watts, claims that the perception that the world is made up of different beings is a mistake made by our minds.

Charlene Spretnak (1997), however, points out the various forms of rejec-tion of "radical nonduality" in Western philosophical movements in modernism and postmodernism, and proposes making room for radical nonduality in an "ecological postmodernism" that does not deny the testimony of contemporary science and human experiences worldwide of the oneness of everything. More-over, Spretnak's (1999) "ecological postmodernism" and David Landis Barnhill's (2001) "relational holism" based on Chinese Huayan Buddhism get at a lot of what Watts wanted to say: that nonduality is not undifferentiated monism, does not obliterate particulars, does not necessarily see a unity as the source that precedes particulars. Watts too saw a unity in the cosmos, but insisted that in this nondual unity the existence and importance of particulars is preserved. This point seems to get lost when Western philosophers unfamiliar with Watts or with non-Western thought and transformative spiritual disciplines reject non-dualism as the way to think about humans in nature and the cosmos.[3]

Another criticism has been raised *contra* the feminist and eco-feminist line of thought. It would also be salient if applied to the thinking of Alan Watts; or, if not the thinking of Alan Watts himself, the thinking of some whom he inspired. This criticism is raised by Donna J. Haraway (1991) in her essay called "A Cyborg Manifesto." She asks whether it is possible for the beings we have become to go back to some spontaneous, natural state, some unity with nature. Have we not become "cyborgs," creatures so dependent on machines, so formed by the mechanical world in our thinking and doing, that we are really already half machine and half human? Haraway suggests that the idea that we can dance with wolves and become earth mothers, that we can at will step out of the whole social order in which we live by committing ourselves to value and care for nature and the natural, deserves to be interrogated. Is there some spontaneous, "natural" man or woman available to us merely by experiencing the realm of spirit that undergirds the world? Are women and men "essentially" any particular thing "by nature"? I think that Watts can answer this criticism; but would he not have to say that that with which we are "one" or "not two" is not solely "nature" but "what is?"

BEYOND POLARITY

Watts' vision of the world as consisting of polarities that unite opposites, including the polarity that unites men and women, would be criticized today as unduly restricting the vast variety of people's sexual natures to only two poles. Feminist thinking starts from the critique that Western philosophy, religion, and culture, as well as those of other global cultures and regions, failed for a very long time to recognize women as human subjects. Against this, women and men feminists began to assert "the radical idea that women are human beings" (that women are also human). Alan Watts, to his credit, got this point; he displays this in *Nature, Man and Woman*. But gender polarity based on the norm of two heterosexual genders has been and still is strongly challenged from several points of view. To make this clear, and to place Watts against a background of contemporary discussion, it will help to give a short history of Western discourse about gender.[4]

Before the second wave of feminism of the 1970s, discourse in the United States generally spoke of two sexes, indistinguishably biological and social, and assumed that both together constituted the humanist category "man," and that men were the typical and normative humans. Second-wave feminists began to use "gender" as distinguished from "sex," to refer to ideas and feelings about sexual difference and identity that do not necessarily reflect biological "reality" but are imposed on and help to constitute human subjects. Although it might remain largely true that there are two biological sexes, feminists argued that "genders" are variously and culturally elaborated (Di Stefano, 1991). "Masculinity" and "femininity" came to be seen as elaborate cultural constructs that did not mirror nature but nevertheless exerted a powerful influence on the identities, behaviors, psychology, and cognition of men and women. Feminists noticed that the generic "man" was "masculine," rather than "human." Feminine "difference" was invoked to make room for women as gendered subjects.

As time went on, critics pointed out that the unity of the gendered "human," that is, the "masculine" or "feminine" subject, was as much a fiction as the universal "man" that gender theory had divided in two (Spelman, 1988). New voices emerged to contest many of the assumptions, biases and limitations of gender theory's assumption that all "women" were fundamentally similar:

for example, lesbians, women of color, third-world and postcolonial women. A wider array of narratives stretched the theoretical "subject" of feminism. "Women" do not mother or have sex: Women of particular races, classes, sexual preferences, ethnicities, and social locations do. As Ann Ferguson (1991) argued, dual gender must give way to multiple genders because factors of race, class, ethnicity, and sexual preference (and potential others) are not qualifiers of a more "basic" gender, which merits theoretical privileging.

With the impact of postmodernism on feminism, the stable or semi-stable "subject" itself disappears, and gender becomes totally a matter of performance in the moment. With the influential voice of Judith Butler, the question has turned from "As women, who are we? Where are we? What do we need?" or, reflecting diversity, "As middle-class lesbian women of color living in the First World, who are we? Etc." to a far more particularist question: "How am 'I' constituted as a provisional and experimental subject through those practices and performances in which I engage?" Biological sex, instead of being seen as something given prior to the socially constructed and learned performance that is gender, is now seen as never prior to gender, and thus to social construction (Butler, 1990).

In light of all this, what do we make of Alan Watts' highly influential discussions of sexual polarity? Oddly enough, Watts' understanding of polarity in general and sexual polarity in particular, although not reflecting this particular line of thought, has some parallels to its end point. Consider Watts' (1969) take on polarity in which he draws, no doubt, on his long interest in Buddhism:

> [Humanity] thinks in terms and therefore divides in thought what is undivided in nature. To think is to categorize, to sort experience into classes and intellectual pigeonholes. It is thus that, from the standpoint of thought, the all-important question is ever, "Is it this, or is it that?" Is the experience inside the class, or is it outside? By answering such questions we describe and explain the world; we make it explicit. But implicitly, in nature itself, there are no classes. We drop these intellectual nets and boxes upon the world as we weave the imaginary lines of latitude and longitude upon the face of the earth and the, likewise imaginary, firmament of the stars. It is thus the imaginary, abstract, and conceptual character of these divisions which renders them polar. (pp. 45–46)

We can certainly see in this statement, if applied to the apparent polarities of sex and of gender prior to the 1970s, a refusal to "naturalize" them, to use today's term. The human mind imposes distinctions, which it then reads onto nature. I believe that Watts would say that this is even true of the human "subject." The reasoning differs between Judith Butler's position and that of

Alan Watts, but Watts escapes from any critique that he has "essentialized" sex—or even, had he thought of it, gender. This is true as long as he remembers this insight.

Nonetheless, when Watts speaks of polarities elsewhere, he emphasizes dualities that he sees as "natural." His vision of the world as consisting of polarities that unite opposites, including the polarity that unites men and women, would be criticized today as unduly restricting the vast variety of people's sexual natures and genders to only two poles. He writes of what he seems chiefly to imagine, that is, the sexual possibilities that await men and women who by nature, when it comes to sex, do not differ in their norms or behaviors according to race, class, culture and social location, and are heterosexual. The possibility that attention should be paid to the wider variety of sexualities and genders that appear in the world and to the subjectivities of persons who experience and perform them rarely enters Watts' discourse.[5]

A more serious problem with Watts' discourse on the polarity of the sexes emerges from reading the French feminist Luce Irigaray. Irigaray proposes that every time sex or gender is imagined as "two," male and female, man and woman, the fact that in our society the male is dominant and normative and powerful means that the "two" actually become "one" (the male). Therefore, for women to come into their rightful place as truly different from men, one should never imagine just two sexes, but rather "at least two" (Irigaray, 1984/1993). Feminist theologian Rachel Muers summarizes Irigaray's perspective when she writes:

> Luce Irigaray's language of "at least two" is helpful in articulating the importance of sexual difference. To say (only) "two" invites a problematic essentialism in the service of a logic of complementarity, or of exhaustive binaries (and hence, in the end, in the service of "the same"); but not to begin with (at least) "two" rather than "more than one" reduces difference to an abstraction. Nor is this simply a strategic move; both gender and sexual binaries and the "exceptions" to them need to be taken into account whatever theory of the relationship between sex, gender, "biology" and "culture" we espouse. (Muers, 2004, p. 2, footnote 5)

Irigaray's insight that when one imagines a binary, an exhaustive binary, the logic of complementarity tends to collapse one pole into the other, the two into "sameness," is a telling point against Watts. We cannot criticize Watts for not having transcended his time. But the fact remains that even when Watts writes of the polarity of male and female, it seems apparent that for Watts these "two" in fact tend to find their real meaning in the male. It is the male that he can truly imagine; as with Derrida, Irigaray's interlocutor against whose imagining of sex she makes this argument, for Watts the male somehow encompasses and encloses the female (Bannet, 1993).

TANTRA AND NEO-TANTRA

Alan Watts contributed very largely to the conversion of Western religion from sex-negative or sex-restrictive/regulative to sex-positive. Indeed, *Nature, Man and Woman* was first published in 1958. The first commercial birth control pill became widely available in the United States in the early 1960s, and the U.S. Supreme Court ruled in 1965 that for the State of Connecticut to ban it would violate a woman's right to privacy. A freer practice of sex became available to many. Nonetheless, Watts' position and lifestyle was considered "bohemian." He may not have been a Beat, the actual number of "Beats" was, after all, rather small, but he certainly knew that his friends Ginsberg, Kerouac, and Gary Snyder totally rejected regulation of sex as part of the business suit-wearing, television-watching "organization-man" prison in which most Americans lived in the 1950s, which stifled spontaneity, real life, creativity, and real freedom. Most of his life he tried to conduct sex within marriage, but he welcomed the idea that socially unregulated sex was a form of sharing of something beautiful and good, and not morally reprehensible because no one is harmed. *Nature, Man and Woman* is a book that, like Watts' other books in the 1950s, is written for an audience of educated, particularly theologically educated, readers who know and can appreciate a treatment of and critique of the history of Western theology and culture. Such readers were open to the idea that sex in Western culture was entirely too regulated, too much made a matter of morality, and conducted with too much hypocrisy.

Watts introduced to a large audience the idea that sex could be done as a spiritual practice through which the sacred, profound unitive nature of reality could be experienced, and still be orgasmic and satisfying to both partners. As someone wrote, "Watts taught us how to do it." Watts drew from the scholarly exposition by Dasgupta (1950) and the less scholarly treatment by Woodroffe (1929) and Coomaraswamy (1957), the basic idea that sex could be done without ego, without a strong sense of the fixed boundaries of the self and what the ego wanted to experience, by doing it as part of contemplation. In contemplation (*kuan*) the participant remains fully an observer, who does not grasp onto results or force or even influence the outcome, but allows things to unfold spontaneously. Thus, we can not only value the unitive, ego-free moment in which self vanishes as a real glimpse into the realm of spirit, into reality, we can prolong the pleasurable feelings of sex by doing it as contemplation.

From a contemporary perspective, there are five problems with Watts' discussion of the tantric attitude toward sex as a route to deep spiritual realization. First, although Watts based his views on a scholarly reading of every book on tantra available in his time, the fact is that then and now we in Western as well as South and East Asian communities of learning still know very little about tantric traditions in general and the tantric traditions that employ sexual ritual in particular. Watts based his identification of what he did or aspired to on a very limited knowledge of "tantra," which is the name of a broad group of texts and by extension of a broad group of nonsexual and a smaller group of sexual practices in South Asia. Apart from Miranda Shaw of the University of Richmond, Virginia, few scholars of Indian Buddhism have studied tantra that uses sexual practices, either in texts or in contemporary communities (Shaw, 1995).

What scholars of Indian religion and Indian Buddhism broadly agree on concerning tantric practice that uses sex includes the following:

- Some tantric groups in their ritual practice of sex refuse orgasm and others do not;

- The exercise focuses on the bliss of arousal in which the tantric yogi realizes that the pleasure is, like everything else, "empty" of substantial existence.

It is also a widespread requirement that the adept visualize his body-in-sex, and that of his partner, as the body of a Buddha-deity. Their virtual bodies are inscribed with mantras, luminous channels, chakras with lotus petals, and mandalas of deities. So it is not the body as body that has tantric sex; it is rather the body as seen in the imagination, as overwritten according to a plan by a set of icons.

What does this mean in the terms that Watts and the countercultural movement set out? Janet Gyatso (2005), a contemporary scholar of Tibetan Buddhism, writes: "Is [tantric sexual ritual practice] more "body-affirming," or less, than [the restraints of celibate] monasticism? Does it allow greater bliss, or does it work to destroy it? I am not able to say. I certainly don't know how to estimate how "repressive" or "liberating" tantric sexual yoga would be" (p. 289).[6] Although Alan Watts no doubt aimed at experiencing the realization that pleasure is empty, judging by his advice to others and his written or oral descriptions of his own experiences in his books, articles, and lectures, it seems unlikely that he visualized his body in the way that tantric yogis often do. We have only his testimony that spirit and matter were unified, and his sexual pleasure was more enriching and longlasting.

Second, one way of thinking about what Watts described and what later proponents of "spiritual sex" advocated, as opposed to what South and East Asians practice, is to call one "neo-tantra," or even "American Tantra," and the other "tantra." Some have argued that one difference between tantra and "neo-tantra" is that the first "sexualizes ritual," whereas the second "ritualizes sex." Hugh Urban (2003) suggests that neo-tantra, into which Watts may not completely fall, but which his writings encourage, is a joint creation of mirroring and mimesis between India and the West (under conditions of colonialism and neo-colonialism) to meet Western cultural goals. Neo-tantra sees great sex as a part of the goal of cultivating concentration and mastering yogic positions. Watts' discussion of the possible union of sexuality and spirituality was never as banal as much of what one finds in neo-tantra; often, in fact, it was profound. But it was more related to the "spiritual sex" of neo-tantra than he no doubt intended.[7]

Third, and related, is the fact that Watts writes in *Nature, Man and Woman* that a modern sexual tantra need not avoid the release of energy in male orgasm, because we do not believe in the theory of the body that underlies such redirection of sexual energy or fluids back into the body of the male. This view dismisses the findings of long enduring traditions of spiritual practice working with sexual energy in India and China. It does not respect what we can and need to learn from these traditions.

Fourth, rather than simply rejecting as wrong all traditions of spiritual training that advocate celibacy, Watts would have done better to realize that there might be good reasons for pursuing a celibate path, reasons just as good as those for pursuing a sexual path to spiritual development. It is not necessarily simply or only a hatred of matter, the body and nature and a desire to believe in the value of disembodied spirit that would lead a spiritual teacher to recommend celibacy to adepts at certain stages of a spiritual path. Watts writes that it is the objectification of the body, and the separation of spirit from body, that leads to the advocacy of celibacy. Although there is no doubt that historically Christianity, perhaps under the influence of Greek and Hellenistic philosophy, opted for a "sex-negative" rather than "sex-positive" view of the spiritual path, in other traditions and cultures worldwide that were not sex-negative it could still be the case that celibacy was preferred as an approach to spiritual training.

Fifth, Watts assumes that ego-free sex is attainable by all just by wishing that one were unattached; he jumps over the problem of how to work with sex if one is not perfectly ego-free; at a minimum, if, in Buddhist terms, one has no experience of "emptiness." In her book *Zen in America,* Helen Tworkov (1994) writes that Watts and others in California in the 1950s and 1960s confused a carefree bohemian way of life with the freedom of mind taught by the Buddhists; they promised liberation through spontaneity. Spontaneity may be one of the fruits of Buddhist liberation, of the realization of "emptiness." But the spontaneity that comes from real freedom of mind is not easily attained. Given Watts' assumption that he himself, without the recommended training, has attained the freedom from ego that would allow him to begin to make judgments on the matter, and given his failure to recommend yogic training to his readers, he may be describing as easily attainable a sexual contemplative practice that is beyond the reach of most, including himself. The need to be aware of and interrogate sexual feelings while on a spiritual path is not only important, it requires in most people complex and multilayered refinements of awareness over which Watts simply leaps.

CONCLUSION

Nonetheless, Watts, along with others in the late 1950s and 1960s, brought about a profound change in how Americans regard the relation between sex and religion, or sex and spirituality. As the former contributor to *The Village Voice* and *Rolling Stone* Robert Levin (2005) writes:

> At bottom the '60s were a reaction to the prospect of total annihila-tion posed by the invention of the hydrogen bomb and they were rooted in the belief that what was wrong, what had brought us to this place, was the denial and suppression of our true selves, of the human beings we were intended to be. . . . The enemy was the superego, the cultural, social and psychological restraints we'd inflicted on our-selves. Destroying the superego would yield the good human beings we were supposed to be. Again, as Marcuse put it, it was a "revolution of unrepression." We wanted to abolish the apparently arbitrary and misbegotten rules that artificially limited us and led to deluded think-ing and behavior. . . . The vanguard figures—like Timothy Leary, Alan Watts, Norman Brown, Allen Ginsberg, Marcuse—envisioned a kind of benign anarchy, a society with no need for governments or police; a society ordered by natural needs, appetites and rhythms and made up of men free of neurosis and in perfect harmony with both nature and other men.

If persons who are free of neurosis and in perfect harmony with nature have sex, and the natural and the spiritual are one, then sexuality and spirit cannot be divided. That this utopian vision convinced many, even those who carry on the traditions such as Christianity that Watts saw as particularly repres-sive in the sexual realm, is more than evident in our religious culture today. For example, Christian theologian and scholar Marcus Borg wrote in his blog, "On Faith," on the *Newsweek/Washington Post* Website the following entry on February 15, 2007:

> Sex is seen as sacred or sinful perhaps for the same reason. Sex has power. Of course, not all sex does. There is great sex, mediocre sex, and bad sex, just as there is great music, mediocre music, and bad music. At its best, sex is ecstatic in the root sense of the word. The Greek roots of the word "ecstasy" mean "to be out of one's self," or "to be out of one's ordinary state of consciousness." Intense religious experience—mystical experience—is also ecstatic in the same sense.

Like mystics, great lovers (and here I am not referring to either technique or number of partners) know something that many people do not know: That there is a way of being, a mode of experience, that makes conventional consciousness seem like living in a cave.

Thus sexual ecstasy has sometimes been seen as a sacrament of the sacred. The union of two people becomes a sacrament of union with "what is," with the sacred. Intense sexual union puts one in touch with a reality that transcends traditional convention.

For some religious orientations, this is threatening. There are forms of Christianity in which the body is mistrusted and seen as a rival to a godly life. And just as there are forms of Christianity that mistrust sexuality, so also there are forms of Christianity that distrust their own mystics.

Great lovers, great artists, great thinkers, and the mystics of all religions know that there is an experience of the sacred that cannot be confined to tradition or domesticated by convention. Such people are dangerous and subversive to the way things are.

In my own experience, sexuality has been a great source of pain in my life and a great source of joy. I suspect this is true for many people. So I understand why religious traditions have seen sexuality as profoundly ambiguous.

But I am also convinced that at its best, it provides us with a taste of union with "what is." It can be a sacrament. (Borg, 2007)

That the widely respected and much read Christian theologian Marcus Borg can write these words in 2007 on a blog sponsored by two major mainstream U.S. publications, words that no one in his position could have written in 1958, shows how far we have come. We owe this to the counterculture movement of the 1950s and 1960s, and particularly to Alan Watts, a rather proper "bohemian" who served as its spokesman and philosopher. Watts' enormous impact in this area was due to the respect he commanded as a learned and widely read intellectual who had something new and welcome to say.

NOTES

1. Rosemary Radford Ruether continues to write on the topic of Christianity and eco-feminism. I believe that she would still endorse this list, but, like many eco-feminists, her position may have changed in nuance in response to the growing diversity among religious eco-feminists, as well as to new work by eco-feminist theologians.

2. Here Ruether draws on Sallie McFague's 1987 book *Models of God: Theology for an Ecological, Nuclear Age.*

3. See also the sharp critique of Watts' thought by Louis Nordstrom and Richard Pilgrim (1980) that is partly on similar grounds.

4. These paragraphs that summarize the history of feminist discourse on gender owe a great deal to Christine Di Stefano (1991).

5. In an article by Watts published in *The Playboy Magazine* of December 1965, called "The Circle of Sex," he deployed a model provided in a book of the same name by his father-in-law Gavin Arthur (1966) that proposed the existence of a dozen or more sexual types rather than two. Here the discussion of sex escapes the heterosexual polarity model. See also Watts' (1979) essay in *The New Gay Liberation Book*.

6. For a different view on this topic by a scholar of Indian Buddhism, see Miranda Shaw (1995).

7. An alternative view is offered by Jeffrey Kripal (2007), who sees Watts' contributions to the "Tantric transmission" in American culture as immensely greater in subtlety and thoughtfulness than is categorically implied by "neo-tantra."

REFERENCES

Arthur, G. (1966). *The circle of sex*. Hyde Park, NY: University Books.

Bannet, E. T. (1993). There have to be at least two. *Diacritics, 23*(1), 84–98.

Barnhill, D. L. (2001). Relational holism: Huayan Buddhism and deep ecology. In D. L. Barnhill & R. S. Gottlieb (Eds.), *Deep ecology and world religions* (pp. 77–106). Albany: State University of New York Press.

Borg, M. (2007, February 15). On faith. Retrieved from http://newsweek.washingtonpost.com/onfaith/marcus_borg.

Butler, J. (1990). *Gender trouble: Feminism and the subversion of identity*. New York: Routledge.

Christ, C. P. (1997). *Rebirth of the goddess: Finding meaning in feminist spirituality*. Reading, MA: Addison-Wesley.

Christ, C. P., & Plaskow, J. (Eds.). (1979). *Womanspirit rising: A feminist reader in religion*. New York: Harper & Row.

Coomaraswamy, A. K. (1957). *The dance of Shiva*. New York: Noonday Press.

Daly, M. (1968). *The church and the second sex*. New York: Harper & Row.

Dasgupta, S. B. (1950). *An introduction to tantric Buddhism*. Calcutta: University of Calcutta Press.

Di Stefano, C. (1991). Who the heck are we? Theoretical turns against gender. *Frontiers, 12*(2), 86–108.

Ferguson, A. (1991). *Sexual democracy: Women, oppression, and revolution*. Boulder, CO: Westview Press.

Gottlieb, R. S. (Ed.). (2004). *This sacred earth: Religion, nature, environment* (2nd ed.). New York: Routledge.

Griffin, S. (1978). *Woman and nature: The roaring inside her*. San Francisco: Harper & Row.

Gyatso, J. (2005). Sex. In D. S. Lopez (Ed.), *Critical terms for the study of Buddhism* (pp. 271–290). Chicago: University of Chicago Press 2005.

Haraway, D. J. (1991). A cyborg manifesto: Science, technology and socialist feminism in the late twentieth century. In D. J. Haraway, *Simians, cyborgs, and women. The re-invention of nature* (pp. 149–182). New York: Routledge.

Irigaray, L. (1993). *An ethics of sexual difference* (C. Burke & G. C. Gill, Trans.). Ithaca, NY: Cornell University Press. (Original work published 1984)

Kerouac, J. (1958). *The dharma bums.* New York. Viking Press.

Kripal, J. J. (2007). *Esalen: America and the religion of no religion.* Chicago: University of Chicago Press.

Levin, R. (2005). *Free jazz: The jazz revolution of the sixties.* Retrieved from http://www.hackwriters.com/freejazz.htm.

McFague, S. (1987). *Models of God: Theology for an ecological, nuclear age.* Philadelphia: Fortress Press.

Merchant, C. (1980). *The death of nature: Women, ecology, and the scientific revolution.* San Francisco: Harper & Row.

Muers, R. (2004). *Keeping God's silence: Toward a theological ethics of communication.* Oxford: Blackwell.

Nash, R. F. (1989). *The rights of nature: A history of environmental ethics.* Madison: University of Wisconsin Press.

Nordstrom, L., & Pilgrim, R. (1980). The wayward mysticism of Alan Watts. *Philosophy East and West, 30*(3), 381–401.

Plaskow, J. (1980). Sex, sin, and grace: Women's experience in the theologies of Reinhold Niebuhr and Paul Tillich. Washington, DC: University Press of America.

Plaskow, J. (1990). *Standing again at Sinai: Judaism from a feminist perspective.* San Francisco: Harper & Row.

Ruether, R. (1975). *New woman/new earth: Sexist ideologies and human liberation.* New York: Seabury Press.

Ruether, R. (1984). Envisioning our hope: Some models for the future. In J. Kalven & M. Buckley (Eds.), *Women's spirit bonding* (pp. 325–335). New York: Pilgrim Press.

Ruether, R. R. (2004). Eco-feminism: Symbolic and social connections of the oppression of women and the domination of nature. In G. S. Gottlieb (Ed.), *This sacred earth: Religion, nature, environment* (2nd ed., pp. 388–399). [Reprinted from C. J. Adams (Ed.). (1993). *Eco-feminism and the Sacred* (pp. 425–436). New York: The Continuum Publishing Company.]

Shaw, M. (1995). *Passionate enlightenment.* Princeton, NJ: Princeton University Press.

Spelman, E. (1988). *Inessential woman: Problems of exclusion in feminist thought.* Boston: Beacon Press.

Spretnak, C. (1997). Radical nonduality in ecofeminist philosophy. In K. Warren & N. Erkal (Eds.), *Ecofeminism: Women, culture, nature* (pp. 425–436). Bloomington: Indiana University Press.

Spretnak, C. (1999). *The resurgence of the real: Body, nature and place in a hypermodern world.* New York: Routledge.

Tworkov, H. (1994). *Zen in America: Five teachers and the search for an American Buddhism.* New York: Kodansha International.

Urban, H. B. (2003). *Tantra: Sex, secrecy, politics, and power in the study of religion.* Berkeley: University of California Press.

Watts, A. W. (1958). *Nature, man and woman.* New York: Pantheon.

Watts, A. W. (1963). The woman in man. In S. M. Farber & R. H. L. Wilson (Eds.), *Man and civilization: The potential of women* (pp. 79–86). San Francisco: McGraw-Hill.

Watts, A. W. (1965). The circle of sex. *Playboy, 12*(12), 134–135.

Watts, A. W. (1969). *The two hands of God: The myths of polarity.* New York: Collier Books.

Watts, A. W. (1979). No more armed clergymen. In L. Richmond & G. Noguera (Eds.), *The new gay liberation book* (pp. 143–146). Berkeley, CA: Ramparts Press.

Watts, A. W. (1995). Religion and sexuality. In *Myth and religion* (M. J. Watts, Ed., pp. 91–107). London: Eden Grove Editions.

Watts. A. W. (1997). The new humanism. In M. Watts & J. Snelling (Eds.), *Seeds of genius: The early writings of Alan Watts* (pp. 45–49). Shaftsbury, UK: Element. (Original work published 1937).

Watts, A. W. (2000). *What is Tao?* Novato, CA: New World Library.

White, L. (1967). The historical roots of our ecological crisis. *Science, 155,* 1203–1207.

Woodroffe, J. (1929). *Shakti and shakta.* London: Luzac.

CHAPTER NINE

Contributions and Conundrums in the Psychospiritual Transformation of Alan Watts

Alan Pope

The writings and lectures of Alan Watts elucidate a vision of psy-chospiritual transformation that is at once comprehensible and profound. Comprised of expositions on Eastern philosophy interpreted through his own Western enculturation, his work sheds light on presuppositions that guide philosophical and psychological inquiry, offering valuable critical perspectives on the nature of personal development and spiritual liberation. Watts' analyses are largely consistent with a proposition that has guided my own research, namely, that personal transformation is essentially a process of *learning to see*. For Watts, the most fundamental transformation occurs when we see the unity out of which duality appears. However, it remains an interesting question as to what extent Watts managed to adopt this vision for himself. Although Watts drew principally from Buddhist, Daoist, and Vedanta literatures to formulate his theoretical frame-work, his experiential understanding derived less from the rigorous application of meditation practices associated with these traditions than from experimentation with psychotropic drugs (Watts, 1960, 1962, 1971). Through psychedelic journey-ing, Watts achieved glimpses of liberation from ordinary, conventional ways of seeing, but others have suggested that he nevertheless held firm to an intellectual appropriation that limited his own vision (Nordstrom & Pilgrim, 1980). The charge is that he interpreted Eastern thought from a functionalist Western sensibility that reduces mysticism to materiality. In this view, as brilliant as many of Watts' ideas were, they often misrepresented the Eastern philosophical traditions on which they were based. This chapter offers both an appreciation of Watts' contributions to our understanding of psychospiritual transformation and a critical appraisal of his attempts to incorporate the Eastern orientation.

WATTS IN THEORY: AN APPRECIATION

The phrase *psychospiritual transformation* implies that the process of personal change and growth involves an intimate interaction between psyche (soul) and spirit. Whereas the realm of spirit had been largely ignored by Western psychology, Watts found in Eastern spirituality a larger context within which Western psychological thought could be situated. This enlarged perspective offered him the critical stance he needed to begin to forge a viable connection between Eastern and Western understandings of the mind and the interrelated connections between psychological and spiritual processes. Watts articulated this attempted union most clearly in his 1961 book *Psychotherapy East and West*, which Eugene Taylor (2003) describes as "possibly one of the most influential texts of the American psychotherapeutic counterculture" (p. 185). This section draws on this and other works in developing a review of some of the major themes that Watts developed in his quest for the "practical transformation of consciousness" (Watts, 1972, p. 247).

EXPOSING THE MYTHS THAT GUIDE HOW WE SEE

In order to learn how to see properly, we must first understand how our vision has been distorted. With brilliance and clarity, Watts articulated the basic myths through which we have historically oriented ourselves and made sense of the world (Watts, 1966, 2004). The *Ceramic Model* of the universe, which arises from Genesis, conceives all material substances as pots created by an external source, God. Just as Jesus was the son of a carpenter, so, too, is God a craftsman, a potter who shapes and breathes life into little clay figurines of which we are each exemplars. But the Renaissance introduced the notion of a mathematical universe, converting the cosmos into a machine holding no place for God. This vision, which Watts calls the *Fully Automatic Model*, comes with two variants—one in which God made the machine and then abandoned it, and another in which God never existed. The universe and everything in it, ourselves included, consists of random combinations of atoms which accidentally have formed the coherence we know as our reality, and the entropy against which we struggle. In Watts' view, the fully automatic model became a scientific dogma that shaped our view of reality and created a tremendous sense of isolation and anxiety.

Watts posited a third alternative to these Western conceptions deriving from the Hindu Vedanta. In the *Dramatic Model* of the universe, God out of boredom makes up disguises in order to play hide-and-seek with itself. We adopt a persona, our egoic identity, as a mask that covers over our true nature as *Atman*, the divine core of human personality that is ultimately none other than *Brahman*, or God itself. It was this myth that captured Watts' imagination and provided the basis for his own way of seeing the nature of self and world. In a sense, we could say that Watts chose the myth that he wanted to live, and he used it as a basis for critically examining ideas and systems that were predicated on the other two.

LANGUAGE, SCIENCE, AND POETRY

In his adoption of the dramatic model as his own personal myth, Watts considered himself first and foremost an entertainer, and, in his capacity as a scholar, a nonacademic philosopher (Watts, 1972). By the accounts of others, Watts had transformed himself from a stuffy, arid intellectual, to a dynamic, playful, rascal (Furlong, 1986; Huang, 1975). A key element in this transformation was Watts' own understanding of the nature and value of poetic language. He possessed an almost unfathomable ability to make the complicated clear and to make the ancient relevant to contemporary life. His capacity for extemporaneous speech was of exceptionally high quality. In his writing, he used words with such a simplicity and lucidity as to draw out the felt sense of that which might otherwise remain mere intellectual abstraction. As he himself said, "much of my work is poetry disguised as prose so that people will read it. As poets value sounds of words above their meaning, and images above arguments, I am trying to get thinking people to be aware of the actual vibrations of life as they would listen to music" (Watts, 1972, p. 5).

Although Watts held reverence for science, he recognized that it could get lost in method, becoming stuffy and dry. His love of poetry reflects his appreciation that the scientific attempt to eradicate ambiguity from language—which Ricoeur (1985) regards as the antithesis of poetic language—eliminated essential possibilities of imagination. Watts thrived on subtlety, moving ever more deeply into nuanced understandings of difficult abstract concepts, searching for truths through a certain embodied resonance that categories alone cannot yield. As such, he held little regard for "the harangues of logical analysts and scientific empiricists against poets and metaphysicians" (Watts, 1972, p. 5). He wanted to reclaim an experiential realm as a source of true knowledge, and as the source of the only knowledge that is truly knowable. In this quest, he recognized that even philosophy was not enough: "I should perhaps add that, for me, philosophical reflection is barren when divorced from poetic imagination, for we proceed to understanding of the world upon two legs, not one" (Watts, 1962, p. xvii).

In addition to utilizing ambiguity—which reflects more faithfully the true nature of ourselves and the world in our immediate experience of it—poetry carries the power to defy the linguistic conventions through which we create a sense of solidity and security. One of Watts' most intriguing insights relates to the manner in which Western languages create through linguistic structure an action (verb) that is performed by an agent (noun). The Chinese written language, he observes, does not follow the same conventions, conceiving action instead as a process without an actor (Watts, 1975). Existentialists, who themselves have favored ambiguity and an experiential approach to philosophy, arrive at a similar conclusion in recognizing the human being as "human becoming"

(May, 1983). The poet's ability to tweak conventional language affords the opportunity to explore new vistas of experience, which Watts suggested includes the ability to describe with words that which cannot be described.

THE NATURE OF PERCEPTION, PLAYFULNESS, AND DEATH

In attempting to express the nondual framework that Eastern thought had introduced to him, Watts adopts a functionalist view in arguing that all our perceptions of the external world are states of the organism (Watts, 1961). Within this framework, he suggests that for any organism there is no *need* to survive, but rather a *desire* to go on living. He repudiates Freud's life-and-death drives as abstract concepts that complicate rather than elucidate our basic nature, quoting Wittgenstein to say, "A necessity for one thing to happen because another has happened does not exist. There is only *logical* necessity" (quoted in Watts, 1961, p. 23). If proof is the province of logic and there is no necessity, only proclivity, then organic life is inherently fuzzy or "wiggly." In line with his personal philosophy and later-life inclinations, he conceived life as most fundamentally directed by playfulness, with no inherently existing causal explanations that we can attribute to it. It is interesting to note how consonant this view is with the attitude of social liberation that emerged during the time in which he lived.

Behind this view of the playfulness of life is the notion that an organism is successful to the extent it is consistent with its environment. As such, the biological organism is most fundamentally a process of transforming food and air into the organism's own pattern. "To say that the organism *needs* food is only to say that it *is* food" (Watts, 1961, p. 23). Our interior life functions similarly:

> More complex organisms, such as human beings, are more complex consistencies, more complex transformations of the environment. Not only are they patterns of transforming food, but their agreement or consistency with the environment changes nuclear vibrations into sound and light, weight and color, taste and smell, temperature and texture, until finally they generate elaborate patterns of signs and symbols of great interior consistency . . . the world is thus transformed into thought in the same way that food was transformed into body. (pp. 23–24)

Hence, Watts views thought as a product of the translation of the world into symbolic representation.

As compelling as Watts' description is, it does not quite accord with Eastern psychology. For example, according to the Buddhist Abhidharma, the philosophical and psychological commentaries on the Buddha's teachings, thoughts and feelings are themselves objects of perception, of no lesser ontological status than any other worldly phenomenon (Govinda, 1961). In this view, the mind is considered an organ of perception, along with the eyes, ears, nose, tongue, and body, forming the *six sense doors* through which the world can be experienced. Including the mind as a sensory organ defies Western common sense because it is not predicated on the Cartesian mind–body split shaping the Western viewpoint. In the Buddhist view, different categories of consciousness arise when a given sensory organ comes into contact with an object of perception. For example, when the eye combines with a form, there arises eye-consciousness. Hence, the Abhidharma identifies eighteen elements—the six sensory organs, their objects, and the consciousnesses associated with each—which form the entirety of our experience of the phenomenal world. Meditation is a process of breaking attachments to any one of these elemental expressions in order to witness the unfolding of what is essentially one vast mandala of experience within which there is no inherent self.

Although Watts' formulation gives priority to materiality and construes the mind as an emergent property rather than a constitutive entity, it represents an attempt tó characterize theoretically the insight gained from Eastern philosophy that there is no inherent self. Throughout his career he was fond of invoking the notion from Vedanta that the true self *is* the cosmos (Watts, 1966). If we are the entire cosmos, then we are deluded in thinking that life-and-death is a problem. Watts understands this faux problem as arising from a primordial repression that he describes as being "that this game is *serious*, i.e., it is not a game" (Watts, 1961, p. 25). This view resonates with the existential idea that our most basic repression is the fear of death (Becker, 1973), although it is characteristic of Watts to reframe an existential concern as a social one. It is interesting that Watts did not advance the same suggestion made more recently by Zen teacher and scholar David Loy (1996)—that a more foundational repression is of the awareness that we don't exist now in the ways that we think we do. From this stance, truly, life-and-death ceases to be a problem, because death itself is an illusion (Nhat Hanh, 2002).

THE ILLUSION OF SELF

Although the theme that the self with which we ordinarily identify is an illusion was central to many of Watts' writings and lectures, as should now be evident, he decried the notion of illusion at the physical level, emphasizing that it resides in social identifications (Watts, 1961). "Very few modern authorities on Buddhism or Vedanta," he writes, "seem to realize that social institutions constitute the *maya*, the illusion, from which they offer release" (p. 47). The intellectual inspiration for this emphasis came from his study of the social psychology of George Herbert Mead (1956). Watts (1961) says of Mead: "he goes on to show that the 'I,' the biological individual, can become conscious of itself only in terms of the 'me,' but that this latter is a view of itself given to it by other people" (pp. 36–37). In other words, the self with which we identify is mirrored to us by others, and we take on their projections and incorporate them into an image of ourselves.

This view accords well with French psychoanalyst Jacques Lacan's (1977) description of the mirror stage of child development. For Lacan, the ego is essentially born in the moment that the child, at the age of about six months, is first able to recognize itself in a mirror. Before this moment, the child gazes on its own body and sees disjointed pieces; afterward, it sees a whole image, a gestalt around which the child can organize ideas about who or what it is. As Lacan points out, however, the child's recognition is a *mis*-recognition. The child is *not* the image, but in identifying itself as such, the child gains the seed potential for entry into the symbolic and social orders. The child acquires the capacity for others to mirror it back to itself in the manner described by Mead, using its new self-image as a way of organizing these self-perceptions, and becoming conscious of itself in terms of "me."

In exploring this social fiction, Watts again quotes Mead: "If mind is socially constituted, then the field or locus of any given individual mind must extend as far as the social activity or apparatus of social relations which constitutes it extends; and hence that field cannot be bounded by the skin of the individual organism to which it belongs" (quoted in Watts, 1961, p. 37). Reinterpreting Mead's use of the word *ego*, Watts (e.g., 1964) would often refer to the "skin-encapsulated ego" as the basic delusion to which we hold ourselves. He saw the promise, however, that we may evolve to the point that we see beyond these narrow conceptions of self: "Yet the time may come when the shock of strangeness turns into the shock of recognition, when looking at the external world as a mirror we may exclaim with amazement, 'Why, that is *me*!'" (Watts, 1961, p. 87).

THE FIELD OF AWARENESS

Watts conceives the nature of reality as a field. When our perceptions of the external world are seen as states of our organism, "the division between 'I' and 'my sights' is projected outwardly into the sharp division between organism and what it sees . . . perception will be known for what it is, a field relationship as distinct from an encounter" (Watts, 1961, p. 81). This division between "I" and "other" or "world" is described in the Mahayana Buddhist school known as Yogācāra, or "Mind Only," as owing to a layer of consciousness called *manas*, or "the creator of duality" (Ray, 2000). Were it not for this function operating within the process of transformation that Watts describes—wherein the actual world is translated into a *grid* or framework that we can use for purposes of reasoning and calculation—our experience would consist of a more nebulous and continuous flow of energy. It is this function within the mind that creates a sense of self and other, of discrete quantities and linear processes, of solidity and stability.

Although Watts does not invoke these deeper layers of consciousness, he nevertheless brilliantly describes the processes whereby the world is transformed into a variety of grids that can be treated in calculative and linear fashion. It begins with the nervous system, the system of discreet neuronal entities that govern the manner in which we make sense out of the world, combining the top–down processes of higher thought function with the bottom–up processing of raw sensory data. At higher levels, mathematics and language are themselves grids that permit us to systematically analyze the world. However, as Watts astutely observes, we can never analyze the world; we can only analyze our grids of the world, for our grids are translations of a field that itself is not linear and discreet, but is dynamic and holistic. "What we call the regularities of nature are the regularities of our grids" (Watts, 1961, p. 29).

In line with Watts' thinking, Romanyshyn (1989) provides a detailed analysis of the birth of linear perspective vision in the Renaissance. At that time, artists began to use an actual, physical grid as an overlay of the subject being artistically reproduced, reducing—or, in Watts' language, *translating*—the whole of the individual to a pattern that becomes an abstraction of the reality being rendered. The result is a cultural shift in how we gaze on the world and ourselves, permanently affecting how we see. Romanyshyn's work is based on J. H. van den Berg's (1961) theory of *metabletics*, which posits that the changing nature of humanity produces changes in the nature of the world, even at the level of materiality. The translation process that Watts describes becomes the element that mediates between inner and outer experience, and that unites the metabletic notion that changes in the world reflect the changing nature of humanity with the idea that there is no essential nature in the human being to change.

The field concept reflects a paradigm shift from the linear thinking of the Renaissance era to an understanding of the world in terms of relationships, organizations, and fields (Combs, 1999; McTaggart, 2002). It also has been formalized as a way of understanding human perception and psychology (Snygg & Combs, 1949) along lines similar to those articulated by Watts. The basic idea of the field is to "explore the nature of human beings and their behavior as field organizations" (Combs, 1999, p. 17) wherein the individual can only be understood with respect to its environment, and vice-versa. The difficulty in our perception arises when we rip the individual out of the larger context within which it is embedded. As Watts (1961) succinctly puts it: "To ignore the context of events is exactly the Buddhist *avidya*, ignorance or ignore-ance, which liberation dispels" (p. 65). Attachment, then, is precisely holding to the figure against the ground as a separable and discreet entity, a perception that always disappears on closer inspection. Consequently, removing attachments is a matter of learning to see with precision what is.

THE NATURE OF LIBERATION

The disjunction between our true nature and what we are told to believe about ourselves through social convention puts us, Watts says, in a double-bind. Specifically,

the members of the [social] game are to play *as if* they were independent agents, but they are not to *know* that they are just playing as
if! It is explicit in the rules that the individual is self-determining, but
implicit that this is so only by virtue of the rules . . . the rules of the
game confer independence and take it away at the same time, without
revealing the contradiction. (Watts, 1961, pp. 37–38)

Watts likens this double-bind to the one hypothesized by Bateson as a
leading factor in the development of schizophrenia. When placed in a situation
in which one is constituted as an independent and responsible entity—in con-
tradistinction to the true nature of reality—and the rules of the game cannot
be called into question, one alternative is to "go crazy," withdrawing from the
game as though involuntarily.

As Watts points out, the other alternative is to consciously see through
the game, to recognize that it is a game, and thereby to not take it seriously;
in other words, to abide with the Dramatic Model of the universe. Watts characterizes the *bodhisattva* of Mahayana Buddhism—the being who forsakes his
or her own enlightenment in order to benefit all beings—as an image of one
who sees through the social ruse and therefore plays the game as game. This
characterization calls to mind a comment by F. Scott Fitzgerald (1936/2000):
"The test of a first-rate intelligence is the ability to hold two opposing ideas in
the mind at the same time, and still retain the ability to function. One should,
for example, be able to see that things are hopeless and yet be determined to
make them otherwise" (p. 139). Even so, this rendering of intelligence holds a
determined resolve that Watts would still find too serious, whereas the bodhisattva, in seeing the world as play, acts out of compassion for those who continue
to suffer by virtue of their own delusion. Once we see the world as play, as a
drama staged for the benefit of our (Atman's) own amusement, the ordinary
problems of life, such as birth and death, cease to be problems.

In the meantime, we suffer to the extent that we do not recognize the
double-bind placed on us by social convention. For Watts, the essence of neurosis is this lack of recognition, reinforced through our absorption in things.
Although I believe he places too much emphasis on social construction, Watts
nevertheless offers a brilliant characterization of both the Zen master and the
psychotherapist as tricksters who exploit the double-bind in effecting an awakening in their students/clients. The Zen master, for example, will demand that the
student deliver a completely spontaneous response to a question. The demand
itself, however, makes spontaneity impossible, just as the societal injunction to
be an independent self, despite the rules governing what it is acceptable for
that self to do or be, creates an unsolvable dilemma. The guru's ruse, then, is
to wake up the student to the bind itself.

Watts characterizes one technique of Zen masters as that of leading their
students to act on their delusions so as to overthrow them by *reductio ad absur-*

dum. He likens this strategy to leading the student to walk in one direction in order to learn, by eventually arriving at the starting point, that the earth is not flat (Watts, 2004). However, this process cannot be forced—it takes time, time that the healer provides. Watts (1961) explains:

> Such trickery is basic to medicine and psychotherapy alike. It has been said that the good doctor is one who keeps the patient amused while nature works the cure . . . it is easier to wait for a natural change when one is given the impression that something is being done to bring it about. What is being done is the trick; the relaxed and rested waiting is the actual cure, but the anxiety which attends a disease makes direct and deliberate relaxation almost impossible. Patients lose confidence in their doctors to the extent that the trickery is exposed, and therefore the art of medicine progresses by the invention of new and ever more impenetrable tricks. (p. 54)

Thus, Watts characterizes the healing arts as a beneficent sham that enables its clientele to let go of the struggle that is their prison so as to live in accord with the way things are.

Watts also characterizes the spiritual guru as deliberately posing, perhaps with the support of the religious establishment, as an exalted figure possessing a (possibly) supernatural power. This is similar to the Lacanian school of psychoanalysis in which it is considered critical that the analyst be the one presumed to know (Fink, 1999). In the case of Lacan, it is equally critical that the analyst not know, that he or she employ Freud's (1912/1963) "even hovering attention" (p. 118). Here the student is placed in the position of wanting to please, yet as Watts points out, "the more you believe that liberation is something that *you* can get, the harder you will have to work" (p. 134). In a famous Tibetan story, Milarepa is instructed by his guru, Marpa, to build and tear down and rebuild the same house over and over again (Lhalungpa, 1977). As Trungpa (1973) expresses it, he eventually has his ambition burned out, reaching a state of genuine openness whereupon he can finally receive his teacher's teachings. This conception of the dynamic differs, however, from the view of Watts, who would see no other teachings as necessary.

WATTS IN PRACTICE: A CRITICAL ASSESSMENT

It is remarkable that for all of Watts' fascination with Eastern philosophical thought, he largely eschewed Eastern spiritual practices. Although he did become an adherent of calligraphy and tai chi, he looked critically on the notion of sitting meditation, pejoratively referring to "the 'aching legs' brand of Buddhism" (Watts, 1975, p. 89). Based on conversations with D. T. Suzuki and R. H. Blythe, Watts claimed that within Zen the emphasis on *zazen* (sitting meditation) was a modern development that the old school would have found laughable. However, it is difficult to find support for this position. Suzuki (1964) himself, writing of the importance of direct experience born of meditation, concluded his introductory book on Zen Buddhism by stating: "The unique position maintained by the Zen sect among the other Buddhist sects in Japan and China *throughout the history of Buddhism* in the Far East is no doubt due to the institution known as the Meditation Hall, or Zendo" (p. 132, emphasis added).

A more direct condemnation of Watts' position on meditation is provided by Zen teacher Philip Kapleau (1967), who claims that it was Watts' discomfort with sitting still that motivated his insistence that meditation is not necessary. Kapleau demonstrates how, in attempting to prove that sitting meditation was not sanctioned by ancient Zen lineages, Watts misappropriated portions of a well-known koan. In this koan, Baso's master asks him why he is sitting daily in zazen. Baso replies, "I am trying to become a Buddha." The master then polishes a tile, claiming he is trying to make a mirror. When Baso objects that polishing a tile cannot make a mirror, his master points out that sitting in zazen cannot make a Buddha. Watts took this statement at face value as evidence that zazen is an ineffective approach to achieving enlightenment. However, placed in the context of the entire koan, Kapleau observes, the point of the story is not to belittle meditation, but rather to show that a Buddha cannot be *made* because Buddhahood does not exist outside of ourselves (i.e., it must be *revealed*). Zazen remains the means by which this revelation is to be effected. It is because Watts himself did not sit that he reached for an intellectual understanding of a story designed to invoke an intuitive realization, thereby, Kapleau claims, "[doing] violence to the whole spirit of the koan" (p. 22).

In addition to Zen's emphasis on sitting practice, there are other Buddhist traditions that as well place tremendous emphasis on practice. For example, the Tibetan tradition's most revered adepts are admired for their long years of intensive solitary retreat in mountain caves. Although Watts' intellectual appropriation, and particularly expression, of Eastern philosophical thought was impressive, it seems likely that his lack of a rigorous and committed sitting practice did indeed incite misinterpretation. In the ensuing critique, I consider Watts in relationship to phenomenological thought, Buddhist philosophy, and the times in which he lived. Finally, in light of these critical considerations, placed alongside his brilliance and influence, I consider the conundrum that Alan Watts represents.

WATTS IN RELATIONSHIP TO PHENOMENOLOGY

Although Watts decried conventional ways of seeing and understanding reality, he at times seemed to exhibit a subtle form of what Husserl called the *natural attitude*, which is the assumption that perceived phenomena have an existence independent of the act of perception (Hammond, Howarth, & Keat, 1991). Interestingly, this viewpoint is in line with the *Fully Automatic Model* that Watts himself critiqued, yet which nevertheless might have continued to inform his way of seeing. Merleau-Ponty (1964) expounded the *primacy of perception* over and against abstract theories of how the brain creates a representation of a separate world. As such, the *phenomenological attitude* regards that which appears as an object to the natural attitude to be, more fundamentally, a phenomenon that is *co-constituted* by the observer and that which is observed. It is only from the viewpoint of our mundane, conventional way of seeing that the phenomenon appears as a separate object. This essential role of consciousness in contributing to the appearance of the world undercuts Watts' contention that thoughts emerge from a passive process of translating the world.

In developing his organic view of the world as naturally unfolding, in contrast to the *Creator Model*, Watts argues that we are not *in* the world; rather we are *of* the world. Although this argument is effective as an initial salvo directed against the *natural* attitude, it falls short of adopting the *phenomenological* attitude. It also betrays an inconsistency with his expressed view that perception is a field relationship distinct from an encounter. Rather, in this instance Watts seems to take literally the idea that we are material beings sprung from a material world without recognizing an ontologically prior order of fundamental relatedness. Martin Heidegger (1927/1962) expressed the relationship of person to world as *Being-in-the-World* in order to convey that simultaneous to our inseparability with the world we also experience ourselves as *thrown* into the world. Being and world co-constitute one another, and arising with that co-constitution is the experience of a felt sense of alienation. This felt sense is part of our existential nature, and to dismiss it as a philosophical error as Watts does is, from the existential phenomenological point of view, to negate an essential aspect of experience, the *prima materia* of contemplative and meditative practice used to effect deep realization.

WATTS IN RELATIONSHIP TO BUDDHIST PHILOSOPHY

At the level of method, Buddhism can be seen as a descriptive phenomenology applied to the mind itself (Olendzki, 2003). Through the disciplined examination of mind in meditation, we discover the nature of phenomenal reality as it appears when we bracket our usual preconceptions and ways of seeing. This bracketing process entails suspending consideration of the *contents* of consciousness in favor of attending to the *process* of consciousness. This approach, gained through a discipline that Watts himself eschewed, has yielded extremely detailed descriptions of the nature of mind and its dynamic processes. As a result, the Abhidharma literature of so-called Source Buddhism provides psychological and philosophical elaborations on the Buddha's teachings, and tells us that what we ordinarily identify as "I" is only combinations of ever-changing physical and mental forces (Rahula, 1959). These aggregates, or *skandhas*—which consist of form, feeling, perception, mental formations, and consciousness—include but one realm of physical phenomena alongside four realms of mental phenomena. We have already examined how Watts did not recognize the mind as an organ of perception, which might favor his suggestion that most Buddhists do not believe in reincarnation. This attribution of belief is curious when one considers, as one example, Tibetan Buddhism's vast, detailed literature on the processes of death and rebirth (e.g., Coleman, Jinpa, & Dorje, 2007) and the reliance on reincarnation as a means of succession within their religious and political system (Mullin, 2001).

Watts prized the term *spiritual materialism* by which he meant that ultimately the mundane and spiritual worlds could not be separated (Nordstrom & Pilgrim, 1980). Consequently, the formation of a sense of "I" is reduced to physical and social elements, as we have seen. Consider by contrast, the explanation of the Mahayana view provided by Khenchen Palden Sherab, a tantric Buddhist master and scholar:

> The "I" exists when we start to form attachments; the "I" is nothing other than the grasping itself. As for what is doing the grasping, it is the mind. Since all notions of a grasping self are developed by the mind, the mind is the most important thing to understand. (Sherab & Dongyal, 2006, p. 10)

Here the social construction of self is but one aspect of a much more basic process that is rooted in what Buddhism calls the *three poisons* of the mind: attachment, aversion, and ignorance (Gunaratana, 1991). If the mind, as opposed to physicality or sociality, is the source of our confusion, then meditation is the primary vehicle for overcoming it. In the Buddhist view, three interrelated elements are essential to training the mind: study, contemplation, and meditation. First we must learn what has been taught in the past, and then we must contemplate it in order to critically evaluate it and relate it to our own experience. Finally, we must suspend conceptual thinking in order to experience the nature of mind directly in meditation.

Watts seemed to think that study and contemplation were enough, and, taken alone, they no doubt were beneficial to him. But can they provide full liberation? Recall Watts' statement about the barrenness of philosophical reflection divorced from poetic imagination—although these two "legs" to walk on suffice for matters of psychological inquiry, from a Buddhist perspective they do not stand up to the task of inquiring into the ultimate nature of reality, which can only be found in transrational investigation of the nature of mind. Study and contemplation provide suitable conditions whereby the act of meditation can lead to direct realization of the nature of reality, but are not in themselves sufficient.

From the Mahayana Buddhist perspective, meditation practice reveals wisdom and compassion to be the two inseparable qualities of our true nature (Ray, 2000). Scholar and meditation master Khenchen Palden Sherab explains that "compassion is the beneficial thought that moves you to help other sentient beings. It arises when you see their misery and pain, and you feel from the depth of your heart that you want to remove that suffering" (Sherab & Dongyal, 2006, p. 51). By contrast, wisdom is the realization of emptiness, the understanding that nothing that arises phenomenally, and to which we ordinarily impute solid, substantial existence, actually exists independently of other factors. By practicing beneficent actions at the relative level, one comes into realization of emptiness, and by practicing on emptiness through meditation, compassion spontaneously grows. "These two natures, the absolute and the relative, are not opposites; they always arise together. They have the same nature; they are inseparable like a fire and its heat or the sun and light. Emptiness and compassion are not two separate elements joined together; they always coexist" (p. 52). In this sense, we could frame wisdom and compassion as the true two "legs" for gaining knowledge. An attempt to gain wisdom without compassion keeps the endeavor lodged in the head, whereas true spiritual realization entails using the head in the service of the heart.

I am reminded of a Zen story about a student who presents his teacher with a flower in attempting to answer a koan. The teacher responds, "Too intellectual." This is my image of Watts—that his spontaneity held residual elements of self-consciousness. In this view, he hadn't fully escaped the double-bind that he so articulately and brilliantly described because he hadn't engaged in paradox at the deepest levels. Perhaps this is why in his writings he often conflated the concepts paradox and contradiction. But a paradox is only a contradiction when viewed from the rationalistic mindset; when that mindset is relaxed, one can examine the situation more deeply and move beyond one's intellectual appropriations. When Watts conflated the mundane and the sublime, reducing the mystical to the physical, he did so in contradiction of the Mahayana view that although at the ultimate level samsara and nirvana are one, at the relative level they are distinct, and these two truths, relative and absolute, are mutually interdependent. Although this formulation of the relative and the absolute are at once different and completely the same is confusing to our duality minds, it is understood to require dedicated practice to resolve this paradox with direct knowledge that lies beyond the realm of intellect (Gyamtso, 1994).

Watts in Relationship to His Times

Perhaps it is largely in light of Watts' upbringing in a strict boarding school, and the intense conformity that marked the era in which he lived, that he construed *maya*, the illusory nature of conventional reality, as a social phenomenon, whereas Mahayana Buddhism understands it as a mental phenomenon. On this point, Watts' writings are more aligned with postmodern than Eastern sensibilities. Clearly, Watts exerted a tremendous influence on the countercultural milieu of the 1960s, helping to galvanize youth rebellion while simultaneously feeding off of it. In fact, he himself suggested that the American Academy of Asian Studies that he co-founded with Frederic Spiegelberg was "one of the principle roots of what later came to be known, in the early sixties, as the San Francisco Renaissance" (Watts, 1972, p. 245). An equally interesting question is what influence Watts' teachings have had on spirituality in the West today.

In 1980, Nordstrom and Pilgrim scathingly observed that "the spiritual climate in America has already significantly changed in a direction away from Watts's wayward way . . . all over the country people are beginning to realize that spirituality is fundamentally a matter of practice, discipline, and effort" (p. 397). Certainly any number of factors could be attributed to this development, not the least of which is the Diaspora of Tibetan lamas to the West following the 1959 Chinese invasion, bringing with them their concentrated practice ethic. In contrast to Nordstrom and Pilgrim's observation, however, is the flourishing of the so-called "New Age" movement in which a fascination with spirituality has replaced the experimentation with drugs and sex of the 1960s. At one level, the New Age movement expresses a continuation of American spirituality rooted in the Transcendentalist movement's rebellion against the orthodoxy of Protestantism (Schmidt, 2005). Even so, such pioneering efforts, like all spiritual seeking, are subject to traps, including the overly selective appropriation of aspects of religious traditions that robs them of the fuller context from which they derive their effectiveness and potency. Although such individualized spiritual exploration can lead to authentic engagement, it can also serve neurotic attachment.

The Tibetan meditation master Chögyam Trungpa recognized this development as soon as he arrived in America to teach, delivering in the early 1970s his famous lectures on *spiritual materialism* (Trungpa, 1973). Here spiritual materialism is meant in a different way than Watts used it, although as Nordstrom and Pilgrim (1980) point out, it is equally applicable. Trungpa's spiritual materialism refers to the tendency of the ego to appropriate the spiritual path to its own purposes, resulting in an inflated sense of oneself as a spiritual person. When we take up only those aspects of a spiritual tradition that appeal to us, we don't face the shadow elements that are also essential aspects of the path. As archetypal psychologist James Hillman (1975) colorfully expresses it, what is omitted is "the thick yellow loam of richly pathologized imagery—demons, monsters, grotesque Goddesses, tortures, and obscenities" (p. 67). Consequently, he continues, "the archetypal content of Eastern doctrines as expressed through the archetypal structures of the Western psyche becomes a major and systematic denial of pathologizing" (p. 67). By pathologizing, Hillman refers to activities that traditional psychology labels pathological, but that are ineluctably part of being human. Like Adam and Eve hiding their sexual organs, we ordinarily repress our pathologizing; in spiritual materialism, we use spirituality as a means of exiling them to the far reaches of the psyche, from which they will find unconscious and potentially pernicious expression. Naturally, we are left to wonder to what extent Watts might have contributed to the spiritual materialism that Trungpa found when he arrived in America.

WATTS AS CONUNDRUM

One conspicuous detail about Watts was his alcoholism, which many have regarded as indicating that he had not achieved realization. If we accept that his alcoholism reflected a neurotic state—suggested by his having once remarked, "But I don't like myself when I am sober" (Huang, 1975, p. 125)—we must ask whether it is the nature of psychospiritual development that psychological health and spiritual realization necessarily always proceed together, or whether they can advance along separate lines. Depending on our view, it is not difficult to portray Watts as having fallen prey to a kind of *spiritual bypassing* (Welwood, 2000), in which he used his intellect to absorb himself in spiritual concerns at the expense of attending to healthy psychological development. Engaging in disciplined meditation practice would have required that he confront his basic anxiety, rather than distracting himself from it by drinking and womanizing. From this vantage point, we could explain Watts' materialistic approach to spirituality (in both senses of the term) as signifying an attempt to *transcend* his situation, rather than to *transform* it. Transcendence without transformation involves a splitting, a leaving behind of something that remains unresolved, as opposed to transforming that which is immanent into something that, through reconfiguration, transcends its earlier structure (Pope, 2006). Therefore, one possible explanation for Watts' questionable behaviors is his own difficulty in facing his personal demons. Rather than inviting those demons in for tea, as did the Indian saint Milarepa (Lhalungpa, 1977), Watts kept them exiled. At least in the abstract, this explanation seems rather plausible. And it may be relatively true.

However, let's consider a similar example with a different conclusion. Tibetan teacher Chögyam Trungpa also was a rascal who drank heavily and slept with female students. Nevertheless, within his tradition, his credentials as an enlightened master are untarnished. His teachings were incredibly profound, he produced many Western students who have become respected teachers and writers (e.g., Pema Chödrön, Reginald Ray, John Welwood, and Han de Wit) and he is revered by his peers as a reincarnate lama who attained the highest realization. Although it is tempting to suggest that Trungpa was a neurotic who was also enlightened, Reginald Ray offers an alternative explanation. Ray (2005) argues that, owing to his training in Tibet, including intensive meditation practice under the tutelage of great beings, Trungpa had become a genuine *siddha*, a *crazy wisdom* master who flouted convention in order to help liberate beings. In keeping with this tradition, Trungpa employed alcohol and sex as skillful means appropriate to working with the wild, spiritually materialistic students that he found when he came to America. Ram Dass (1989), in having worked through his own initial judgments of Trungpa's behaviors, entertains a similar conclusion:

> Trungpa Rinpoche had taken [his students] through their obsessions and on to deeper practices. He was not afraid, while most of the other traditions avoided such risks for fear that someone would get lost along the way. A Tantric teacher is not afraid to lead us through our own dark side. Thus you never know whether the Tantric is an exquisite teacher or hung up on his or her own obsessions. (p. 183)

And it seems we find ourselves at a similar crossroads with Alan Watts.

Granted, Watts was not recognized as a reincarnate lama, and certainly he did not engage in intensive meditation practice. Although Trungpa himself was something of an iconoclast, he nevertheless depended on the very traditions that had brought him to the point that he could, as a crazy wisdom yogi, transcend traditional forms, similar to the Buddhist adage that the teachings are a raft to the other shore and are not to be an encumbrance once you get there. Is it possible that Watts achieved the other shore through his experimentation with psychotropic drugs, only to have abandoned them once he got there? In his autobiography he famously remarked: "My retrospective attitude to LSD is that when one has received the message, one hangs up the phone" (Watts, 1972, p. 347). Was this medium, this "phone," an adequate technology to bring him to the same point as someone like Trungpa?

In a passage from his biography of Zen master Shunryu Suzuki, David Chadwick (1999) observes that Watts "had interpreted Zen to millions and helped to open the minds of a generation, yet Suzuki's simple presence could make him feel off balance" (p. 381). One evening late in Suzuki's life, Watts paid the master a visit at Tassajara Zen Center. During a long conversation, Suzuki and his wife were mostly silent while, according to Chadwick, Watts "lost his cool," and was "chatting nervously" (p. 381) while periodically excusing himself to fetch more alcohol. The next day, one of Suzuki's students who had been present commented of Watts: "We used to think he was profound until we found the real thing" (p. 381). To that comment, Suzuki suddenly declared with great intensity: "You completely miss the point about Alan Watts! You should notice what he has done. He is a great bodhisattva" (p. 381).

Shunryu Suzuki's appreciation of Watts balances the negative view offered by Kapleau earlier. However, whereas Kapleau's criticism of Watts offered evidence leading to a definite conclusion, Suzuki's spontaneous assessment, as reported from a biographer's memory, is unclear and open to a variety of interpretations. Maybe, for example, Suzuki was intending to cut through his student's arrogance. Maybe he spontaneously was defending a friend and bene-factor. Maybe he was speaking from the perspective of his own pure vision. However, if we take at face value the notion that Watts was a great bodhisattva, then Suzuki's wording is significant: "You should notice what he has done." I understand this to mean that we should not look at the man in all of his flaws; rather, we should look at his accomplishments. And, as Suzuki's biographer says, Watts did indeed turn millions onto Eastern thought as he "helped to open the minds of a generation." After all, a bodhisattva is regarded as one who is not yet enlightened, but devotes him or herself to the task of liberating others nonetheless.

If Watts operated from the materialistic mindset indicated earlier, perhaps that was appropriate to his times. The post-1950s American era was primed for and receptive to an interpretation of liberation as freedom from stifling conformity. That Watts was raised in a stifling British boarding school envi-ronment contributed to making him the right man for the job. He entered into and deepened the current of American spiritualism with its individualist ethic, creating his own unique fusion of various traditions in such a way that the types of misinterpretations for which he has been criticized perhaps were inevitable. In this way, he promoted his own rendering of the *perennial philoso-phy*: "Taking the premises of Christian dogmatics, Hindu mythology, Buddhist psychology, Zen practice, psychoanalysis, behaviorism, or logical positivism, I have tried to show that all are aiming, however disputatiously, at one center" (Watts, 1972, p. 4). Ferrer (2002) compellingly argues that "most universalist visions distort the essential message of the various religious traditions" (p. 71). With its subtle form of Cartesianism, the perennial philosophy makes a priori assumptions, privileges a nondual monistic metaphysics, and is geared toward an objectivist epistemology. Although such an approach might succeed in free-ing oneself of conventional thinking at one level, there may be additional, more subtle conventions to break through. Still, Watts made no pretenses to being anything other than an entertainer, albeit a gifted and brilliant one who, indeed, influenced a generation.

CONCLUSION

Alan Watts contributed to our understanding of psychospiritual transforma-tion by applying the broad perspective of Eastern spiritual thought to Western psychology. With this influence, he understood that personal transformation is first and foremost a process of learning to see: to see in new ways and to see what ultimately is. He was an effective and exciting translator and transmitter of distant cultures who helped to foment and reflect the radical social move-ments in 1960s America. Watts' use of Eastern thought to deconstruct social influence represents an effective response to the stultifying conformity of his own era in the same way that Freud's emphasis on sexual repression reflected the Victorian culture within which he lived. As with Freud, Watts' influence is profound and far-reaching, and the movement that follows him, and that he largely inspired, is deepening and refining engagement with the philosophies he introduced. Trungpa famously predicted that "Buddhism would come to the West as a psychology" (Goleman, 2005). Today this prediction seems quite prescient, and Alan Watts stands out as one of its earliest and most intriguing forerunners.

REFERENCES

Becker, E. (1973). *The denial of death.* New York: The Free Press.

Chadwick, D. (1999). *Crooked cucumber.* New York: Broadway.

Coleman, G., Jinpa, T., & Dorje, G. (2007). *The Tibetan book of the dead: First complete translation* (Deluxe). New York: Penguin Classics.

Combs, A. W. (1999). *Being and becoming: A field approach to psychology.* New York: Springer.

Dass, R. (1989). Promises and pitfalls of the spiritual path. In S. Grof & C. Grof (Eds.), *Spiritual emergency: When personal transformation becomes a crisis* (pp. 171–187). Los Angeles: Jeremy P. Tarcher.

Ferrer, J. N. (2002). Revisioning transpersonal theory: A participatory vision of human spirituality. Albany: State University of New York Press.

Fink, B. (1999). *A clinical introduction to Lacanian psychoanalysis: Theory and technique.* Cambridge, MA: Harvard University Press.

Fitzgerald, F. S. (2000). The crack-up. In J. C. Oats & A. Atwan (Eds.), *The best American essays of the century* (pp. 139–152). New York: Houghton Mifflin. (Original work published 1936)

Freud, S. (1963). Recommendations for physicians on the psychoanalytic method of treatment (J. Rivieri, Trans.). In P. Rieff (Ed.), *Therapy and technique* (pp. 117–126). New York: Macmillan. (Original work published 1912)

Furlong, M. (1986). *Zen effects: The life of Alan Watts.* Boston: Houghton.

Goleman, D. (2005). Foreword. In C. R. Gimian (Ed.), *The sanity we are born with: A Buddhist approach to psychology.* Boston: Shambhala.

Govinda, L. (1961). *The psychological attitude of early Buddhist philosophy.* London: Rider.

Gunaratana, V. H. (1991). *Mindfulness in plain English.* Boston: Wisdom.

Gyamtso, T. (1994). *Progressive stages of meditation on emptiness.* Auckland, New Zealand: Zhyisil Chokyi Ghatsal.

Hammond, M., Howarth, J., & Keat, R. (1991). *Understanding phenomenology.* Oxford, UK: Blackwell.

Heidegger, M. (1962). *Being and time.* San Francisco: HarperCollins. (Original work published 1927)

Hillman, J. (1975). *Re-visioning psychology.* New York: HarperCollins.

Huang, C. (1975). Foreword. In A. W. Watts, *Tao: The watercourse way* (pp. vii–xiii). New York: Pantheon.

Kapleau, P. (1967). *The three pillars of Zen: Teaching, practice, and enlightenment.* Boston: Beacon Press.

Lacan, J. (1977). The mirror stage as formative of the function of the I as revealed in psychoanalytic experience (A. Sheridan, Trans.). In J. Lacan (Ed.), *Écrits: A selection* (pp. 1–7). New York: W. W. Norton.

Lhalungpa, L. P. (1977). *The life of Milarepa.* New York: Penguin.

Loy, D. (1996). *Lack and transcendence: The problem of death and life in psychotherapy, existentialism, and Buddhism.* Amherst, NY: Humanity.

May, R. (1983). *The discovery of being: Writings in existential psychology.* New York: W.W. Norton.

McTaggart, L. (2002). *The field.* New York: HarperCollins.

Mead, G. H. (1956). *The social psychology of George Herbert Mead* (A. Strauss, Ed.). Chicago: University of Chicago Press.

Merleau-Ponty, M. (1964). *The primacy of perception: And other essays on phenomenological psychology, the philosophy of art, history, and politics.* Evanston, IL: Northwestern University Press.

Mullin, G. H. (2001). *The fourteen Dalai Lamas: A sacred legacy of reincarnation.* Sante Fe, NM: Clear Light.

Nhat Hanh, T. (2002). *No death, no fear: Comforting wisdom for life.* New York: Riverhead.

Nordstrom, L., & Pilgrim, R. (1980). The wayward mysticism of Alan Watts. *Philosophy East and West, 30*(3), 381–401.

Olendzki, A. (2003). Buddhist psychology. In S. R. Seagall (Ed.), *Encountering Buddhism: Western psychology and Buddhist teachings.* Albany: State University of New York Press.

Pope, A. (2006). *From child to elder: Personal transformation in becoming an orphan at midlife.* New York: Peter Lang.

Rahula, W. (1959). *What the Buddha taught.* New York: Grove Press.

Ray, R. A. (2000). *Indestructible truth: The living spirituality of Tibetan Buddhism.* Boston: Shambhala.

Ray, R. A. (2005). Chögyam Trungpa as a Siddha. In F. Midal (Ed.), *Recalling Chögyam Trungpa* (pp. 197–219). Boston: Shambhala.

Ricoeur, P. (1985). The power of speech: Science and poetry. *Philosophy Today, 29,* 59–70.

Romanyshyn, R. (1989). *Technology as symptom and dream.* London: Routledge.

Schmidt, L. (2005). *Restless souls: The making of American spirituality.* San Francisco: HarperCollins.

Sherab, P., & Dongyal, T. (2006). *Opening to our primordial nature.* Ithaca, NY: Snow Lion.

Snygg, D., & Combs, A. W. (1949). *Individual behavior.* New York: Harper.

Suzuki, D. T. (1964). *An introduction to Zen Buddhism.* New York: Grove Press.

Taylor, E. (2003). Buddhism and Western psychology: An intellectual memoir. In *Encountering Buddhism: Western psychology and Buddhist teachings.* Albany: State University of New York Press.

Trungpa, C. (1973). *Cutting through spiritual materialism.* Boston: Shambhala.

van den Berg, J. H. (1961). *The changing nature of man: Introduction to a historical psychology.* New York: W.W. Norton.

Watts, A. W. (1960). *This is it: And other essays on Zen and spiritual experience.* New York: Pantheon Books.

Watts, A. W. (1961). *Psychotherapy east and west.* New York: Random House.

Watts, A. W. (1962). *The joyous cosmology: Adventures in the chemistry of consciousness.* New York: Vintage Books.

Watts, A. W. (1964). *Beyond theology: The art of godmanship.* New York: Random House.

Watts, A. W. (1966). *The book: On the taboo against knowing who you are.* New York: Vintage Books.

Watts, A. W. (1971). *Does it matter? Essays on man's relation to materiality.* New York: Random House.

Watts, A. W. (1972). *In my own way: An autobiography 1915–1965.* New York: Pantheon.

Watts, A. W. (1975). *Tao: The watercourse way.* New York: Pantheon Books.

Watts, A. W. (2004). *Out of your mind: Essential listening from the Alan Watts archives.* Boulder, CO: Sounds True.

Welwood, J. (2000). *Toward a psychology of awakening: Buddhism, psychotherapy, and the path of personal and spiritual transformation.* Boston & London: Shambhala.

CHAPTER TEN

Buddhist Wisdom in the West: A Fifty-Year Perspective on the Contributions of Alan Watts

Kaisa Puhakka

As a student of Indian and Comparative Philosophy in the mid-1960s, I witnessed the encounter between Asian wisdom and American culture from a particular perspective—that of the scholar and philosopher in the Academy. At conferences I listened to philosophers and linguists discoursing on topics like "knowledge" and "reality" and the epistemological implications of "enlightenment" in the Sanskrit and Tibetan texts of Vedanta and Buddhism. Yet I often found myself wondering about these scholars, whether they really knew what they were talking about. Arrogant thoughts from a graduate student to be sure, but I could not help but feel that something was missing in these learned and highly technical discourses.

The prevailing attitude in the Academy was that scholarly objectivity could only be maintained if one did not get personally involved in the traditions one was studying. "Involvement" meant taking up a practice, such as medita-tion, the prescription of which seemed to be the conclusion of many of those scholarly texts. On occasion, there were hushed rumors in those circles about so-and-so having a secret "practice," and oh, how scandalous! The paradox in the situation did not escape me: These fine scholars were studying texts about reality and about knowing reality that said you have to change your usual ways of knowing to actually know what the texts were saying. They were drawn to these texts no doubt by that very challenge yet thought they should not undertake the disciplined practice necessary to meet it.

I took up meditation practice in the Buddhist tradition. For twenty-five years, mine was a solo practice in which I was initially guided by my renegade scholarly mentor. My sense of being alone in my practice was reinforced by my belief that Buddhism and Asian wisdom in general could not break through the barrier I had seen in the Academy to make a real impact on American culture. Certainly, philosophy, linguistics, or religion as understood and taught in the Academy were not the door through which Asian wisdom would enter into the general American culture.

As it turned out, I was wrong about Asian wisdom not being able to make an impact on the American culture. There was already then a movement afoot known as the Counterculture, and it was bringing Buddhism and especially Zen to the American popular consciousness. Alan Watts (1915–1973) was a key figure in this movement. He had written his first book about Zen that stirred his Western audiences already in the 1930s (*The Spirit of Zen*, 1936/1955a) and had written voluminously on the subject after that time (Watts, 1940/1970, 1948, 1955b, 1957/1989b). Watts' mission was to bring Zen and Asian wisdom to people in the streets of America. And his unique talents allowed him to be remarkably successful at this mission. By the end of the millennium, Zen had become a household word if not in mainstream America, certainly in the Counterculture and the subsequent New Age popular movements.

But I was right in thinking that religion, philosophy, and linguistics were not the door through which Asian wisdom would enter into the general American culture. There was another door, and it was psychotherapy. Alan Watts had discovered it. In the opening lines to his *Psychotherapy East and West* (1961/1975), Watts said: "If we look deeply into such ways of life as Buddhism and Taoism, Vedanta and Yoga, we do not find either philosophy or religion as these are understood in the West. We find something more nearly resembling psychotherapy" (p. 3).

Those words struck me when I read them in the mid-1960s, and they continued to resonate with me several years later when I left philosophy to study psychology and psychotherapy. I found a natural fit between the Buddha's practical emphasis and intent to alleviate suffering and the profession of psychotherapy. This fit had been entirely missed in the Academy where the lines were sharply drawn among disciplines. Academic psychology, having extricated itself from philosophy, was busy trying to be objective and scientific, and there was no room in it for Eastern thought or Buddhism. Psychotherapy, however, mostly takes place in the world outside of the universities where the objective scientific posture tends to soften and fade into irrelevance in the face of the myriad forms of real-life suffering for which people seek help from the profession.

Alan Watts articulated this natural fit between Western psychotherapy and Asian wisdom, particularly Buddhism and Zen. But he did more than that: His lucid, down-to-earth exposition of Zen resonated with the Western psyche and jump-started the integration of Zen and other Asian wisdom traditions with Western psychotherapy that is still under way. Today there are areas of research and practice in the interface of Buddhism and psychotherapy not envisioned by Watts. There are also problematic ways in which the integration has proceeded in the popular culture and the profession of psychotherapy that were anticipated by Watts and on which his insights continue to challenge as well as inspire. In this chapter, I reflect on Watts' contributions to the integration of Buddhism and other Asian wisdom traditions into American popular culture and into psychotherapy, and his continued relevance to these areas.

WATTS' APPROACH TO THE TRANSMISSION
OF ASIAN WISDOM AND ZEN

Watts had illustrious friends among both scholars and practitioners of Zen, some American and others teachers who had come to America from Japan in the 1950s and 1960s. Among these friends were such influential figures as Christmas Humphreys, J. Krishnamurti, D. T. Suzuki, Sokei-an Sasaki, and Ruth Sasaki. Although he certainly learned much from these people, Watts never entered a formal discipleship with them. Nor did he sit at the feet of a Master of any of the traditions or take up a disciplined practice of any sort other than learn Chinese language and calligraphy (Stuart, 1983). He also did not travel to Asia to learn firsthand from the culture and practitioners there until the 1960s, after he had already written his most influential works on Zen and Eastern wisdom.

Watts relied on his own decidedly Western lens for interpreting Asian wisdom, and he did this with a confidence that had not a trace of apology in it. He was interested in the kind of Zen that would capture the minds and hearts of his audiences and revitalize their vision for life. He had little patience and perhaps even a little contempt for the traditionalists who were concerned with preserving the authentic Asian forms of disciplined training associated with Zen, and apparently, he did not think it necessary for people to undertake a study of the original texts of these traditions to the depth and extent he had done himself. For Watts, there was the "essence" and "spirit" of Zen that had nothing to do with the cultural forms in which it was embedded, either Asian or Western. It was this "essence" that he was interested in transmitting.

CAPTURING THE ESSENCE

Zen is famous for defying clear exposition and remains inscrutable by most accounts even today. The practitioners of Zen often claim to "do" Zen while admitting they don't really understand what they are doing. And most add that when it comes to Zen, understanding is not necessary and is likely to be an obstacle, anyway. While there may be a certain truth to this, when adopted as a *position* of anti-intellectualism, such a view can become a license for promoting confusion and even dullness that may in the end become an even greater obstacle for the practitioner. Watts was aware of this trap and stayed clear of it. He had an almost uncanny ability to capture and make accessible the most profound and at the same time most elusive essence of the Mahayana Buddhist and Zen teachings. His language was down to earth and his illustrations stunning in their hominess, yet his words rarely missed the subtlety of the teachings. On the contrary, they distilled the teaching to a simplicity that seemed intrinsic to the teaching itself. Over the years and decades, the words got simpler and simpler, and he was eventually criticized by friends and associates of repeating himself, of losing his edge (Stuart, 1983). Yet when it was there, the distillation had the diamond quality of depth and clarity.

In this regard, I find a lecture posthumously published (Watts, 1965/1999) quite remarkable. Delivered on a tour to Japan in the mid-1960s, it expounds on a phenomenon he had discussed extensively in his other writings (e.g., Watts, 1966/1989a) known as the "double-bind." The double-bind manifests in the intractable conflicts and impasses that result when trying to be or do something negates the very thing one is trying to be or do (i.e., the bind: you are not what you are supposed to be; the double-bind: you should try to be it, but trying will guarantee that you will not be it). The double-bind is ubiquitous in the exhortations of religion ("Thou shalt love the Lord, thy God") and in the familial and societal expectations we deal with every day (you should "be spontaneous," "act naturally," "love yourself," "be genuine," etc.). The double-bind associated with spiritual practice can be particularly intense ("you should be enlightened, wise," or "the loving being you truly are"). Watts took the double-bind to the deepest existential levels and showed how Zen addresses it there. The double-bind that is deepest in all of us, he said, is "You must go on living." This and similar exhortations, often unconsciously operating within us, arrest the natural flow of life. According to Watts (1965/1999), "The purpose of Zen is to make this double bind visible, so that you can see how stupid it is" (p. 62).

Anyone who has undertaken a rigorous study of Zen, especially involving *koan* practice, will recognize in this a succinct and accurate statement of the purpose of Zen and of the paradoxical nature of the entire endeavor of Zen practice (Puhakka, 1998). A koan traps the practitioner in a double-bind that is, as Lin Chi, the founder of Rinzai Zen put it, like a red hot iron ball stuck in your throat that you cannot swallow and cannot spit out (Watson, 1993). Many people object to the harshness of Zen discipline, especially as it is done in the Rinzai tradition. But Watts who neither practiced nor advocated it understood the motive behind such a practice: "The Zen teacher will be well aware of everything he is doing and what tricks he is playing on you, but he will play them anyway, because behind it all he has the compassionate intent of getting you into such a fierce double bind that you will see how stupid it is and let go of it" (Watts, 1965/1999, p. 63).

MAGIC WITH WORDS

A feature of Watts' approach that may strike especially contemporary students of Zen as being peculiar is that it relied entirely on words. Nonverbal activity such as disciplined training or practice was absent from Watts' teaching arsenal. As mentioned before, he did not take up such a practice himself nor recommended it to his audiences. In my early readings of Watts, this aroused in me the same reservation I had with the scholars in the academy: I wondered if Watts *really* knew what he was talking about.

The conviction with which he spoke and wrote certainly made it sound as though he did know what he was talking about. He believed he could cut to the chase of the deep layers of human conditioning with his insightful analyses of the workings of the double-bind. In this belief, Watts took sides in a controversy as old as the Eastern practice traditions themselves regarding the role of disciplined practice in liberation or enlightenment. On one side of the controversy is the "Sudden Enlightenment" school, which maintains that enlightenment or liberation is an unconditioned state and therefore, no amount of practice (conditioned activity) can bring it about. On the other side is the "Gradual Enlightenment" school, which maintains that enlightenment comes bit by bit with patient and diligent practice. Watts was a passionate advocate of Sudden Enlightenment, and for this he drew support from some of the most celebrated Buddhist teachings from schools of Indian Mahayana Buddhism that flourished in the second through fifth centuries, C.E. and are regarded by most scholars as foundational to Zen and Tibetan Buddhism. These were the Madhyamika and Yogacara, and they included such thinkers as Nagarjuna, Chandrakirti, Asanga, and Vasubandhu (Kalupahana, 1986; Lindtner, 1997; Padmakara Translation Group, 2004). These sages expounded a radical teaching aimed particularly at practitioners with great intellectual prowess and a strong attachment to such prowess. Theirs was an uncompromisingly deconstructive teaching that exposes the self-contradictory nature of all views or assertions about reality. This teaching silences the thinking mind by shattering its foundational beliefs. It was called "Middle Way" because it eschewed both extremes of affirming and of denying any and all views or beliefs. Enlightenment itself is a construct of the thinking mind, and when that construct (and the "self" that is attached to it) is finally let go, the original, already and always enlightened state would spontaneously shine forth. In this sense, enlightenment is said to be "sudden"; nothing needed to be—or even could be—done to bring it about.

An introduction to the Madhyamika, Yogacara, and the subsequent Hua-yen School in China form a center piece of Watts' most important work on Zen, *The Way of Zen* (1957/1989b). The crispness and lucidity with which he discusses the subtleties of the Middle Way and Hua-yen teachings is unsurpassed by anything written about them since for popular audiences. In fact, not much is available about these elusive but foundational teachings in the popular literature.

A point that Watts appears to have missed—or glossed over—about the Middle Way teachings is that they do not endorse a position "for" or "against" practice. If there is anything they are "for," it is silence. Watts, by contrast, liked talking and believed in the power of words. This belief appears to be more a matter of temperament and personal inclination than of a misunderstanding of the Middle Way teachings. I return to it briefly toward the end of this chapter.

But Watts clearly wanted to do more than talk; he wanted to bring people to Zen, to have them taste its essence directly. And he did with his words what the dry scholarly expositions of the experts had not been able to do: open the hearts and minds of his audience, wake them up from their slumber, nudge them toward insights. His words seemed to almost touch the things he talked about and promised enlightenment, not down the road of arduous discipline but right here and now. In fairness, he never claimed to deliver enlightenment to his readers or listeners. But at times he seemed to bring it intoxicatingly near. At the very least, he wielded magic with words.

Watts' gift of gab was legendary. But I believe that his magic had also much to do with the psychological orientation of his approach and his penchant for drawing parallels as well as pointing out differences between Western psycho-therapy and Eastern wisdom (Watts, 1940/1970, 1961/1975). He explored topics such as the search for the "true self" that seemed to intersect the two worlds in a language that felt familiar yet opened a door to expansive insights beyond the familiar (Watts, 1940/1970, 2003). He named the most secret and yet most pervasive pain of his listeners. Ours is the "Age of Anxiety," he declared in the title to the opening chapter of *The Wisdom of Insecurity* (1951) and, diving right into the deepest existential pain of the meaninglessness and futility of our lives, he deftly exposed the illusions by which we keep it at bay. Yet he also managed to get a laughter and perhaps cathartic relief from his readers. He did this with vivid images that are poignant and funny and amazingly effective in driving the point home. Thus he would disarm his listeners by saying:

> I may not, perhaps, be forgiven for introducing sober matters with a frivolous notion, but the problem of making sense out of the seem-ing chaos of experience reminds me of my childish desire to send someone a parcel of water in the mail. The recipient unties the string, releasing the deluge in his lap.(p. 13)

Watts' point being that the futility has to do not with life itself but with "the task of trying to get the water of life into neat and permanent packages"(p. 14).

BUDDHISM AND ZEN IN CONTEMPORARY AMERICA

Buddhism and Zen in America have changed in many ways in the half a cen-tury or so since Watts along with a few other notable Buddhist scholars and practitioners introduced it to the Counterculture. Opportunities for learning about Zen and for trying out various practice traditions abound today, not just in California's Bay Area but in large and even middle-sized cities throughout America. The teachers now are "second generation," even "third generation," mostly Americans whose teachers were either Asian transplants, mainly from Japan but also from Vietnam and Korea, or Americans who studied with Asian-trained teachers.

The audiences whose hearts and minds Watts captured in the middle decades of the twentieth century were, for the first part, new and fresh to the message, perhaps one could even say naïve, and no doubt they were more susceptible than audiences today to the exciting feeling that enlightenment is just around the corner. The essence of Zen that Watts sought to transmit paid little attention to the differences in approaches and interpretations found within the Asian traditions. Some informed critics of his time characterized Watts' Zen as a generic "Zen-lite" (Stuart, 1983), but most of his audience, having really nothing to compare it with, were probably oblivious to such criticism or at any rate failed to see it as anything more than academic hair-splitting.

There is today a more sophisticated understanding of the differences and unique approaches among the various Zen traditions, and some of this under-standing has seeped into the popular, if not mainstream, culture. Also, with the influx of Tibetan Buddhism and the variety and richness of its traditions into the popular culture, Zen is now positioned as one among several Buddhist traditions and no longer the major Asian wisdom tradition as it was for Watts.

But by far the most significant feature of the contemporary scene is the psychological sophistication with which teachers and students alike approach the study and practice of Zen and of meditation and spiritual practice in general. Watts was certainly instrumental for preparing the soil for the meeting of Western psychotherapy and Buddhism, and this meeting has now borne fruit in many ways. There is today much talk about integrating Buddhism and psychotherapy. Even though Watts was busy doing it, in his time it was not talked about as "integration." The effort to integrate today is self-conscious and deliberate, and often has a specific meaning or application. There is now abundant literature on integrating Buddhist approaches including Zen into psychological theory and practice (Aronson, 2004; Claxton, 1986; Prendergast, Fenner, & Krystal, 2003; Segall, 2003; Welwood, 2000) and on applying techniques from Buddhist practice traditions to treating specific psychological problems (Germer, Siegel, & Fulton, 2005; Linehan, 1993; Segal, Williams, & Teasdale, 2002). And these developments are taking place not just in the fringes of culture but in its mainstream (Walsh & Shapiro, 2006). Also, lessons have been learned from the excesses of the early days, from the promises of liberation not delivered, and from the psychological casualties of reaching too far too fast, whether with drugs or with meditation (Engler, 1986; Vaughan, 1995). It appears that the understanding and practice of Zen and other Buddhist traditions in America have matured into a cultural form with a distinctive psychological twist that reflects the uniqueness and complexity of its new host culture.

The lens through which Americans interpret teachings and practices from Asian and other traditions has also changed somewhat. Today, Americans are more multicultural, not just in terms of their ethnic composition but in their thinking and worldviews as well. There is a greater awareness of the influence of culture in everything people do, including even the ways in which they express their spiritual aspirations. There may be even greater self-awareness of one's own cultural biases (see, e.g., Usatynski, 2001). Most importantly, there is a general feeling that cultural influence reaches deep into what might be taken as essence—that perhaps there is no such thing as universal essence but all essences are culturally constructed.

WHAT BUDDHISM IN TWENTY-FIRST-CENTURY AMERICA CAN LEARN FROM WATTS

I now address the value of Watts' contributions to the contemporary scene as outlined in the previous section. Fifty years after he wrote them, his books and lectures are reissued in paperback and widely read. His message still has appeal because it addresses the deep and enduring problems of humanity in a hopeful and up-beat manner that enlivens the spirit of optimism in the American psyche. But I believe that the greatest significance of Watts' contributions may lie in his offering a counterbalance or corrective to problematic developments in the contemporary integration of Asian wisdom traditions. There are two such developments I address here. One is the effect of constructivism on popular culture. The other is the excessive emphasis on the psychological, or what might be called the "psychologizing tendency." Both have direct impact on the understanding and practice of Buddhism and Zen (as well as other forms of Asian and indigenous spirituality) in contemporary America.

Constructivism

Constructivism is "in," especially in the social sciences and humanities. Its popularity has spilled over into the general culture where it looks more and more like crass relativism. Subjectivity is celebrated even as it is being reduced to the cultural, social, and linguistic forces (*context* is the preferred term) that construct it. In its extreme form, this relativism is evident in contemporary politics and media where truth and falsehood can no longer be easily told apart because they both depend on where the speaker (or listener) may be "coming from"—which is rarely revealed or openly and frankly discussed. In the Academy, constructivist discourse is more sophisticated, but the end result is much the same—no conclusions can be drawn about anything that don't ultimately come down to a reference to context. Context has become the new sacred cow.

Religious fundamentalists certainly take exception to the claims of constructivism. A discussion of their viewpoint, however, is beyond the scope of this chapter. But the other group more relevant to our concerns that also finds constructivism in its extreme form troubling are those with serious, even if nondoctrinal, spiritual aspirations. These include practitioners of Buddhism and other Asian wisdom traditions. Such people quest after a spirituality that transcends culture and the everyday self-experience or "ego" that is—as they are likely to concede to constructivism—culturally constructed. The champions of the spiritual viewpoint in the Academy have been Transpersonal Psychologists who, since the late 1960s, have been studying spiritual phenomena in human experience and spiritual development beyond the socially adjusted personality (Brown, 1986; Hart, Nelson, & Puhakka, 2000; Walsh & Shapiro, 1983; Washburn, 1988; Wilber, 1981). Mostly, however, their affirmations of transcendence appeal to nonordinary personal experiences and perhaps also to a metaphysical vision called the "Perennial Philosophy" (Huxley, 1945; Rothberg, 1986)—neither of which is considered acceptable by mainstream psychology and certainly fail to persuade constructivists who would point out that such personal experiences and visions are all culturally constructed.

But there is a more rigorous approach to meeting the challenge of constructivism that appeals to neither personal experience nor metaphysics. It is found within the Buddhist teachings of the Middle Way discussed earlier. This approach deconstructs the very constructs to which constructivism would reduce human experience. From the point of view of the Middle Way teachings, constructivism in its extreme forms where it becomes relativism is self-contradictory because its own claim that "all truths are relative to context" or "all truths are contextually constructed" is asserted as context-free and absolute. The Middle Way teachings demonstrate again and again that there really is nothing that can be claimed as absolutely true. Watts understood that such a demonstration is the very essence of the Buddhist and Zen teachings, and this understanding gave him a freedom to speak clearly and boldly without bowing before the sacred cow of cultural and social context but cutting right through it. His analyses of the double-bind intend to expose the very cultural constructs that shape the experience of his listeners.

This last point takes me to the second contribution of Watts' that I believe has great relevance today. This is his insight that Buddhism is, first and foremost, a social and cultural critique. To fully appreciate the significance of this, however, we must consider the other major trend in contemporary American culture, the "psychologizing tendency." This tendency is largely responsible for the aforementioned insight of Watts' getting lost in contemporary popular culture.

THE PSYCHOLOGIZING TENDENCY

Along with constructivism and relativism, a distinguishing feature of contemporary American culture (and increasingly the global consumer culture) is a tendency to refer whatever is going on in society to psychological states or experiences of individuals. This "psychologizing" tendency is most evident in, and may indeed have begun with the advertising and promotion of consumerism, but it is nowadays pervasive in arts, politics, and social interactions of all sorts. Culturally, we are more comfortable than ever airing out publicly what used to be considered private matters, such as feelings and experiences and individual life stories. This trend was already in evidence in Watts' time, and by going for what personally mattered most to people, he may well have contributed to it. But we have moved way past Watts' time when students at universities were clamoring for greater personal relevance. Today, teachers accept without question that things are meaningful only to the extent that students can relate to them with their personal feelings and associations. Critical analysis, debate, and simply cramming information—the tried and true ways in which teachers and students used to go about the business of learning—have given way to an activity that increasingly resembles psychotherapy. In the contemporary classroom, the creation of a safe and comfortable environment is of prime concern and the aim is to "facilitate" the students' own process. In short, whether in the giving or receiving end of transactions in contemporary society, we find ourselves being psychologized and can hardly help psychologizing in turn.

This psychologizing tendency has influenced American Buddhism as well. To be sure, the influence is not all negative. As I noted earlier, thanks to it attention is now given to the psychological complexities that had been overlooked by, or perhaps more likely were not relevant, in the Asian cultures that hosted Buddhism before it reached the shores of America and other Western countries. The pervasive influence of the psychologizing tendency continues to inspire research on the psychological effects of spiritual practice and on adaptations of Buddhist and other spiritual practices into psychotherapy. The psychologizing tendency may also contribute to the greater openness people today seem to have to gaining insight into their own personal issues. Bringing a sophisticated understanding of human psychology into Buddhism may indeed be the distinctive contribution of the West to Asian Buddhism.

But on the negative side, there is a popular tendency to reduce Buddhist and Zen teachings to psychology. Buddhist practitioners in America, for example, often see "enlightenment" as an experience or attribute of the human self to be attained in a narrowly personal quest. Meditation teachers tend to tailor their "dharma talks" to the psychological needs and experiences of their students and are hesitant to touch what may be deeper and more subtle teachings in the Asian texts for fear that they may seem too impersonal to their Western audiences. Psychotherapists often see Buddhism as something that offers techniques or approaches for their work with clients. In short, the wisdom of Zen and other forms of Buddhism in contemporary popular culture tend to become a sort of applied psychology, a diffuse "psychobuddhism" that has lost much of the depth and revolutionary power of the original.

THE WATTSIAN ANTIDOTE

The same Alan Watts who opened the psychological door to Asian wisdom in the West also offers an antidote to the tendency to assimilate Buddhism into psychology. His language was replete with popular psychological terms, to be sure. But far from using such words to assimilate Buddhism into psychology he saw in the former an opportunity to stretch the limits of psychology.

For Watts, Buddhism was, first and foremost, a critique of culture and society. In his own words, "Buddhism, in common with such aspects of Hinduism as Vedanta and Yoga, and with Taoism in China, is not a culture but a critique of culture, an enduring nonviolent revolution or 'loyal opposition' to the culture with which it is involved" (Watts, 1961/1975, p. 4). When Watts talks about these wisdom traditions as being "not a culture but a critique of culture," he is talking about a critique that does not simply represent a different cultural standpoint but one that deconstructs any and all such standpoints. This point bears emphasizing, for today cultural critique is most often understood in cross-cultural or multicultural terms where the presuppositions of one culture are implicitly affirmed while those of another are being questioned. All cultural presuppositions are, in principle, questioned in Buddhism, but first and foremost, those of the culture in which the Buddhist practice happens to be embedded, for it is this culture that constructs the practitioner's sense of self and world. It is this culture also—at least in the West—that spawned the field of psychology and the profession of psychotherapy, and thus the kind of cultural critique Watts advocated and drew from Buddhism can also be a critique of psychology and psychotherapy.

In seeing Buddhism as first and foremost a critique of the culture with which it is involved, Watts clarified what today has become a rather confused picture of the relationship between psychotherapy and Buddhism. Today there is a tendency in the popular culture, including the profession of psychotherapy, to view Buddhism and psychotherapy either in a symmetrical relationship where the two are equivalent alternatives that can be "mixed and matched" depending on what the situation requires, or in an asymmetrical relationship where psychotherapy is the more encompassing term and Buddhism serves as an "adjunct" that can add to the arsenal of specific techniques in psychotherapy. Watts saw and, I believe, correctly articulated an asymmetrical relationship between the two wherein Buddhism encompasses and extends beyond psychotherapy. Psychotherapy, especially as practiced in America, does not present a serious "loyal opposition" to its own culture. Post-Lacanian psychoanalysis (Deleuze & Guattari, 1977/2003), known and practiced in Europe and certain South American countries but virtually unknown in North America, is the only exception of which I am aware. Contemporary American psychotherapy, by contrast, tends to be a "loyal supporter" of the basic values of its own culture. Its capacity to alleviate the suffering of its clients is obviously limited by the extent to which it subscribes to the same cultural premises that they do.

Buddhism can offer a critique of psychotherapy's limiting premises, in a "loyal opposition" that is not out to destroy but to take psychotherapy to another level of depth. This intent to stretch psychotherapy rather than destroy or find fault with it is evident in Watts' discussions of the various psychotherapeutic approaches, including the Freudian and the Jungian theories (Watts, 1961/1975). Whether his interpretations of the psychoanalytic and other approaches he discusses are faithful to the originals in every respect may be arguable, but what allowed him to even attempt such stretching was a larger perspective that exposed the cultural premises of the psychotherapies he discussed. This larger perspective was provided by his understanding of Buddhism and Zen.

For the past decade or more I have taught psychotherapy to graduate students preparing themselves for the profession. I have also taught courses on Buddhism and psychotherapy to such students. The automatic inclination of many of the students is to "adapt" Buddhist meditation techniques to their therapeutic toolbox, thus betraying the psychologizing tendency of their culture. Trying to reorient their understanding of the relationship between psychotherapy and Buddhism often has been an uphill battle. But eventually at least a few students are persuaded to drop their quest for applicable techniques, and once they drop that quest, they begin to see that Buddhism has much more to offer to them and their client. They discover that they can take the deconstruction of the ego—including and especially their own—much farther than their psychotherapeutic work has so far allowed them to do and that they can move to an altogether new level of openness, understanding, and acceptance of their clients' as well as their own issues. I see Buddhism not as an adjunct to psychotherapy but as the larger container that can embrace and support (and challenge as well) the therapist and his or her work in containing, supporting, and challenging the client. In this, I have found much support from Watts' writings on the relationship between Buddhism and psychotherapy.

CONCLUSION: ALAN WATTS—MAGICIAN OR ILLUSIONIST?

The image of a teacher as a magician is apropos the Middle Way teachings. Nagarjuna, the founder of this school whom Watts held in high esteem, has been called the Great Magician (Lindtner, 1997). He was not, however, in the business of casting spells but rather just the opposite; he sought to wake people up from their spells, to dispel their illusions (Puhakka, 2003). Watts certainly did magic with words and dazzled his audiences with insights. But did he liberate them from spells or perhaps cast his own, more enticing spells? I believe he did some of both. To be a magician in the Nagarjunian sense would have eventually led him to give up talking and writing—at least his attachment to them—for he would have seen that all such activity is, in the final analysis, just casting spells. Watts did see this—judging from his writing—but he could not bring himself to give up talk. Earlier, I suggested that this was due to personal bias. The personal nature of his bias is evident in the following words he spoke, relatively late in life, to his audience in Japan:

> If I were to give you a truly proper and educated talk about Zen, I would gather you around and sit here in silence for five minutes and leave. This would be a much more direct exposition of it than I am

going to do instead, which is to talk about it. I am afraid that you would feel disappointed and somewhat cheated if I just left after five minutes of silence, though. (Watts, 1965/1999, pp. 50–51)

Watts loved to talk, and he hated to disappoint his audiences. He considered himself an entertainer, perhaps even more than a teacher of Zen. He even regarded himself as "part charlatan" (Stuart, 1983, p. 224), as if he was aware of casting spells to allure and entertain where silence might have been called for. Thus for all the insights and awakenings of his magic, Watts was also an illusionist whose spells shroud the silence into which they might dissolve.

In conclusion, we have come full circle to the edge of the silence where Watts brought many of his readers and listeners. There he stood himself, one might imagine, ready to jump off the edge, yet reluctant to do so. Being an entertainer cannot be enough for someone as struck by the wisdom of Zen as was Watts. I did not know Watts personally, nor am I privy to his intimate feelings and thoughts about himself in his solitude. I do know that his biographers were puzzled by the complexity of his character (Furlong, 1986; Stuart, 1983) and that toward the end of his life he drank to excess and apparently could not stand himself when sober. Especially the latter sentiment suggests that he was torn by conflict, caught in a double-bind that for him must have been made all the more unbearable by the fact of his recognition of his own predicament. Knowing better than to talk, he must have at times felt phony about talking. It seems as though life itself had become a *koan* for Watts, a red hot iron ball that was stuck in his throat that he could neither swallow nor spit out, and so he lived a tormented life in the midst of pleasure and enjoyment.

What could be viewed as Watts' personal failure is, paradoxically, testimony to the depth and clarity of his understanding. Without such understanding, he might have been at peace, satisfied that he had captured all there is to the wisdom of Zen. But he knew better, and because of this his writings are alive— dangerously alive, one might add—with a magical power to evoke insights in readers, today as much as half a century ago.

REFERENCES

Aronson, H. (2004). *Buddhist practice on Western ground: Reconciling Eastern ideals and Western psychology.* Boston, MA: Shambhala.

Brown, D. (1986). The stages of meditation in cross-cultural perspective. In K. Wilber, J. Engler, & D. Brown (Eds.), *Transformations of consciousness: Conventional and contemplative perspectives on development* (pp. 219–284). Boston: Shambhala.

Claxton G. (Ed.). (1986). *Beyond therapy: The impact of Eastern religions on psychological theory and practice.* London: Wisdom Publications

Deleuze, G., & Guattari, F. (2003). *Anti-Oedipus: Capitalism and schizophrenia.* Minneapolis: University of Minnesota Press. (Original work published 1977)

Engler, J. (1986). Therapeutic aims in psychotherapy and meditation. In K. Wilber, J. J. Engler, & D. Brown (Eds.), *Transformations of consciousness: Conventional and contemplative perspectives on development*. Boston: Shambhala.

Furlong, M. (1986). *Zen effects: The life of Alan Watts*. New York: Houghton Mifflin.

Germer, C., Siegel, R., & Fulton, P. (Eds.). (2005). *Mindfulness and psychotherapy*. New York: Guilford.

Hart, T., Nelson, P. L., & Puhakka, K. (Eds.). (2000). *Transpersonal knowing: Exploring the horizon of consciousness*. Albany: State University of New York Press.

Huxley, A. (1945). *The perennial philosophy*. New York: Harper & Row.

Kalupahana, D. J. (1986). *Nagarjuna: The philosophy of the Middle Way*. Albany: State University of New York Press.

Lindtner, P. (Trans. and studies). (1997). *Master of wisdom: Writings of the Buddhist master Nagarjuna*. Berkeley, CA: Dharma.

Linehan, M. (1993). *Cognitive-behavioral treatment of borderline personality disorder*. New York: Guilford.

Padmakara Translation Group. (2004). *Introduction to the Middle Way: Chandrakirti's Madhyamakavatara with commentary by Jamgon Mipham*. Boston: Shambhala.

Prendergast, J., Fenner, P., & Krystal, S. (2003). *The sacred mirror: Nondual Wisdom and psychotherapy*. St. Paul, MN: The Paragon House.

Puhakka, K. (1998). Dissolving the self: Rinzai Zen practice at an American monastery. *The Journal of Transpersonal Psychology, 30*(2), 135–160.

Puhakka, K. (2003). Awakening from the spell of reality: Lessons from Nagarjuna. In S. Segall (Ed.), *Encountering Buddhism: Western psychology and Buddhist teachings* (pp. 131–142). Albany: State University of New York Press.

Rothberg, D. (1986). Philosophical foundations of transpersonal psychology. An introduction to some basic issues. *The Journal of Transpersonal Psychology, 18*(1), 1–34.

Segal, Z., Williams, J. M., & Teasdale, J. (2002). *Mindfulness-based cognitive therapy for depression: A new approach to preventing relapse*. New York: Guilford.

Segall, S. (Ed.). (2003). *Encountering Buddhism: Western psychology and Buddhist teachings*. Albany: State University of New York Press.

Stuart, D. (1983). *Alan Watts*. New York: Scarborough House.

Usatynski, T. J. (2001). Hidden assumptions of modern Western contemplative cultures. *The Journal of Transpersonal Psychology, 33*(2), 131–150.

Vaughan, F. (1995). *Shadows of the sacred: Seeing through spiritual illusions*. Wheaton, IL: Quest Books.

Walsh, R., & Shapiro, D. H. (Eds.). (1983). *Beyond health and normality: Explorations of exceptional psychological well-being*. New York: Van Nostrand Reinhold.

Walsh, R., & Shapiro, S. (2006). The meeting of meditative disciplines and Western Psychology. *The American Psychologist, 61*(3), 227–239.

Washburn, M. (1988). *The ego and the dynamic ground: A transpersonal theory of human development*. Albany: State University of New York Press.

Watson, B. (Trans.). (1993). *The Zen teachings of master Lin-Chi*. Boston: Shambhala.

Watts, A. W. (1948). *Zen*. Stanford, CA: Delkin

Watts, A. W. (1951). *The wisdom of insecurity*. New York: Pantheon.

Watts, A. W. (1955a). *The spirit of Zen*. London: Murray. (Original work published 1936)

Watts, A. W. (1955b). The way of liberation in Zen Buddhism. *Asia Study Monographs*, No. 1. San Francisco: American Academy of Asian Studies.

Watts. A. W. (1970). *The meaning of happiness*. New York: Harper & Row. (Original work published 1940)

Watts, A. W. (1975). *Psychotherapy East and West*. New York: Vintage Books. (Original work published 1961)

Watts, A. W. (1989a). *The book: On the taboo against knowing who you are*. New York: Vintage Books. (Original work published 1966)

Watts, A. W. (1989b). *The way of Zen*. New York: Vintage Books. (Original work published 1957)

Watts, A. W. (1999). Buddhism in dialogue. In A. Watts, *Buddhism: The religion of no religion* (M. Watts, Ed., pp. 49–65). Boston: Tuttle. (Original work presented 1965)

Watts, A. W. (2003). *Become what you are*. Boston: Shambhala.

Welwood, J. (2000). *Toward a psychology of awakening*. Boston: Shambhala.

Wilber, K. (1981). *Up from Eden: A transpersonal view of human evolution*. Garden City, NY: Doubleday.

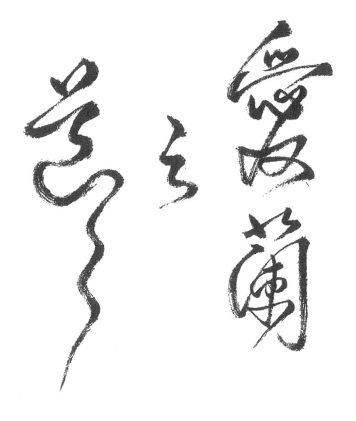

The Tao of Alan (the person who Loves Orchid~cultivation)

The Tao of Alan Watts by Chungliang Al Huang

CHAPTER ELEVEN

Watercourse Way: Still Flowing with Alan Watts

Chungliang Al Huang

After nearly a decade of collaborative teaching at various seminars and retreat centers with my mentor and friend, Alan Watts, I was honored to help on his book devoted to the essence of Daoism (Watts, 1975). It was a most inspiring and joyous period of our kindred sharing as close colleagues. I had long admired his genius of writing about the unwritable. Alan's insights were so lucidly accessible to a general readership in all his brilliant books on Asian philosophy and comparative religion. He had touched on many aspects of Dao philosophy in his previous writings, particularly in *Nature, Man and Woman* (Watts, 1958) and in his many essays during his later years compiled under the title *Cloud-hidden, Whereabouts Unknown* (Watts, 1973a).

At the time of our partnership on his new book, Alan was focused on researching and penetrating deeper into the realm of Dao philosophy and its teachings, exploring the core aspects and multiple dimensions of meaning. While engaged in this process, Alan was interested in my own elucidations of primary Chinese-language Dao texts. We shared an enjoyment for translating intricate verses chock-full of ambiguous meaning and overloaded with decodable variations. We examined the available interpretations, deliberated their accuracy, processed our conclusions, placed them aside, and subsequently began anew, trying for alternative understandings to suit our intuition (Huang, 1975a).

Also, Alan had asked me to illustrate the cover and chapter headings with cursive brush art of designated symbols appropriate to each of the chapters. As the pages lengthened we began to entertain the idea of a title for the book. Although we both shared the joy of exploring this venerated flowing practice of penmanship, it occurred to us that the very process of dipping brushes in ink to allow the symbols to appear, gliding across the paper, was indeed the "watercourse" way. Voila, "Tao: The Watercourse Way!" The title came into being. After that *"Satori"* moment, the rest of the book seemed to flow effortlessly. As I said in the foreword to the text, "Alan was going to allow this book on Taoism to write itself. He knew, as a scholar, that he was turning out another of his famous themes-and-variations on the meaning of East and West. But as a man of Tao, he also realized that he must give up controlling it intellectually" (Huang, 1975a, pp. vii–viii).

Auspiciously, during our research, Alan received a cordial reply from the eminent Cambridge University sinologist, Joseph Needham, to congratulate us on our endeavor, and with a referral to a colleague for certain specific inquiries regarding our project. To our totally unexpected delight, the colleague Needham had referred was my long-lost uncle, Professor Kai-loo Huang, who was teaching Daoist economics at Moravian College in Pennsylvania. Synchronicity and serendipity of this kind would continue until the process was temporarily suspended when Alan left for Europe for what turned out to be his final lecture tour.

During Alan's absence, I had helped to organize a weeklong series of seminars on comparative philosophy and religion in Toronto, Canada, where I was a visiting professor at York University. Alan was scheduled to preside over this eagerly awaited conference soon after returning from his European tour. Alas, it was not to be. Alan returned to his Muir Woods cottage in California completely exhausted. I spoke with him on the phone on his last evening to find him drained in energy but euphoric during a gathering of friends in his "Mandala" house (reconstructed from a circular wine vat). "Wish you could join us dancing Tai Ji tonight . . . we are playing with helium balloons. . . . I feel my spirit is flying up with them, . . ." were his last words to me. The next morning, his wife Mary Jane (Jano), awoke to find Alan gone peacefully during the night, joining other Daoist immortals in the celestial kingdom.

Alan passed on with unfinished manuscripts, mere outlines of further concepts to be explored. As already said in the foreword of the eventually published book (Watts, 1975), when all fingers pointed to me to undertake the completion of the manuscript, I simply surrendered to the wisdom from the first line of the *Tao te Ching*, paraphrasing, "The Tao that can be completed is not the Tao." However, I managed a foreword and an afterword to frame this open-ended book, and bowed to and allowed the "Watercourse Way" to naturally be in the eternal flux of becoming.

Thirty-six years later, a worthy tribute is being paid to Alan Watts' unique genius in transmitting the ineffable. More than ever, his teachings and writings in comparative philosophy, religion and psychology have continued to provide mind-shifting foundations for an ever-evolving continuum of Dao learning, further along the "Watercourse Way!"

My wish and hope in this humble contribution is to provide some balance to the scholarly and analytical essays from other colleagues by telling a few personal stories of Alan Watts, the person, his ways (Dao) of being, to illustrate his unique talents as the magically inspired teacher, the philosophical entertainer, a proud title he often claimed for himself. As friend and co-conspirator, I have experienced many joyous rides along this "Watercourse Way" with him. I am eternally grateful.

OUR FIRST ENCOUNTER

When I first met Alan Watts, he was possibly the most celebrated countercultural guru in America due to his influence on the San Francisco Renaissance about which Alan wrote the following in his autobiography:

> I know only that between, say, 1958 and 1970 a huge tide of spiritual energy in the form of poetry, music, philosophy, painting, religion, communications techniques in radio, television, and cinema, dancing, theater, and general life-style swept out of this city and its environs to affect America and the whole world, and that I have been intensely involved with it. It would be false modesty to say I had little to do with it. (Watts, 1973c, p. 284)

Beyond the admiration of the 1960s Flower Children who flocked to him in thousands wherever he appeared, he was immensely sought after by young professionals and the thoughtful intellectual elites.

My introduction to Alan was by a successful Santa Barbara attorney, Boyd E. "Buck" Hornor, who, with a few of his equally bright and "tuned-in" (but not "dropped out") colleagues in the legal profession, had formed a not-for-profit organization called The Foundation for the Study of Law and Philosophy. One of their righteously gratuitous services was to bail out marijuana inhalers and help free these hip and slightly indulgent "consciousness seekers" who were clearly delving much too deeply into their experimentations, interpreting freely and flying high with Aldous Huxley's (1954) *Doors of Perception* and Alan Watts' (1962) *Joyous Cosmology*.

Buck Hornor was married to Mary Crawford, one of my UCLA dance students. He visited my tai ji classes and handed me a copy of Watts' (1961) book, *Psychotherapy East and West*. Until then, I was strictly a sheltered academic and confined in my "well frog's view" from my dancing career. I had not heard of Alan Watts, and truthfully, had never wanted to be exposed to those countercultural social conventions, let alone inhaling—we were much too arrogant to forego our artistic clarity and pure visions; no way we would be tainted by mind-expanding drugs!

When Buck subsequently invited me to participate in a seminar by Alan Watts at the Hope Ranch in Santa Barbara, I was ready and eager to meet the man. I arrived early, and joined Buck to meet Alan at the airport. Watts was in his favorite Asian attire, a Japanese coat with beads and medallions around his neck and rosaries on his wrist, very much the look of the time, in sharp contrast to my conservative young professor's sports jacket with suede elbow patches. (To my chagrin now, both clichés of the time!!)

Alan was delighted to meet a new Asian friend, and he suggested that we dine at the one and only decent Japanese restaurant on State Street. After we sat down at a tatami-matted booth, a young Asian waitress approached us. I could see Alan's face light up, and he proceeded to order in Japanese, with great vanity, apparently trying to impress me. "Sorry, I don't speak Japanese" demurred this third-generation young woman. Much too human and obviously flustered, Alan's crest-fallen disappointment was palpable and endearing. I instantly found him a lovable, kindred spirit.

HUMAN POTENTIAL

Spontaneously, and easily, I began collaborating in Alan's teaching that very first week of our meeting. From then and there Alan helped usher me into the circle of all the "human potential" growth centers everywhere he went. With my respectable lineage and seemingly authoritative understanding of the Chinese classics and expertise in tai ji, and being the co-leader with Alan Watts, overnight I was given the position of a reluctant countercultural luminary! Teaching in concert with Alan, my learning on how to synthesize Eastern philosophy with Western psychology began. Alan Watts was my first mentor and guide on this new journey that changed my life.

Alan was a pioneer in the field of human growth and potential. He began leading seminars on Asian philosophy and the meaning of happiness after his move to New York City from London in 1939, well before there was any such phenomenon as the Human Potential Movement. His reputation grew significantly during the 1940s while serving as the Episcopal chaplain on the campus of Northwestern University. Robert Ellwood (1979) wrote that Alan's religious services during that time attracted participants from nearby places and distant locations "to a rich liturgical splendor embellished with a sense of playfulness and to the incomparable mystical sermons of he who then as later could induce with words a sense of spiritual experience and of being on the 'inside' of some cosmic secret" (p. 155).

When Alan joined the faculty of the American Academy of Asian Studies in the early 1950s, he found students seeking the illumination of a transfigured mind awakened from a spiritual slumber. "In retrospect," Alan wrote in his autobiography, "one can see that the Academy of Asian Studies was a transitional institution emerging from the failure of universities and churches to satisfy important spiritual needs" (Watts, 1973c, p. 315). He considered the Academy as a bridge to the emergence and proliferation of facilities such as Esalen Institute and other centers for personal and spiritual exploration.

Two students at the American Academy of Asian Studies, Michael Murphy and Richard Price, would eventually found the Esalen Institute at Big Sur,

California, and Alan offered the first-ever seminar on its premises in 1962. He returned repeatedly to Esalen because he felt the institute was "doing something absolutely important for the future of education and religion" by concerning itself with "matters fundamental to life . . . our relations to each other, to ourselves, and to cosmic experience (Watts, 1973c, p. 344).

Alan and I cooperatively offered seminars at Esalen and other retreat centers. In these seminars, Alan would speak eloquently on the philosophy of Dao and I presented its practical expression in the form of tai ji movement. In the midst of our final collaborative teaching at Esalen, we completed an afternoon gathering that left everyone in high spirits, and while returning to the lodge afterward:

> Alan turned to me and started to speak, ready to impress me with his usual eloquence about our successful week together. I noticed a sudden breakthrough in his expression; a look of lightness and glow appeared all around him. Alan had discovered a different way to tell me of his feelings: Yah . . . ha . . . Ho . . . Ha!Ho! . . . La Cha Om Ha Hom . . . Te Te Te . . . We gibbered and danced all the way up the hill. (Huang, 1975a, p. ix)

EAST AND WEST

My first experience teaching with Alan at Esalen Institute occurred shortly after my return from a year's research work at the Academia Sinica at the College of Chinese Culture in Taiwan. For a Chinese and a typical academic, Esalen was, at first, not an easy fit. I was much too conservative and disciplined to mix with the "let it all hang out" free-spirited countercultural searchers. Alan's sagely advice was: "Simply be yourself, and teach what you know." In other words, be *"Tze-Jan,"* spontaneously "Self-So" in the true Daoist fashion.

I was keenly aware of the incongruity in Alan's subconscious wish to be and sound Asian, but his passionate desire to transcend the limitations of his Caucasian/Christian bondage, to fully embrace the Asian philosophy and spiritual essence, became my inspiration and guide to finding my personal Dao. To be both Chinese and Western, genuinely, without contradictions and ambivalence, I began, slowly, to discover and rediscover my way, to tread gently and thrive solidly, finding a balance in my East–West heritages. Alan's teaching and his genius to transmit this harmonious unity of East and West were the perfect guides and inspiration along "my own way." Indeed, my calligraphy entitled *Tze-Jan and Feng Liu* is inspired by Alan and dedicated to his enduring spirit.

It was always my tendency to wear clearly Western attire when Alan and I jointly guided seminar programs. Given Alan's routine appreciation for Eastern style, I surmised that one Asian retreat host among the pair of us was adequate to our task. At one event, where my role was to talk about and exhibit the

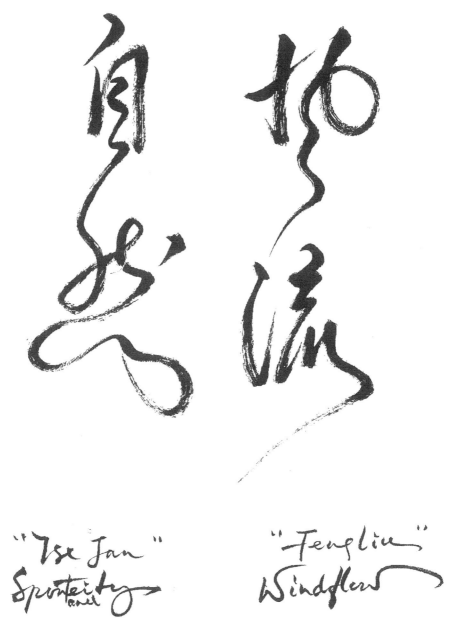

Tze-Jan and Feng Liu by Chungliang Al Huang

artful process of Asian tea ceremonies, I showed up in my Western garb, decked out thoroughly with cowboy hat and boots. Fittingly, the only props available for that particular retreat session were a coffee maker, grunting and snorting, and plastic spoons and cups. "We found great pleasure in the incongruity of his green-eyed Zen-master and my yellow-skinned cowboy meticulously going through the ritual of creating 'beauty and essence' in spite of mixed-up cultural juxtapositions" (Huang, 1991, p. 79).

Alan used to say that Asian spiritual practices should be incorporated into the Western culture by informal and casual means, likening the process to how Americans drink tea, because it can be more effortlessly digested that way. He saw this as similar to the Zen masters of ancient China who were steeped like tea in the Tao philosophy of life.

"They saw every creature and every experience is in accord with the Tao of nature just as it is. . . . Their Zen was *wu-shih*, which means approximately 'nothing special' or 'no fuss'" (Watts, 1960, p. 109).

It was a great honor to have Alan Watts write the foreword to my book, *Embrace Tiger, Return to Mountain* (Huang, 1973). By then, we had shared much time with each other, exploring the scholarly and hands-on aspects of Dao philosophy. Alan said that he and I "have come to a consensus of understanding and feeling about it such that I can say of the relationship between us that East and West have undoubtedly met—and, for me, this is no small matter" (Watts, 1973b, p. 1). He went on to write:

> To work with Huang is to learn to move with wind and water—not only in the t'ai chi exercises, but also in the course of everyday life. In going by "the watercourse way" he is as fresh as a mountain stream, with all its bubbles and babbles, and, way down below, as deep and powerful as the Yang-tze Chiang. (p. 2)

Thank you, Alan, for your kind and loving sentiment.

THE WISDOM OF INSECURITY

Through my collaborations with Alan Watts, I came to appreciate that subjective feelings of inadequacy and doubts in the midst of transition make only mild obstacles along the way of life if they are accepted and embraced with an open heart. In his younger days, Alan was basically inhibited and quite critical of himself, yet he developed into a colorful and outgoing man in later years. His delight with life was founded on his willingness to acknowledge the faults underlying his footing in the world. He was a clay-footed Buddha, but those feet of clay were positioned directly on the path of life.

I admired many of Alan's books, particularly the title of *The Wisdom of Insecurity* (Watts, 1951). It alone can be a potent tai ji lesson to us all. This book was ostensibly addressed to a mid-twentieth-century readership experiencing the onset of the nuclear "cold war" in the aftermath of World War II. Yet Alan's pithy writing flowed out of his own personal crises at the time. His first marriage had collapsed, he resigned his positions in the Episcopal Church and at Northwestern University, and had yet to secure his faculty post at the American Academy of Asian Studies in San Francisco.

My comprehension of *The Wisdom of Insecurity* (Watts, 1951) was merely conceptual until he expressed the gist of the text to me in a very direct manner. He was adamant in suggesting that I not only accept my insecurity with the English language but use it to advantage. Alan once said to me:

> Don't you dare improve your Chinese-English. Look at me. I am so clever with words that I trick myself all the time. I can turn it off and on, like a taped message, always slick and perfect. No, you just keep fumbling. The essence is better conveyed that way. (quoted in Huang, 1991, p. 59)

The obvious point of Alan's suggestion is that we must make allowances for our imperfections and insecurities if true peace of mind is to be experienced. It is not the disappearance of the problem that matters most, but rather it is the process of living in its presence that is the imperative call.

Alan and I wanted to do a joint seminar in Big Sur on this wonderful Dao concept to synthesize the contradiction of these polar opposites, "equanimity" and "insecurity," in tai ji practice. We decided to add a subtitle, "Shangri-la on the San Andreas Fault." What a brilliant juxtaposition! But the Esalen Institute's management at the time did not think it wise to draw attention to the well-known fault line that was in close proximity to the retreat center, and they edited our title to *The Wisdom of Insecurity: Shangri-la at the Edge of the Sea*! Alas, the whole point was lost. Exit, Dao wisdom; enter, innocuous pacifier! Alan was furious!

Alan's encouragement to discover the wisdom of my own insecurity with the English language provided an auspicious reassurance to trust my style of expression as I was just about to embark on a particularly fearful journey—trying to write my first book.

Through the living example of Alan's Dao wisdom I wrote the following in 1973:

> Insecurity and uncertainty are everywhere. If you don't let it become part of your flow, you will always be resisting and fighting. If the ground here suddenly shakes and trembles, can you give with it and still maintain your center? The joy in surfing and skiing and so many other sports is in being able to do this. If you stiffen up and fight the wave, then you will never learn; you have to give in to the waves in

order to ride them. If you can become fluid and open even when you are standing still, then this fluidness and openness makes you able to respond to changes. You will be able to play the changes and enjoy them. (Huang, 1973, p. 179)

DAO CALLIGRAPHY

In due course I was able to reciprocate a gift of reassurance to Alan. He loved Chinese writing, especially the art of brush calligraphy. He diligently practiced the art through his later life and was pleased with his accomplishments that were much admired and sought after by his friends and followers. But clearly, as someone who began practicing late in adulthood without formal discipline and guidance, his efforts, although admirable, were far from excellent. The best way I had tried to compliment his work was "very strong in Chi, and in character, but with a distinctive foreign accent!"

When approached by a trendy art gallery in the Bay Area to have an exhibition of his brush calligraphy, Alan was flattered and excited. He sought my advice and support. With a proposed date to open the exhibit, Alan was eager to buckle down to relearn the basics and correct all his obvious mistakes. I said to him, "If you try too hard to improve and correct your faults, the best you might achieve would be a relatively fault-free, bland, and uninteresting hand" (Huang, 1991, p. 111). Very quickly he agreed with me that if he had a choice to be "simply an average, properly correct brush calligrapher" or "a one-of-a-kind, unique, eccentric brush artist with character and a distinctive Chi-full foreign accent," which is he to be? He definitely preferred to be the latter.

We conducted a workshop many years ago in which the participants determined that Alan and I should engage a conversation by using calligraphy. Employing the *Tao te Ching* as a textual point of departure, we brushed wide swaths of outsized figures on hefty spools of paper. This process of dialogue grew more and more animated with the increasing pace of our call and response. We brushed in a fast and sinuous style, and Alan's cursive script became so improvisational that, all of a sudden, neither he nor I knew the linguistic meaning of our brush strokes. We were not focused on the subject matter, but instead were simply moving freely with the suppleness and grace of the calligraphic process.

As we continued unrolling the spools and putting brush to ink to paper, a workshop participant started a drumbeat, and almost immediately the entire gathering was doing a spontaneous jig down the edges of our masterpiece. The dancing became more full of life, and the paper started shredding underneath the bouncing feet. In a very short time, tattered paper was strewn all over and the entire room was a cyclone of action and oomph!

When I was doing the calligraphy for Alan's book, I would set up the brush and black ink and contemplate, in my native language, the spirit of Alan's thoughts and expressions, the whole time sensing their bodily inspiration to the point where they were no longer "separate from the dance." Continuing with the dancing process, I would unroll the calligraphy paper and allow the procedure to unfold, the brush, ink-laden, moving non-stop and without thinking. Notes on my calligraphy in Alan's book say the following:

> The Watercourse Way is not one man's way. It is the universal way. The calligraphy done by me is not really mine exclusively; it is also Alan Watts's, for so much of his spirit-energy had been embodied within me when I wrote these cursive words. It is yours, too, our reader when you are in tune with us in this watercourse way. (Huang, 1975b, p. 128)

"Om" and "Yes!" the Perfect Dao Answers to Everything

Alan Watts was a genius at public speaking. He had a special knack for capturing and holding the attention of an audience with his spontaneity and quick wit. Alan's friend, Sandy Jacobs, offered this description of his oratory skills:

> He didn't *prepare*. He had a fine library, of course, and he did extensive research for his books, but for his lectures? No way. He would just wander in to an auditorium someplace—some college town. He'd walk up on the stage, and he'd say, "Let's see, today were going to discuss, say Ramakrishna." Right away, some totally brilliant opening would suggest itself to him, he'd gather up the audience with some incredible beginning which would draw people in. There'd be this long, rambling middle, which would keep people's interest—jokes, laughs. He had a mental watch which said, "Hey! It's fifty minutes," and then he'd draw it all in, and come up with this cliffhanger, a conclusion, but it was a pregnant moment where everybody would say, "God, that's fantastic!" (quoted in Furlong, 2001, pp. 161–162)

A true Daoist and Zen master, Alan Watts is also "the Buddha with feet of clay," human and imperfect. He loved life in all aspects—food, wine, people, and all the joyful fun in everyday life. He could be excessive and out of bounds, but always instinctively marvelous, living in the moment and always present, despite everything. Here we have two stories of "Being Alan Watts":

Alan's gregarious hosting was well known. Prior to his big lecture at the University of California in Berkeley, Alan gave a dinner party in a fine Sausalito restaurant. He had much too much to drink and was quite inebriated and cotton-mouthed as we ushered him to the auditorium stage, late. He sat down facing a packed house of eager listeners for his usual wisdom and his famously perfect British baritone delivery. Instead, he picked up his brass bowl in front of him, rang it to let the sound reverberate into the hall and began chanting "OM," Gong! "OM," another Gong! Soon the large crowd began chanting with him. "OM" "OM" . . .

We "OM"ed all night long until Alan finally sobered up. But there was no more need for words. Just "OM," and all the floodgates of the Heart Chakras opened wide! The crowd was happy and clearly enlightened for that brief and miraculous night! To this day, whenever some of us present that night try to reminisce, it was and still is, agreed, one of the best transcendental evenings of "Zen and Tao" (Then and Now!) we could have ever experienced!

Another occasion in Chicago, prior to a major conference's panel discussion, Alan again had a little too much to drink on the previous night. Still groggy on stage as the panel convened, Alan succumbed to a short catnap. A long-winded and complex question was put forth to Dr. Watts by a man—the kind who loved to hear his own voice—expounding endlessly. Not awake in time to hear this specific question, Alan suddenly realized that all eyes were on him, awaiting his wise response. Unruffled, with a brief pause, Alan nodded his head with an emphatic "YES!" "Thank you, thank you, Dr. Watts, thank you!!!" shouted the satisfied and most grateful seeker of truth.

Alan Watts was my mentor. I once defined mentoring as the capacity to lead and follow at the same time. "You need to have as much enthusiasm to learn from your students as you do to teach them. If you just teach, its only half of the yin/yang tai ji circle" (Huang, 1996, pp. 126–127). Alan learned tai ji with me. He exuded a childlike enthusiasm for the tai ji dance movements. Learning how to dance was something he had not done in his early life, and the times when he was affectionate and embraceable were usually after we had been dancing. But a few alcoholic beverages were often required to experience the ease and joy of the dance. It seemed to me that Alan used alcohol to transcend the heavy intellectual burdens of his writing and lecture schedule. In my epilogue to *Tao: The Watercourse Way* I wrote:

> Through his theatrical talents and game-plays, Alan was able to forgo many of his Victorian inhibitions and create for himself and others a curious kind of balance which somehow sustained him. In later life, he depended more on his external need to perform and to receive support from his audience. Constantly pulled by outside demands, he was too successful to stop—and too brilliant to submit to his own nature. He became the perfect example of the Western man as victim of the *yang*-dominant world. He revealed the crux of this tragedy shared by most men in this unbalanced time by admitting, "But I don't like myself when I am sober," as he surrendered to another shot of vodka at a time when he knew he need not and should not rely on it any more. (Huang, 1975b, p. 125)

THE DAO OF ALAN WATTS

When Alan was writing his autobiography, only in his middle fifties at the time, he shared with me his manuscript, which was full of marvelous anecdotes and adventures, deeply fascinating to one who had come from a totally opposite cultural background. Particularly amazing was his metamorphosis from British boarding school student, Christian upbringing, and brief Anglican priesthood to become the darling of the counterculture in America. His book *The Way of Zen* (Watts, 1957) was already a modern classic. His list of mentors, colleagues in the fields of Zen, alternative higher education, and the "Human Potential Movement" were most impressive. Also, in the new circles of Humanistic, Transpersonal and depth psychology, Alan shared his authenticity and brilliance with all the outstanding pioneering "Original Minds" of the era.

For a long period of time, Alan was fixated with the title of "Out of My Mind" (in order to extend "into my body and higher and deeper into personal consciousness") for his autobiography. But his publisher rejected it for fear of the link with his fascination in the mind-expanding drug culture. The other alternative was to be "Coincidence of the Opposites," which we both thought was very Daoist but somewhat pretentious. Again, vetoed by his publisher.

I remember the fluidity and flow of our many discussions on our life's callings and our true paths, ranging from the sayings of Confucius to Joseph Campbell's "journey of the mythic hero" and "following one's bliss," on to Dao, the Way, and our personal Dao. "*In My Own Way*" was finally accepted to be the title of his autobiography. Alan actually gave seminars at Esalen Institute entitled "Being in the Way," which explored the multiple meanings of this expression, from the sense of obstruction to feeling one with the stream of life (see Watts, 2002a, 2002b).

In his foreword to my book on tai ji, Alan commented on the notion of *wu-wei*, describing the "spirit" of its meaning "is to make turns with curves instead of crick-crack angles, and for this reason the whole biological world is curvaceous—water being its main component. As Lao-Tzu said, although water is soft and weak it invariably overcomes the rigid and hard" (Watts, 1973b, p. 2). In similar spirit, Alan wrote an essay entitled "The Watercourse Way." He said:

> When I stand by the stream and watch it, I am relatively still, and the flowing water makes a path across my memory so that I realize its transience in comparison with my stability. This is, of course, an illusion in the sense that I, too, am in flow and likewise have no final destination—for can anyone imagine finality as a form of life? My death will be a disappearance of a particular pattern in the water. (Watts, 1973d, pp. 15–16)

Yet it seems that new patterns and undulations of Alan's legacy continue to appear in the flowing Dao waters of contemporary life. Indeed, Alan Watts lived on a vessel in the waters off Sausalito, California. On that houseboat, the S. S. Vallejo, in 1975, I created the *Lan Ting Institute* in memory of Alan. The institute is an experiential learning process using poetry, music, philosophy, brush calligraphy, and tai ji movement to enrich our lives-in-progress. "Lan," the second syllable of Alan's name, means "orchid" in Chinese, and represents the budding of humanity's primal realization, our "Original Self." Out of the Lan Ting Institute blossomed *The Living Tao Foundation*, a not-for-profit education project. In 2007, we celebrated our thirtieth anniversary of sharing seminars, workshops, and training programs oriented toward inspiring creative consciousness and supportive relationships among people. At our old Big Sur stomping grounds, Esalen Institute, I presented two seminars in 2008. One was entitled "That was Zen, This is Tao: Watts up when East meets West" (Huang & Walter, 2008b), the other was called "Creative Tai Ji Practice: Play and Improvisation in Tao Living" (Huang & Walter, 2008a), and both were inspired by, and in honor of, my dear friend, Alan Watts.

Here and now, writing these words of reflection on Alan as I knew him years ago and sensing the flow of his legacy embodied through my life and work in this new century, he reminds me that the present moment:

> is everything that there is. . . . It contains the whole of time, all past, all future, everything. You never have to hold on to it. If you can feel that, then realize that the movement of the Tao is exactly the same thing as the present moment—that which we call *now* is the same thing as the Tao. The Tao, the course of things, the eternal now, the presence of God, anything you want to call it—that is *now!* And you cannot get out of it. There is no need to get with it because you cannot get away from it! That is beautiful. You just relax, and you are there. (Watts, 1983, p. 88)

REFERENCES

Ellwood, R. S. (1979). *Alternative alters: Unconventional and Eastern spirituality in America*. Chicago: University of Chicago Press.

Furlong, M. (2001). *Zen effects: The life of Alan Watts*. Woodstock, VT: Skylight Paths.

Huang, C. (1973). *Embrace tiger, Return to mountain*. Moab, UT: Real People Press.

Huang, C. (1975a). Foreword. In A.W. Watts, *Tao: The watercourse way* (p. vii–xiii). New York: Pantheon.

Huang, C. (1975b). Once again: A new beginning. In A.W. Watts, *Tao: The watercourse way* (pp. 123–128). New York: Pantheon.

Huang, C. (1991). *Quantum soup: Fortune cookies in crisis*. Berkeley, CA: Celestial Arts

Huang, C. (1996). Living your Tao. In S. Towler (Ed.), *A gathering of cranes: Bringing the Tao to the West* (p. 110–130). Eugene, OR: Abode of the Eternal Tao.

Huang, C., & Walter, R. (2008a, March). *Creative Tai practice: Play and improvisation in Tao living*. Seminar presented at Esalen Institute, Big Sur, CA.

Huang, C., & Walter, R. (2008b, March). *That was Zen, This is Tao: Watts up when East Meets West.* Seminar presented at Esalen Institute, Big Sur, CA.

Huxley, A. (1954). *Doors of perception.* New York: Harper

Watts, A. W. (1951). *The wisdom of insecurity.* New York: Pantheon.

Watts, A. W. (1957). *The way of Zen.* New York: Pantheon.

Watts, A. W. (1958). *Nature, man and woman.* New York: Pantheon.

Watts, A. W. (1960). Beat Zen, square Zen, and Zen. In A. W. Watts, *This is It and other essays on Zen and spiritual experience* (pp. 76–110). New York: Vintage.

Watts, A. W. (1961). *Psychotherapy East and West.* New York: Pantheon.

Watts, A. W. (1962). *The joyous cosmology.* New York: Pantheon.

Watts, A. W. (1973a) *Cloud-hidden, whereabouts unknown.* New York: Pantheon.

Watts, A. W. (1973b). Foreword. In C. Huang, *Embrace tiger, Return to mountain* (pp. 1–3). Moab, UT: Real People Press.

Watts, A. W. (1973c). *In my own way.* New York: Vintage.

Watts, A. W. (1973d). The watercourse way. In *Cloud-hidden, whereabouts unknown: A mountain journal* (pp. 15–23). New York: Pantheon.

Watts, A. W. (with Al Huang) (1975). *Tao: The watercourse way.* New York: Pantheon.

Watts, A. W. (1983). Chuang-Tzu: Wisdom of the ridiculous. In *The way of liberation: Essays and lectures on the transformation of the self* (M. Watts & R. Shropshire, Eds., pp. 73–88). New York: Weatherhill.

Watts, A. W. (2002a). Being in the Way I. In *Taoism: Way beyond seeking* (M. Watts, Ed., pp. 51–70). Boston: Tuttle.

Watts, A. W. (2002b). Being in the Way II. In *Taoism: Way beyond seeking* (M. Watts, Ed., pp. 71–90). Boston: Tuttle.

Contributors

Michael C. Brannigan is the Pfaff Endowed Chair in Ethics and Moral Values at The College of Saint Rose and holds a joint appointment at the Alden March Bioethics Institute, Albany Medical College. Along with numerous scholarly articles on ethics, Asian thought, and cross-cultural studies, his books include *Everywhere and Nowhere: The Path of Alan Watts*; *Cross-Cultural Biotechnology*; *Healthcare Ethics in a Diverse Society*; *Ethical Issues in Human Cloning*; *Striking a Balance: A Primer in Traditional Asian Values*, and *The Pulse of Wisdom: The Philosophies of India, China, and Japan*. He received his PhD in philosophy and MA in religious studies from the University of Leuven, Belgium.

Peter J. Columbus is a research psychologist working in the phenomenological tradition of human inquiry. He is published in a range of academic venues including *The Humanistic Psychologist, British Journal of Medical Psychology, Journal of Fluency Disorders, Journal of Engineering Education*, and *Journal of Sport Behavior*. Co-editor (with Don Rice) of *Psychology of the Martial Arts*, he holds a PhD in experimental psychology from The University of Tennessee-Knoxville and an MA in humanistic psychology from the University of West Georgia. He has held faculty appointments at Assumption College and Union College (Kentucky), and is presently serving as administrator of the Shantigar Foundation located in the Berkshire Hills of Massachusetts.

Ralph W. Hood Jr. is professor of psychology at the University of Tennessee-Chattanooga where he teaches courses on psychology of religion and philosophical psychology. He is author of *Dimensions of Mystical Experience: Empirical Studies and Psychological Links*, coauthor of *The Psychology of Religion: An Empirical Approach* (with Peter C. Hill and Bernard Spilka) and *Psychology of Religious Fundamentalism* (with Peter C. Hill and W. Paul Williamson), editor of the *Handbook of Religious Experience*, and founding editor of the *International Journal* *for the Psychology of Religion.* He is a fellow of the Society for the Scientific Study of Religion and the American Psychological Association, past president of APA's division on Psychology of Religion, and recipient of its William James Award. His PhD is from the University of Reno-Nevada.

Chungliang Al Huang is a philosopher, performing artist, and internationally renowned Dao master. He is the founder-president of the Living Tao Foundation and the international Lan Ting Institute in the sacred mountains of China, and on the Oregon coast. He is a research scholar of the Academia Sinica, a fellow of the World Academy of Art and Science, and an assembly member for the Council for a Parliament of the World Religions. He received the highest rated Speaker's Award from the Young Presidents' Organization, the New Dimension Broadcaster Award, and the prestigious Gold Medal from the Ministry of Education of the Republic of China. He is author of numerous best-selling books, including the classics *Embrace Tiger, Return to Mountain*; *Quantum Soup*; *Essential Tai Ji*; and *The Chinese Book of Animal Powers*; and co-author with Alan Watts of *Tao: The Watercourse Way*; and with Dr. Jerry Lynch of *Thinking Body, Dancing Mind.*

Alan Keightley is the former head of religious studies at King Edward VI College in Stourbridge, England, and adjunct professor at the University of Birmingham where he offered courses on wisdom traditions and mystic teachers. His writings and book reviews are published in *Theology*, the *Journal of Beliefs and Values*, and the *British Journal of Religious Education*. His books include *Wittgenstein, Grammar, and God; Religion and the Great Fallacy;* and *Into Every Life a Little Zen Must Fall: A Christian Philosopher Looks to Alan Watts and the East*. He studied at Wesley Theological College and Bristol University where he obtained an honors degree in theology before earning his PhD at the University of Birmingham in 1974.

Stanley Krippner is Alan W. Watts Professor of Psychology at the Saybrook Graduate School and holds faculty appointments at Universidade Holistica Internacional (Brazil) and Instituto de Medicina y Technologia Avanzada de la Conducta (Mexico). Formerly, he was director of the Kent State University Child Study Center and the Maimonides Medical Center Dream Research Laboratory. A fellow of the American Psychological Association and the Society for the Scientific Study of Religion, he is author, co-author, or editor of numerous books, including *Extraordinary Dreams*; *Varieties of Anomalous Experience: Examining the Scientific Evidence;* and *The Psychological Impact of War on Civilians: An International Perspective*. His PhD is from Northwestern University.

Miriam L. Levering is professor of religious studies at the University of Tennessee-Knoxville. She was a visiting scholar at the Fairbanks Center for East Asian Studies at Harvard University for 2005–2006, and served as Numata Visiting Professor of Buddhism at McGill University during fall semester of 2008. She is involved with several translation projects including "The Biography of Miaozong" published in the *Zen Sourcebook: Traditional Documents from China, Korea, and Japan*, and *The Letters of Chan Master Dahui Pujue Zonggao.* Author of many articles on religion in China, Zen Buddhism and Japanese religion, and women in Zen, she is editor of *Rethinking Scripture: Essays from a Comparative Perspective,* and *Zen: Images, Texts and Teachings.* Her PhD is from Harvard University.

Ralph Metzner is professor emeritus of psychology and former academic dean at the California Institute of Integral Studies. His many books include *The Well of Remembrance: Rediscovering the Earth Wisdom Myths of Northern Europe; The Unfolding Self: The Varieties of Transformative Experience; Green Psychology: Transforming Our Relationship to the Earth,* and two edited collections on the science and phenomenology of *Ayahuasca* and *Teonanácatl.* He is co-founder and president of the Green Earth Foundation (see www.greenearthfound.org), holds a BA in philosophy and psychology from Oxford University, and earned a PhD in clinical psychology from Harvard University where he worked with Timothy Leary and Richard Alpert (Ram Dass) on the Harvard Psychedelic Research Project.

Alan Pope is associate professor of psychology and member of the graduate faculty at the University of West Georgia. Following advanced graduate studies in computer science and artificial intelligence, he received his PhD in clinical existential-phenomenological psychology at Duquesne University. He has been a student and practitioner of Vajrayana Buddhism since 1991. His research generally aims to elucidate the processes of psychospiritual transformation resulting from involuntary suffering and from disciplined spiritual and creative practice. His graduate seminars include Buddhist Psychology, Psychology of Loss, and Explorations into Creativity. He is author of *From Child to Elder: Personal Transformation in Becoming an Orphan at Midlife* (2006).

Kaisa Puhakka is professor of psychology at California Institute of Integral Studies where she teaches courses on psychotherapy, Buddhist thought and meditation, and transformation of consciousness. She holds MA degrees in philosophy and psychology, a PhD in experimental psychology from the University of Toledo, and a postdoctoral diploma in clinical psychology from Adelphi University. She is co-editor (with Tobin Hart and Peter Nelson) of *Transpersonal Knowing: Exploring the Horizon of Consciousness,* a former editor of *The Journal of Transpersonal Psychology,* and author of some fifty articles and book chapters in the fields of comparative philosophy, phenomenology, and psychotherapy. For more than thirty years, she has been a student of a variety of Buddhist practices, including monastic Rinzai Zen.

Donadrian L. Rice is professor and chair of psychology at the University of West Georgia. He is co-editor (with Peter Columbus) of *Psychology of the Martial Arts*, and a former editor of the newsletter of the Transpersonal Psychology Interest Group of the American Psychological Association. He has published/presented more than fifty papers on martial arts, dreams, hypnosis, organizational development, psychotherapy, and mind–body studies. His writings and reviews appear in numerous journals and edited volumes including *Contemporary Psychology*; *Somatics*; *The Humanistic Psychologist*; *Humanistic and Transpersonal Psychology: Historical and Biographical Sourcebook* (D. Moss, Ed.); and *Existential-Integrative Psychotherapy: Guideposts to the Core of Practice* (K. J. Schneider, Ed.). He holds a PhD from Saybrook Graduate School in San Francisco, received training from R. D. Laing at the Philadelphia Association Clinic in London, and is a licensed psychotherapist.

Index

.

Made in the USA
San Bernardino, CA
26 August 2014